THE CROOKED LADDER

THE CROOKED LADDER

Gangsters, Ethnicity, and the American Dream

James M. O'Kane

Transaction Publishers
New Brunswick (U.S.A.) and London (U.K.)

First paperback printing 2003
Copyright © 1992 by Transaction Publishers, New Brunswick, New Jersey.

This book is printed on acid-free paper that meets the American National Standard for Permanence of Paper for Printed Library Materials.

Library of Congress Catalog Number: 91-28923
ISBN: 1-56000-021-X (cloth); 0-7658-0994-X (paper)
Printed in the United States of America

Library of Congress Cataloging-in-Publication Data

O'Kane, James M.
    The crooked ladder : gangsters, ethnicity, and the American dream / James M. O'Kane.
        p. cm.
    Includes bibliographical references and index.
    ISBN 0-7658-0994-X (alk. paper)
    1. Criminals—United States—History. 2. Minorities—United States—History. 3. United States—Ethnic relations. 4. Organized crime—United States—History. I. Title.

HV6197.U5043 1992
364.1'06'0973—dc20   91-28923
                                                             CIP

To my wife, Marge,
and my children,
J.B., Dan, Pat, Joe, and
Mary Rose

Want is not the sole incentive to crime. Men also wish to enjoy themselves and not be in a state of desire—they wish to cure some desire going beyond necessities of life, which preys upon them . . . and therefore they commit crime.

—Aristotle, *Politics*

I'm telling you . . . Joxer . . . th' whole worl's . . . in a terr . . . ible state o' . . . chassis.
—Captain Boyle, in Sean O'Casey's *Juno and the Paycock*

Contents

Acknowledgments   ix

Introduction   1

1. Newcomers vs. the Established Society   7

2. The Climb from the Bottom   25

3. Ethnic Organized Crime: Historical Dimensions   51

4. The Decline of the Italians and the
   Rise of the New Ethnic Criminals   79

5. Individual and Group Mobility in Crime   111

6. The Future of Ethnic Organized Crime   139

Appendix—The Criminal in American Ballad and Film   159

Bibliography   177

Index   187

Acknowledgments

I wish to record my sincere appreciation to the many people who have assisted me in completing this book.

Special thanks goes to my wife Marge, and my children—J.B., Dan, Pat, Joe, and Mary Rose—who patiently endured my suppertime monologues on Dutch Schultz, Chinese tong violence, crack homicides, Irish rebel ballads, Prohibition, and other diverse topics touched upon in this book. I'm grateful to my mother, Matilda O'Kane, and to my sisters, Helen Grubbs and Bernadette Moran, who alerted me to our family's immigrant heritage and to the part crime and ethnicity played in the communities in Brooklyn where we had lived and matured. Without this personal background I probably never would have been interested in the relationship between ethnic crime and upward social mobility.

To my collegues at Drew University I also owe a special debt. My two "tertulia" comrades—Tom Oden and John Ollom—who constantly encouraged me in this labor of love as they read chapters, critiqued them, and offered constructive advice. So also did Phil Jensen, Jim Mills, Al Lee, David Cowell, George de Stevens, Jonathan Reader, and Lydia Ledeen. Each helped me to focus my arguments as each analyzed various parts of the work and supplied generous suggestions as to how I could better state my thesis. Other Drew collegues assisted me by providing pertinent information when I needed it. Here I would like to acknowledge Neal Riemer, John Copeland, Paul Wice, Kathy Gray, Roxanne Friedenfels, Luiz Barbosa, Hans Morsink, Mike Meagher, Evelyn Meyer, Roger Wescott, Rebecca Hodgkins and Jean Marie Madorran. So also did my brother-in-law, James Gray, of American University.

Those receiving special thanks should also include my dean, Paolo Cucchi, who made possible the support services necessary, and Mitzi Pappas, Lois Conant, Sue Bennett, Lydia Feldman, Jean Ruch, and

Paula Massa who endured tedious hours at their word processors typing various versions of the manuscript. Without their assistance, there literally would be no book.

I'm grateful to others who never read any of the manuscript but whose ideas permeate my thesis. I would single out Will Herberg, now deceased, who had been a collegue of mine at Drew University; over many a cup of coffee we debated the topics of ethnic crime and subsequent mobility. Richard Cloward of Columbia University also deserves special mention, for he was the first professor I encountered who alerted me to the manner in which ethnic groups really "make it" in American life.

To the members of various law enforcement departments I also express my gratitude. Special thanks go to Jack Hughes, a close friend and a former sergeant of the New York City Police Department who opened my sociological eyes to the realities of urban crime. Without him, my views on crime would still be text book oriented, devoid of any real connection to the actualities of crimes. Other NYPD detectives, both retired and active, who worked in the Brooklyn and Queens NYPD homicide divisions—Paul Weidenbaum, Al Cachie, Bob Alongi, Mike Fella, Lenny Ayers, Joe Titus, Lou Savarese, Bob Gabriel—as well as Brooklyn North's Robbery Investigating Program's Rich Conforte, and Bob Creighton, the chief investigator for the district attorney's office of Suffolk County, New York, alerted me to current trends in organized crime and continued tutoring me in what really goes on in the streets. Finally, I would like to acknowledge the late Manny Ayers, Drew University's past security department head and former police chief of Leonia, New Jersey, who further assisted in formulating my ideas about criminal careers, as did my brother-in-law, Tom Moran, of the Palm Beach, Florida, police department. Without the generous input of all of these dedicated police officers I would still be in the "ivory tower" of sociological theorizing.

Also, I would like to thank Jean Hutson of the Schomburg Center for Research in Black Culture for her assistance in helping me with background documentation. Finally, I would like to thank those friends connected neither with academia nor law enforcement who assisted me with their ideas, and advice as well as critical reviews of rough drafts of various chapters of the manuscript. These include Steve Huvane, who critiqued the entire book, as well as George S. Johnston, Addie Mae Kelly, John Caporasa, and Rafael Francia who assisted me with their insights.

To all of the above, I am deeply endebted.

Introduction

This book represents an attempt to describe how ethnic minorities coming to America's shores and cities have utilized organized crime as one vehicle of upward mobility, removing themselves from lower-class status, advancing to middle-class power and respectability.

Ethnic organized crime has largely been ignored by social scientists and historians alike. The phenomenon constitutes the "dust" of American social history, a curious footnote in the odyssey of ethnic and racial minorities seeking to "make it," a subject not to be taken too seriously by those researching the mobility patterns of either their own ethnic ancestors, or current minority newcomers.

But those of us from such ethnic backgrounds know better, for our lives have witnessed the salience and resilience of organized crime in lower-income and working-class communities. The ethnic gangster constitutes a ubiquitous fixture in such communities and—contrary to the often distorted media presentations—he often is admired by many, his actions emulated and romanticized by his ethnic brethren. Were the bookie, the loan shark, the racketeer, the bootlegger, the vice lord, the crack dealer, the prostitute, and pimp truly despised and hated by the communities in which they flourish, they would have disappeared long ago, for the public would have no interest in, or need for, their services. Historically, such has not been the case nor is it currently the case, for communities are in fact ambivalent towards their ethnic gangsters, fearing them and supporting them simultaneously.

How did I become interested in such an area of inquiry which strikes many as "off the beaten track" of traditional sociology and criminology?

My lifelong interest in ethnic organized crime most likely stems from two factors: my upbringing as a second-generation Irish Catholic and my early life residing in the Bedford-Stuyvesant section of Brooklyn in a lower-middle class, soon-to-be-lower-class, neighborhood.

From immigrant family members, particularly my mother and grandmother, I discovered that resistance to legal authority constituted an integral part of their lives as Catholics in late-nineteenth- or early-twentieth-century County Derry in Northern Ireland. I still recall stories and tales told by them as they recounted their deeds during the "troubles" in Ireland following the 1916 Easter Rebellion. I recall their terror of, and resistance to, the "Black and Tans" (the British rabble sent to Ireland to suppress the rebellion), of their admiration of Irish rebels and fighters who resisted oppressive landlords, police, and so on. From my mother I also learned how this distrust of legal authority embedded itself in verse and song. She often would sing songs, such as "The Wild Colonial Boy," a ballad that romanticizes the Robin Hood character of Jack Duggan, an Irishman who emigrated to Australia to pursue his dreams of fame and fortune through criminal means:

> There was a wild, colonial boy
> Jack Duggan was his name
> He was born and raised in Ireland
> In a place called Castlemane
>
> At the early age of sixteen
> He left his native home
> And to Australia's sunny shore
> He was inclined to roam
>
> He robbed the rich, he helped the poor
> He shot James McAvoy
> A terror to Australia
> Was the wild colonial boy. (Various verses)

Another of her favorite ballads, "The Phoenix Park Murders," heralded the exploits of Dan Curley, the Irish nationalist who in 1882 assassinated England's Lord Frederick Cavendish and his under secretary T.H. Burke in Dublin's famed Phoenix Park. Curley was turned into the authorities by James Carey, an informer. The ballad does not treat this informer well, and I remember my mother's songful disdain for traitors such as Carey:

> James Carey, that false heart informer and traitor
> May the ground he walks on, may the grass never grow
> While he lives on earth let his name be detested
> And shunned by mankind wherever he goes.

May his wife die a widow and his children driven,
Wandering from Erin's green shores.
May the curse of the widow and orphan light on him. My
husband, Dan Curley I'll never see more.

It was by his orders the deeds were committed
Lord Cavendish and Burke were both laid in the gore
To escape from the gallows he turned and informed,
My husband Dan Curley I'll never see more.

Ah, but as my mother recalls, James Carey himself was assassinated by Pat O'Donnell who avenged his betrayal. O'Donnell's retribution was heralded in the ballad, "Pat O'Donnell."

My name is Pat O'Donnel,
I came from Donegal
I am you know a fighting foe
To traitors one and all.

For the shooting of James Carey
I was tried in London Town
And on the scaffold high
My life I must lay down.

I wish that I was a free man
And could live for another year
All traitors and informers
I would make them quake with fear.

I would make them fly before my eyes
Like the hare before the hound
On the twenty-second of December
My life I must lay down.

Ballads such as these as well as other noteable ones recalled by my mother such as "The Boston Burglar" and "Jesse James " awakened in me a curiosity about criminals, particularly the folk-hero types who resisted traditional authority, who believed that one didn't get far in life by doing things "normally"—the way "they" wanted them done—who decided early in life that they would "make it" on their own terms, and so on. Long ago, I wondered whether such romanticized criminals were not, in fact, models for the lower classes who saw in them admirable traits, different from the despicable ones noticed by the middle classes. Surely these gangsters must serve some societal need, for why else would we write songs honoring them, author books depicting their lives, create films lionizing their infamous deeds, and compose legends about them, making their names household terms? Perhaps, in sociological parlance, crime served some useful function in American society as it enabled its practitioners to realize their peculiar version of the American Dream.

My upbringing in the multi-ethnic/racial Bedford-Stuyvesant section of Brooklyn in the 1940s and 1950s likewise influenced my interest in ethnic organized crime. A rich assortment of different groups resided on my block—Jefferson Avenue: Irish, Italians, Jews, Germans, African Americans, and Puerto Ricans; our street even had a Spanish family from the Canary Islands. All of us "rubbed elbows" with each other, trusting and distrusting each other, liking and disliking each other. Those of us of Irish descent thought it peculiar that the Italians ate pasta rather than potatoes, that the Germans always seemed to be washing their apartment stoops, and that Puerto Ricans loved loud vibrant music. These ethnic differences were omnipresent and taken for granted, so much so that most of us never really knew that there were people without an ethnic identity, "those people"—people who in the 1960s would be termed WASPs—White Anglo-Saxon Protestants. My world was populated with Catholics and Jews, and the dominant Anglo-Saxon Americans were people I had heard about, a peculiar group that was "out there" beyond the confines of New York City. In my formative years I tended to view "them" as a minority group, for they played but a minor role in my life and the lives of those around me. It was not until I reached graduate school at Columbia University that I made my close friendship with such an "oddity"— Don Schmidt, hailing from North Dakota. Likewise, he formed his friendship with this "oddity"—a Brooklyn-born Irish Catholic.

In this stable, ethnic Brooklyn neighborhood, crime—both organized and unorganized—was not uncommon. Illegal gambling—"the numbers"—existed in many of the small businesses in the area, particularly in "mom and pop" groceries, luncheonettes, barber shops, and bars. Certain individuals in the neighborhood were reputed to be involved with organized crime and my friends and I both feared and were fascinated with such "mafiosi."

Violent street crime also existed, and as I approached adolescence,

I could see that such crime became the norm. At that point Jefferson Avenue was fast becoming a slum, and the ethnic stability quickly disappeared. By the mid-1950s violent street gangs dominated the scene with the "El Quintos," the "Stompers," and the "Chaplins," killing each other for "turf," "honor," and "rep." These gangs quickly subdivided along ethnic and racial lines, with alliances and treaties made and broken within the same day, with "war counselors" and "warlords" appearing and disappearing in an equally short interval of time. Unlike the current drug wars in our inner cities, the gang wars of that era centered on status and "rep," with narcotics such as heroin playing a minor role. Sadly, the next generation witnessed the almost complete disintegration of blocks such as Jefferson Avenue, and my latest trip to the area in 1991 shocked me into realizing how the collapse of the lower-income family structure, the presence of ubiquitous crack dealers, and the disintegration of a viable community spirit, have destroyed the stable pattern I once remembered. Even the organized criminals have abandoned the area, leaving it to the drug dealers, robbers, burglars, murderers, pimps, and prostitutes. In my entire youth I recall no more than five murders taking place in the vicinity of Jefferson Avenue. But my police friends, Rich Conforti, Paul Weidenbaum, Al Cachie, Bob Alongi, and Mike Fella, detectives at New York City's 90th Police Precinct, reminded me that one street corner not far from Jefferson Avenue had been the scene of six separate murders in a one-month period in 1988; in a ten-year period they estimated a hundred homicides on that same corner, virtually all related to drug dealing.

I guess it's this sort of upbringing which has interested me in the question of urban crime. Why have streets such as Jefferson Avenue changed? Why have the Irish, Jewish, and Italian populations moved on, and their criminals with them? What does the future portend for the current African Americans and Hispanic residents and criminals of the Jefferson Avenues of America? Is there a pattern in the use of criminal activity by various ethnic groups? Do they succeed each other and use crime as a means of "making it" in America? Will the current chaos in the drug wars in our inner cities produce an imposed truce, *Pax Caponeana*, with the equivalent of an Al Capone, a Dutch Schultz, or a Carlo Gambino emerging to assert his authority over this latest criminal enterprise? Is there a regular cycle in all of this wherein current African-American, Hispanic, and Asian criminals are transversing the well-worn road pioneered by Irish, Jewish, and Italian syndicates?

The forthcoming chapters attempt to answer these questions and describe the role of organized crime in the life of the lower-class ethnic immigrant and migrant community, and how these ambitious gangsters coexist with other ambitious newcomers seeking to "make it" through other routes of upward mobility (i.e., unskilled and skilled labor, the clergy, the professions, entertainment, small businesses, politics, etc.). By ethnic organized crime I mean the following: An organization formed by individuals of the same or similar ethnic backgrounds for the purpose of securing income, power, and prestige through illegal means.

Little in these chapters is surprising, for scholars such as Herbert Asbury, Daniel Bell, Richard Cloward, Will Herberg, and Francis Ianni, have set forth integral segments of the position which I espouse and I am sincerely indebted to their works in helping me focus on the issue.

What I have attempted to do is pull together much of what these scholars and others have done previously with the intention of offering a plausible account of how ethnic minorities "make it" in American life, and how ethnic organized crime plays a logical and integral part in this process, creating, as Louis Winnick would conclude, "a crooked ladder to achievement" (Winnick 1988).

1

Newcomers vs. the Established Society

Arrival of the Newcomers

In the course of American history, millions of newcomers have entered the nation's mainstream. They left their homelands for varied reasons: enslavement; social, economic, religious or political pressure; or most often, whether peasants, townfolk, or urbanites, simply because of dissatisfaction with their lives. With the exception of those enslaved, these expatriates embarked on their odyssey to America's cities and plains with the vague realization that their new lives would be immeasurably different from and superior to their old ones.

And so they came—slaves and free men, colonists and gentry, contract laborers and artisans, farmers and townsmen, rich and poor, dreamers and realists—approximately 40 million strong, shaping and transforming American society.

Louis Adamic, a Slovenian immigrant, differed little from most immigrants. In his autobiography he wrote about his new homeland: "In America one could make pots of money in a short time, acquire immense holdings, wear a white collar, and have polish on one's boots like a *gospod*—one of the gentry—and eat white bread, soup, and meat on weekdays as well as Sundays, even if one were but an ordinary workman to begin with" (Adamic 1932, 5).

Like millions of fellow immigrants, Adamic marvelled at what America might bring him. In his native village of Blato, he witnessed with awe those immigrants who had returned to visit family and friends:

Five or six years before . . . the man had quietly left the village for the United States, a poor peasant clad in homespun, with a moustache under his nose and a bundle on his back; now, a clean-shaven *Amerikanec* he sported a blue-serge suit, buttoned shoes very large in the toes and with india-rubber heels, a black derby, a shiny

7

celluloid collar, and a loud necktie made even louder by a dazzling horseshoe pin, which, rumor had it, was made of gold, with his two suitcases of imitation leather, tied with straps, bulged with gifts from America for his relatives and friends in the village. In nine cases out of ten, he had left in economic desperation, on money borrowed from some relative in the United States; now there was talk in the village that he was worth anywhere from one to three thousand American dollars. And to my eyes he truly bore all the earmarks of affluence. (Adamic 1932, 3)

Upon their arrival, the vast majority of these newcomers settled at the bottom of the social hierarchy. Impoverished and illiterate, devoid of any real knowledge of urban-industrial life, they quickly comprised the bulk of the lower classes, the great "unwashed masses" of the eighteenth, nineteenth, and early twentieth centuries.

Generations later, the descendents of many of these groups have "made it" into the middle class. With nostalgia they talk of their ancestors' plight as railroad men, canal diggers, domestics, sweatshop operatives, factory hands, and homesteaders—people who earned scarcely enough to keep body and soul together. With justifiable pride they recount the journey of their families up the ladder of American success.

How did such a phenomenal transition ever take place? Did it occur as simply as many of the newcomers' descendents would have us believe? How could entire groups in the space of two or three generations move from the lower-class to middle-class affluence and respectability? Equally important, will those currently defined as lower class repeat and reenact this same upward mobility trek?

Traditional View of Newcomers' Upward Mobility

The idealized rendering of American social history suggests that the newcomers achieved this remarkable transition to middle-class status via the Horatio Alger route. Alger, a late-nineteenth-century New England novelist and moralizer, authored numerous books for young boys that embodied the themes of success and achievement. His characters, generally orphans, rose to prominence through hard work, intelligence, sobriety, and virtuous living. This rags-to-riches theme eventually became the blueprint to instruct those seeking to better themselves. Furthermore, it became the accepted version of how successful newcomers pulled themselves out of the lower classes: they worked hard, attended night school, mastered the English language, and made themselves respectable in the ever-present eyes of the dominant society. Their character embodied the Puritan Ethic. They struggled, and as America witnessed their determined efforts, it rewarded them with economic, political, and social acceptance. Initially viewed with suspicion, they soon adopted American ideals and took their places next to their fellow Americans. The assimilation process was relatively simple and the newcomers blended into the mainstream without disrupting the dominant American way of life. (Hartmann 1948, 14).

Social scientists refer to these newcomer groups as *ethnic groups*, those groups that share similar cultural characteristics, values, physical characteristics, and styles of life. Thus racial groups (e.g., African Americans, Asians, etc.) and religious groups (e.g., Jews) are included and considered ethnic groups in the broad sense of the term. Social scientist also refer to dominant groups, those diverse groups— both middle and upper class—belonging to the mainstream of American society in the era under investigation (in the 1840s, the dominant groups comprised essentially of white Protestant groups of Northern and Western European origins; in the current era, they would include those groups characterized by middle- and upper-income socioeconomic status.)

If these newcomers wished to "make it," they would quickly shed their foreign, lower-class life-style and emulate the behavior of the established middle class, the group to which they aspired. They would go to school, work at respectable jobs, industriously save their modest wages, shun disreputable companions, and lead sober, exemplary lives. In substance, these ethnic groups would conform to the expectations of the dominant middle-class and upper-class groups, fulfilling their role in a diligent and enthusiastic manner. The dominants, in turn, would see their obvious worthiness and invite them into their midst for, in America's view, "they are people just like ourselves."

This typical interpretation of how these ethnic groups "made it" in American life consequently viewed ethnic mobility as a process wherein all groups conformed to the expectations and norms of the established society. This conformity allowed the ethnic group to move up the social class ladder, a move largely dependent upon the benevolence and good will of the dominant established society. This dominant society, through its economic, political, educational and religious spokes-men, set the ground rules in the form of both norms and laws, and the ethnic minorities were expected to follow the predetermined game plan.

The Horatio Alger Route: Myth or Reality?

Is such an interpretation of ethnic upward mobility accurate? Did each of the lower-class minorities "make it" by following the script set forth by the large American society?

Undoubtedly significant numbers of the newcomers *did* climb the success ladder in the accepted fashion, for our history books are filled with countless examples of such men and women from every group. These newcomers achieved the American Dream in a manner ap-plauded by both their fellow ethnics and the larger society. They have been presented as models worthy of honor and emulation, with biog-raphies scarcely different from those of Horatio Alger's fiction.

Yet these heroes comprised only a small segment of their respective ethnic groups. The vast majority of their fellows struggled with the daily realities and disappointments of lower-class life. Even though the heroes may have been admired by these fellows, there was little chance that their life experiences could be repeated by those less fortunate. Those ethnic heroes had been singled out for respect and praise, their lives representing a startling contrast to the lives of their ethnic breth-ren. It was as though the dominant society had said, "Here, follow the example of these men and women; they have made something of themselves by doing what we have suggested. You do likewise instead of living in the degradation of poverty and social chaos."

The vast majority of these newly arrived lower-income groups did not move swiftly from the lowest rungs of the status ladder. Their upward mobility was slow and tedious, their stay in the lower class far longer than ethnic sentimentalists care to admit. The textbook heroes were clearly exceptional cases. The bulk of their struggling brethren did not, and indeed could not, follow the accepted avenues of mobility laid out by the dominant middle-class American society, for these socially approved routes bore little semblance to the daily realities of lower-class life. Gladly did America accept the newcomer if he had economic means or possessed valued work skills. If he did not, his arrival was received with suspicion and disdain, with a welcome more appropriate to an intruder than to a desired guest.

Hostility to Newcomers

Periodically, violent methods were used to control the newcomers, political movements constituted to oppose them, philosophical ideologies devised to dehumanize them, and legislation enacted to exclude them. Violence and hatred were natural sequels to these conditions. So it was with the immigrants, whether African Americans, Germans, Scandinavians, Jews, Slavs, Greeks or Italians; so it is with contemporary migrants and immigrants whether blacks, Mexicans, Puerto Ricans, Haitians, Venezuelans, or Cubans. Regardless of their national origins, low ethnic status and lower-class status have precluded the social acceptance of newcomers in America who often were considered the "scum of the earth" (Burgess 1913, 186).

Yet not all immigrant newcomers were in fact lower class. Thus, German Jews who immigrated to America in the 1840s were predominately middle class, as were many political refugees of various ethnic groups in recent times (for example, significant numbers of Jews in the World War II era, Cubans in the 1960s, Filipinos in the 1970s and 1980s). However, the bulk of newcomers to America's farms and cities have been lower class.

Prejudice and discrimination prevented equal access to decent jobs, education, and eventual social respectability. Commonly in the 1850s, "Jobs available—Irish need not apply," signs faced the Irish and subsequently, each succeeding minority. On one hand, the larger society offered the opportunity of advancement beyond the lower class through job opportunities; on the other hand, it prevented access to the occupational route by discrimination, whether blatantly as with the early immigrants or subtly as with current minority groups. The dominant ideal was one that gave with one hand, yet in practice took away with the other.

Established Americans often feared those who were different from them. Those with alien traits, suspect religious beliefs, different skin color, peculiar political traditions, strange languages, and strange customs were ostracized. This hostility to outsiders was expressed in the early colonial period wherein settlers slaughtered Indians, exiled Catholics, and generally discriminated against anyone who differed from them in culture or religious belief. In the Massachusetts Bay Colony, for example, Quakers were beaten and driven from the community; in Connecticut, one had to be a Congregationalist to vote. This pattern continued after the founding of the Republic as many Americans remained ambivalent towards newcomers. Even though the new nation's culture developed patterns distinctly American—not English, Huguenot, or whatever—it still remained Protestant in its traditions and moral outlook, remaining hostile to those immigrants who differed from these patterns. (cf. Glazer 1978, 5) Some fear probably was justified, since the established Americans saw their most cherished Anglo-Saxon beliefs threatened by newcomers whom they stereotyped as Papists, drinkers, socialists, anarchists, and misfits. They came in large numbers. How would their institutions ever survive the tidal wave of newcomers? How could the American Republic avoid the onslaught of millions who simply had never been exposed to a democratic way of life? For some, fear converted itself into prejudice and hatred of the newcomers, impeding and frustrating assimilation.

In the 1840s events reached the crisis point with the massive waves of Irish Catholic immigrants, newcomers who shared few of the Anglo-Saxon ideals of the native American groups. These Irish arrived with their alien religion and their open hostility to British social and political institutions that had oppressed, disenfranchised, and humiliated them for centuries in Ireland. Their resentment of everything English was fueled by the deplorably slow and fainthearted reaction of the English to the Great Famine in Ireland in the mid-1840s. The Irish understandably had little desire to embrace an American Creed so accepting in its beliefs of English values.

Violent Nativism

Fear of the newcomer gradually evolved into discriminatory and retaliatory movements such as nativism—ideologies that favored the native inhabitants of the United States as against the newcomers. Generally the nativism of the established middle class remained nonviolent surfacing mainly in a vague resentment of both immigrants and the lower classes. However, lower-class nativism began to take on a more virulent form in the 1840s and 1850s with violent attacks on immigrants, starting with Irish Catholics and encompassing most incoming lower-income groups since. Sporadic as the violence was, the resentment against the newcomer was ever present.

Many of the these attacks took the form of nativistic riots—violent disorders wherein specific ethnic groups were attacked by members of the socially dominant groups (O'Kane 1975, 231). American social history is replete with dozens of examples of such disorders, for virtually every ethnic group had been subjected to violence. A partial list would include the victimization of the Irish in Boston in 1834 and in Philadelphia in 1844, the Germans in Louisville in 1855, the Chinese in Los Angeles in 1871, blacks in Vicksburg in 1874, the Italians in New Orleans in 1891, blacks again in East St. Louis and Chicago in 1919, and in Detroit in 1943, the Mexicans in Los Angeles in 1943. (Graham and Gurr 1969, Cp. 2; Hofstadter and Wallace 1970.

The fear also spawned political movements to destroy the newcomers growing demographic and political power. In the 1840s and 1850s, the American Native Party—the so-called Know-Nothings— politicized much of the resentment of the newcomer in platforms that were not only antiforeigner, but also anti-Catholic, and antiblack. The Know-Nothing Movement sought to oppose the entrance of the ethnic minorities into the mainstream through both legal and illegal means. Often the illegal methods gained the upper hand, for many communities had nativistic gangs who were "supporters" of the Know-Nothing Movement.

During election time, these gangs were used to harass newcomers. Irish Catholics in the 1850s were the primary victims of such violence. One Baltimore gang, the Blood Tubs, developed a particularly graphic method of intimidating Irish-Democratic voters. The members of the gang would fill large basins with blood collected from local butchers. They would then find some unsuspecting Irishman, strip him, and throw him in the basin, drenching him with blood. Following this, with drawn knives they would chase the victim through the Irish district. Needless to say, any Irishman on his way to the polls to vote would have second thoughts after witnessing such a terrifying act (Hofstadter and Wallace 1970, 93).

German newcomers were also subjected to similar harassment from nativists groups such as the Know-Nothings. In 1855 in Louisville,

Kentucky, twenty people were killed and several hundred injured after nativists marched and rioted in the German neighborhood.

The sympathy with the nativists' resentment of "foreign groups" extended to the highest echelons of American life. E. Digby Baltzell points out that Abraham Lincoln had many political and personal friends who were Know-Nothings. His wife once stated that his "weak woman's heart felt the necessity of keeping foreigners within bounds." However, it is quite apparent that Lincoln did not support the philosophy or programs of the Know-Nothings (Baltzell 1964, 25).

This type of raw violence did not continue for any extended period simply because the newcomers grew more numerous, more demographically concentrated, and thus more powerful. As they did, particularly in the cities of the northeast, they retaliated against the nativists and their surrogates, initiating what might be termed "ethnic reactive riots," disorders wherein the riot involved the active reaction of the ethnic minority to its treatment by the dominant social groups (O'Kane 1975, 231–32). The reactive riot represented a reversal of the nativistic riot, for the reactive rioters now became the attackers and controlled the riot.

The behavior of the Irish illustrated this point. The pattern of being victimized in scores of riots was reversed in the 1863 New York City Draft Riot, the worst such civil disorder in American history. In this riot the Irish were fully retaliatory and retributive towards the dominant groups in society. Much of the violence was initiated by Irish gangs, and for the duration of the riot they were largely in control. A week after the Union Army's victory at Gettysburg, federal troops were ordered by President Lincoln to New York by forced march to quell the riot. The Draft Riot proved to be the transition point for the Irish, since it signified the first of the large-scale reactions of subordinate groups to harassment. From this point on the Irish rarely suffered from direct nativistic attacks.

In substance, as the Irish became numerically strong in America's cities, and as they became aware of their ethnicity and their subcultural position, they no longer permitted nativist harassment. The reactive stance of the Irish in the 1860s depended upon this demographic factor, for without a "demographic critical mass"—a population size substantial enough to ward off violence—they could not have prevented nativistic attacks, nor have initiated their own reactive pattern. This critical mass helps us understand not only the Irish pattern, but the pattern of other ethnic group riots as well, particularly those of the blacks in the 1960s where the ethnic-reactive pattern repeats itself in dozens of urban riots (O'Kane 1975, 233ff).

The Draft Riot served as a transition point in New York City and after it the old native American and Irish relationships were never quite the same, for the Irish would no longer accept the violence of the dominant groups. Subsequent to this role reversal, the incidence of riots involving the Irish noticeably declined. Their growing demographic power, combined with their increasing dominance of the urban political system, constituted a substantial deterrent to those who in former decades might have attacked them, even though anti-Irish incidents occurred sporadically (e.g., in Al Smith's 1932 presidential campaign).

Ideological Attacks

As incidents of violence waned and came to be perceived as counterproductive, the opposition to the nation's ethnic minorities changed its focus. In the twentieth century, intellectual and ideological weapons increasingly replaced physical violence. These weapons included efforts to demonstrate scientifically that the newcomers were of inferior racial stock, that they were less human and less developed than the dominant groups, and consequently that they should be subordinate to the majority. This evolving "scientific racism" proposed the thesis that some races (i.e., the caucasian) are inherently superior to other races. In addition, the supposed inherited superior physical traits are accompanied by superior intellectual, moral, and cultural traits.

In the early 1900s this thesis attracted to its ranks some of the foremost representatives of established society, men and women of widespread influence with impeccable social and academic credentials who viewed large-scale immigration as a real threat to the American way of life with its Anglo-Saxon traditions. The basic dilemma revolved around the fact that virtually all of the newcomers, with the exception of German and some Scandinavian groups, shared little and cared even less about this Anglo-Saxon scenario for acceptance. The German immigrants arrived at approximately the same time as the Catholic Irish, but their presence constituted less of a threat to the dominant ethos. Though they did differ substantively from the native Americans on certain themes (e.g., a more liberal political outlook, an antitemperance position, a more liberal religious viewpoint, etc.) they had much in common with respect to social and political issues (Handlin 1979, 136ff).

The shock encountered by the native Americans over the arrival of millions of poverty-stricken alien Irish repeated itself constantly in mid-nineteenth- and early-twentieth-century America: massive numbers of African Americans migrated to northern areas with scarcely any appreciation of things Anglo-Saxon; millions of Jews, Slavs, Italians, and Greeks did likewise, bringing with them political ideas, social customs, religious beliefs, and life-styles increasingly abhorrent to the nativist.

Similar to other new arrivals to America's shores in the 1880s, Jewish immigrants encountered the sting of resentment and exclusion. In his discussion of the problems faced by Jewish newcomers, Irving Howe quotes the *New York Herald* of that era that viewed Jews as "obstructing the walks and sitting on chairs at the New York's Battery Park. They are filthy in their habits and most obstinate in their mode of living. They persist in keeping live fowls in their rooms." The *Tribune* reported that Jews "were accustomed to taking only one bath a year." Furthermore, "they are utter strangers to soap and water and are on social terms with parasitic vermin" (quoted in Howe 1976, 396).

Similar accounts depicted Italian immigrants of this same era:

> By his tongue and his ways, the Italian is felt to be a "foreigner" . . . he has a low standard of living, and that is ever an unpleasant consideration to those who wish to live better. His crowding and dirt are assumed to be his own choice. . . . His children are too numerous, and perhaps his low standard of living shows nowhere so plainly as in that pressure of baby cart upon push cart which makes the Italian streets of New York picturesque. (Forester 1919, 407–08)

By the end of the 1880s many in the dominant classes had despaired of assimilating these "unwashed masses," of America achieving a melting pot whereby all of these diverse groups would blend together, producing a new American race, superior to anything before it (Gordon 1964, Ch. 5). Crevecoeur's earlier dream of a melting pot wherein "individuals of all nations are melted into a new race of men, whose labors and posterity will one day cause great changes in the world" had, by the 1880s become a nightmare to a significant proportion of the leadership of the American establishment (Crevecoeur 1782).

By the 1900s the negative feelings against the newcomers became more intense throughout American society. The newcomers were now considered intruders and the economic instability induced by recurring financial panics created the social climate wherein the immigrants were viewed as the source of the nation's troubles. Even the advocates of assimilation of all newcomers began to lose confidence in their dream, for everywhere it appeared that the "hordes" of immigrants from Southern and Eastern Europe would overwhelm democracy and the American social system.

Caste and Racism

Largely abandoning any hope that the newcomers would assimilate into American society according to *their* ideas, significant segments of the native upper class hardened their positions and became what Baltzell has termed the "upper caste" (Baltzell 1966, 8ff). They feared that the massive arrival and intermingling of so many different groups would produce a bastardized American race, far different and grossly inferior to anything that either they or the Founding Fathers had ever envisioned or wanted.

Forsaking Anglo-conformity, fearing a real melting pot, they vigorously embraced xenophobic policies. By the latter part of the nineteenth century, increasing numbers of intellectuals and ideologists now joined the nativist in a "sophisticated" condemnation of the ethnic minorities, particularly those represented in the "new" immigration (1870–1914—Jews, Italians, Slavs, Greeks, etc.).

African Americans were similarly castigated, characterized as less than human. Melville Herskovits cites a quote by H.W. Odum, a respected writer of his time who in 1902 wrote:

> The Negro has little home conscience or love of home. . . . He has no pride of ancestry . . . has few ideals . . . little conception of the meaning of virtue, truth, honor, manhood, integrity. He is shifty, untidy, and indolent . . . the migratory or roving tendency seems to be a natural one to him. The Negro is improvident and

extravagant; . . . he lacks initiative; he is often dishonest and untruthful. He is over-religious and superstitious . . . his mind does not conceive of faith in humanity—he does not comprehend it. (Herskovitz 1958, 22)

It should be mentioned that Odum's position in 1902 was viewed as one of the more sympathetic ones vis-à-vis African Americans!

Increasingly some members of the elite groups of American society promoted the notion of the innate superiority of the Anglo-Saxon over other "races." This self-comforting view enabled them to characterize themselves as dedicated defenders of the dominant cultural ethos, one which many of them sincerely believed was being overwhelmed by the massive waves of newcomers of inferior racial stock who were "mongrelizing" the nation. With such firmly entrenched views, it is not difficult to see why they so ardently embraced organizations such as the eugenics movement that sought to improve the "American race" by selective breeding of preferred males and females and formed groups and associations such as the Immigration Restriction League that would lobby for the cessation of immigration. Nor is it coincidental that the rise and growth of violent, xenophobic organizations such as the Ku Klux Klan occurred and reached their zenith of power in this same era following the end of World War I.

Immigrant Restrictions

The first successes at controlling the influx of immigrants occurred on the west coast, with numerous punitive actions directed at the Chinese in the 1870s and 1880s and the Japanese in the early 1900s. Following the Civil War, nativist groups and their sympathizers who often were themselves second- and even first-generation Americans attacked Chinese immigrants in a number of riots in California and Wyoming. Nativist fears centered on potential economic competition from the Chinese and Japanese, along with the resentment of their "alien" customs, language, and manners. Like other ethnic minorities on the east coast, the oriental newcomers were regarded as inferior and dangerous and it was held that their immigration to America should thus be prohibited. Roy Garis presents this position, stating, "For America, the Japanese are non-assimilable people, as are all Asiatics, and little could be gained by the continuance of a policy contrary to

America's interests and which removed from our control a universally recognized domestic problem" (Garis 1927, 352).

In responding to nativist fears and pressures, Congress enacted legislation to restrict oriental immigration. In 1882 the Chinese Exclusion Act effectively cut off Chinese immigration. Though this legislation sought to exclude the entry of Chinese laborers, its provisions were soon expanded to other ethnic groups. In 1917 Congress prohibited immigration from additional areas in Asia, restricted immigration on the basis of national origin from other areas of the globe, and mandated a literacy test requirement for all immigrants.

The restrictions continued in 1921 and 1924 with the further limitation of all immigration via the quota system based on the national origins of those seeking entry to America. What had started as local legislation to prohibit Asian immigration on the west coast had now evolved into federal law effectively curtailing mass immigration of those ethnic groups least likely to approximate the Anglo-Saxon standard of the nativist. Even groups that previously had been favored were now excluded. In 1934, the Philippines, a United States protectorate, had its immigration quota set at fifty per year; in 1946 following independence, this quota was raised to one hundred! The nation would have to wait decades before these restrictive rules were liberalized.

Liberalization of Immigration Policy

The move to liberalize the restrictive immigration policies of the 1920s culminated in the passage of the 1965 Hart-Cellar Act that abolished the quota system based on national origins and that opened American doors to those groups previously denied admission — Chinese, Indians, Greeks, Colombians, Haitians, Koreans, Nigerians, Filipinos, and so on. Filipinos, for example, entered the United States in large numbers 276,000 between 1967 and 1976, and the 1980 census estimates that 750,000 legal Filipinos reside in the United States.

Gradually, the restrictive ethos of nativism and xenophobia gave way to a fairer system of immigrant selection and these new groups coming to America's shores eagerly tackled the American Dream. Frequently settling in inner cities, many of them have already made their mark on American life. As Louis Winnick states,

Most of today's new immigrants are strivers with a higher participation rate in the labor force than native Americans. Many of them exhibit a work ethnic that shrinks the exalted Protestant ethic to indolence. Others, like their predecessors, climb a crooked ladder to achievement—the Chinese teenage extortion gangs, the Colombian hidalgos of cocaine and, yes, the Odessa mafia of Brighton Beach. Many burden the schools with formidable teaching problems while others carry away, with astronomic regularity, all the glittering prizes. In weighing pluses and minuses, we find the latest wave (of newcomers) to yield a wide margin of benefits. (Winnick 1988)

For the most part, these latest newcomers settle near the bottom of our class ladder, setting up their green groceries, clothing stores, and car repair shops; working as janitors, short-order cooks, hotel attendants, gardeners, factory hands, and assembly line workers; servicing the economy and the middle classes. The more fortunate newcomers enter the professions, capitalizing on their previous backgrounds as nurses, doctors, lawyers, accountants, and teachers. Each though encounters a new life with its hopes and perils and each must come to terms with the demands and rewards of the American Dream.

Inadequacy of Existing Theoretical Explanations of Ethnic Assimilation

The historical findings cited suggest that the Anglo-conformity and melting pot approaches are inadequate explanations of the ethnic upward mobility of newcomers in American life. Perhaps the Anglo-conformity position—the viewpoint that things British were the goals to which newcomers should aspire—had been operative and viable before the 1840s; after that, it ceased to serve as a realistic assimilation model simply because the millions of newcomers to America's cities—Irish Catholics, Germans, Chinese, Slavs, Italians, Jews, Greeks, blacks, Hispanics—possessed few British "traits," beliefs, or inclinations. After the 1840s there remained little realistic hope of America becoming a carbon copy of Mother England and the Anglo-conformity approach endured only as a wishful fantasy of older stock Americans rather than a blueprint to be followed by new arrivals.

The melting pot approach likewise remained a dream, for the lessons of the past 150 years of American social history clearly indicated that a true melting pot has not yet occurred. America is, if anything, a compilation of a myriad of ethnic, regional, religious and socioeconomic subcultures. As many social scientists have previously pointed out, there may in fact be a multiplicity of "pots," each significantly different from the other in essential aspects (Kennedy 1944). Will Herberg presents the argument that the solvent for the melting pot is religion, which has become the common denominator in the assimilation process in America. People marry *within* the confines of Protestantism, Catholicism, or Judaism, embracing the cultural and moral convictions of that specific faith (Herberg 1955, 34). Lee argues persuasively that there are actually four melting pots—white Protestant, white Roman Catholic, white Jewish, and nonwhite—and that the assimilation which takes place occurs *within* each group more so than between each group (Lee 1966, ch. 17). A future single melting pot there may be, but the contemporary evidence argues against those who dream of "a biological merger of the Anglo-Saxon peoples with other immigrant groups and a blending of their respective cultures into a new indigenous American type" (Gordon 1964, 85). What may be taking place is a gradual assimilation and blending of different groups, reflected in intermarriage among Protestants, Catholics, Jews, American Indians, and blacks.

The remaining prominent theoretical explanation of ethnic and immigrant assimilation—the cultural pluralism approach—argues that incoming ethnic groups preserve their language, communal institutions, religious heritage, and family patterns. They simultaneously adopt the English language and participate in the economic and political life of America. They have not become Anglo-Saxon, nor have they "melted" into a new "race." Horace Kallen, the foremost proponent of this position, saw that the newcomers preserved much of their old culture and added much more from the new. To Kallen, these multitudinous ethnic subcultures exist side by side with each other in America's cities, each considering itself as American as the next. American democracy represents a harmony of these different groups, who together created and orchestrated the unity of the nation (Kallen 1924; see also Gordon 1964, ch. 6).

Yet as an explanation of how groups assimilate into the middle-class mainstream, the cultural pluralism position is deficient. Distinctive ethnic minorities may coexist, yet this thesis says nothing of the manner by which different newcomer groups remove themselves from the lowest steps of the socioeconomic ladder and take their places at the

center of American life, nor does assimilation necessarily involve upward mobility. This approach remains more a descriptive analysis of
the heterogeneity of American life than a predictive model of the
assimilation process. Milton Gordon examines the cultural pluralism
thesis in depth and concludes that a much more important concept is
structural pluralism (Gordon 1964, 81, 158).

Here we see how Gordon branches off from the usual rendering of
cultural pluralism theory. His work, however, doesn't dwell on the
actual process of ethnic mobility; it relates more directly to the main-
tenance of ethnic identification and structural assimilation. As with its
Anglo-conformity and melting pot forerunners, cultural pluralism fails
to represent adequately the upward mobility process and assimilation
of ethnic minorities.

The Anglo-conformity, melting pot, and cultural pluralism approaches say little of the social conflict evident between newcomers
and the more established groups in America. These interpretations
treat the assimilation process as a demographic phenomenon impervi-
ous to social and political conflicts. Each assumes that the absorption
of newcomers took place in a benign manner, that tensions between
new and old groups were minimal, if not nonexistent, and that the
passage of time alone accounted for the absorption of the newcomers
into the social, economic, political, and cultural mainstream. Simply
stated, conflict, whether it be in the form of prejudice and discrimination, or of violence, is minimized in these theories.

A cursory reading of America's social history clearly illustrates the
presence of such conflict as an important factor in the subsequent
behavior of both established groups and newcomers. A more realistic
stance is required that accounts for the movement of ethnic minorities
out of the bottom of society. Included in it should be an analysis of the
broader issue of social conflict, and how that conflict influenced the
social and political ways in which ethnic minorities perceived their
chances of upward mobility and subsequently acted upon these per-
ceptions.

The Newcomer's Paradox

Considering this sociohistorical picture, it is not difficult to unveil
the suspicion and, at times, outright hostility directed against the new-

comers, past and present. Their movement into the mainstream of American life has been and continues to be infinitely more complicated than the Horatio Algers would have it; (see O'Kane 1969). Indeed the climb from the bottom is exceedingly difficult, with the higher status groups—whether they be native Americans or former ethnic minorities—impeding the lower-class newcomers every step of the way, denying them access to respectable jobs, formal education, and social respectability. Deprived of these prerequisites, the ethnic minorities have little chance of achieving their own upward mobility exclusively through the conventionally accepted routes. If significant upward mobility is to take place, alternative avenues of advancement have to be considered and, if appropriate, utilized as additional vehicles in the climb from the bottom.

2

The Climb from the Bottom

What were the means or routes that newcomers used in pulling themselves from the bottom rungs of the American social class ladder? How did they deal with what they had been promised in life and what actually was available to them?

Others have specified what the routes of upward mobility used throughout American history may have been. I recall a graduate lecture in 1963 at Columbia University when Richard Cloward, a professor of sociology, indicated that labor, crime, and politics comprised the key routes used by immigrant minorities in climbing the status ladder. In these lectures he frequently referred to the work of another sociologist, Daniel Bell, in underlining the importance of one of these routes— crime (Bell 1960, 128ff). Bell has, of course, become somewhat famous in identifying crime as a "queer" avenue of success in America, so much so that in his estimation, crime is literally an American way of life.

E. Digby Baltzell also indicates the availability of alternate routes to success and respectability: "As the traditional ways to wealth and respectability were more or less monopolized by Protestant Americans of older stock, many of the more talented and ambitious members of minority groups found careers in urban politics, in organized crime or for those of the Catholic faith, in the hierarchy of the church" (Baltzell 1966, 49). In addition, Will Herberg speaks of the importance of the interrelationship of ethnicity and religious affiliation and the role of the ethnic clergy in leading ethnic minorities from the bottom of the class ladder (Herberg 1960, 160). Herberg and I were colleagues at Drew University and spent many rewarding hours discussing various routes, with Herberg focusing attention on how each of the alternative routes interrelated with the others. Arthur Schlesinger has also commented on the importance of marginal occupations for incoming groups in nineteenth-century America (Schlesinger 1969, xxiv).

In this analysis, I would like to utilize the works of Robert Merton, Richard Cloward, and Lloyd Ohlin in outlining how ethnic minorities climb the ladder of success, and what role crime plays in this trek.

Robert Merton provides a model through which we can understand what newcomers do when confronted with a situation wherein they desire all that America offers but are unable to utilize the means necessary to achieve their desires because of the hostility of the established society. He identifies four such responses or adaptations to this dilemma, considering each of them deviant responses since they are condemned by the larger society. These are: innovation, ritualism, retreatism, and rebellion. The innovator seeks to attain the dominant social goals of American society (e.g., success, wealth, etc.) but uses illegitimate means to accomplish these goals; the ritualist abandons these goals but continues slavishly to use the legitimate means for their attainment; the retreatist forsakes and abandons both the goals and means to them; the rebel substitutes new goals and new means for the conventional ones.

Innovation as an Adaptive Response

Of the four adaptations, innovation fits best in explaining the response of both former and contemporary ethnic minorities to the assimilation dilemma. They greatly desired success and upward social mobility, yet the hostility and prejudice of the larger society prevented the easy attainment of these cultural goals.

With respect to innovation, newcomers wanted what America offered. The cultural goals were clearly set forth, and the newcomers had little difficulty identifying with these. The *means* to these goals created the ethnic minorities' dilemma, for the open access to these means was largely denied them. Because of their social, economic, political, and religious ostracism, the newcomers developed new ways of removing themselves from lower-class poverty using additional modes of mobility other than those approved and offered by the large American society. To gain a toehold in the higher, more affluent classes, they had but one viable option—that of circumventing the established routes of upward mobility denied them. In turn they pioneered new routes, some of which proved to be unacceptable to the dominant society. In this sense, the ethnic minorities made an "end run" around the conventional, accepted social expectations rather than directly and abortively confronting them. Inevitable conflict with the larger society resulted, a conflict over some of the *means* to the society's ends and goals. Innovation constituted the primary response of the newcomers' paradoxical manner of "making it" yet further analysis beyond the Mertonian interpretation is needed to demonstrate how it functioned.

Legitimate and Illegitimate Opportunities—Richard Cloward and Lloyd Ohlin's Contribution

Richard Cloward (1959) takes Merton's analysis one step further. He advances the idea of differential opportunity structures: not only are there differentials in access to social goals through *legitimate means*, but also through *illegitimate means*. Cloward and Ohlin (1960) extend this concept of illegitimate means to an explanation of delinquency. They argue that delinquency and crime result from the discrepancy between what lower-income youths desire and what is realistically available to them. They want what American society offers and expects of all—success—yet they are prevented from legitimately achieving this goal because of opportunity blockage, that is, poverty and discrimination. Blocked from legitimate means to success, unable to modify their goal of success, these youths turn to illegitimate means of achieving it. However, these illegitimate means are also differentially distributed, for the attainment of success in the deviate realm encounters the same impediments of poverty and discrimination found in the conventional world. Thus Cloward and Ohlin go on to specify the forms that this illegitimate access to socially approved success goals take: the criminal subculture, the conflict subculture, and the retreatist subculture (Cloward and Ohlin 1960, chs. 6 and 7).

Cloward and Ohlin's fruitful analysis of the forms that illegitimate means may take advances the work of Merton. Their work likewise assists our analysis of the ethnic minority's situation for the newcomers also encountered the blockages of poverty and discrimination in their quest for the socially expected goals of economic success, educational achievement, and so on.

But how did the new arrivals to America's industrial cities deal with this opportunity blockage? How did they react to the poverty and discrimination that effectively precluded their success? How did they adapt to these conditions? What routes of mobility did they take in attempting to attain the American Dream?

In an earlier work I identified only three of these routes: unskilled labor, ethnic politics, and ethnic crime, yet these routes do not encompass sufficiently the actual experience of upward mobility (O'Kane 1969). The addition of the four routes outlined below seems to approximate the reality more closely.

Ethnic minorities utilized at least seven core routes of mobility from the lower classes to the middle classes. These are (a) unskilled and semiskilled labor; (b) retail small business; (c) the professions; (d) the clergy; (e) entertainment; (f) urban politics; (g) organized crime. The first five routes describe legitimate, acceptable avenues to America's goals since the larger dominant society considers them to be more or less "normal" pursuits of incoming ethnic minorities. The sixth route— urban politics—can be considered to be a semilegitimate mode of upward mobility since the established society is ambivalent towards ethnic politicians; it accepts them as legitimate actors performing their parts in the normal democratic process within the nation, but oftentimes is fearful and hostile to the actual ways in which they perform their roles. The final route—organized crime—is clearly illegitimate, for the larger society views the ethnic criminal's behavior as outside the pale of normal conventional behavior, something to be shunned and controlled.

These seven routes of upward mobility constitute ideal types, but different ethnic minorities used different combinations of them. The lower-income Irish of a century ago used unskilled and semiskilled labor, the clergy, politics, and crime; all of which comprised key paths to their success. For the Jews, labor, retail businesses, the professions, entertainment, and organized crime comprised main vehicles to success. African Americans have used and continue to use labor, entertainment, the clergy, politics, and organized crime. Each group tends to channel maximum effort into one of these routes, while giving secondary emphasis to the remaining ones. Thus, the Irish tended to emphasize urban politics; Jews, the professions; Italians, Greeks, Koreans, and Armenians, small businesses; African Americans, religious leadership, and so on. Thus, each incoming group does not utilize all seven of the modes of mobility with equal frequency. Each group also had to contend with other ethnic minority members who were entrenched in these routes as well, and the conflict between ethnic groups often was more intense than that between the ethnic newcomers and the dominant established mainstream groups: Jewish and Italian politicians had to confront Irish politicians; African-American musicians and athletes had to break into entertainment and sports domains dominated by white ethnics, and so on.

Legitimate Routes

The five legitimate routes created circumstances conducive to the gradual upward social mobility of the nation's ethnic minorities. The larger society regarded favorably those newcomers pursuing legitimate channels of advancement, viewing them as fulfilling the accepted version of the American Dream through hard work, clean living, industriousness, individualism, and proper respect for those in higher social positions. Let us examine each of these legitimate routes.

Labor

The unskilled and skilled labor route provided the newcomer with a relative degree of economic security. Lacking the prerequisite background necessary for higher positioning in an industrial society, newcomers found themselves relegated to the dirtiest and most menial of jobs—farming and farm labor, working in sweatshops and factories, digging canals, laying railroad track, working in low-skilled construction trades, and engaging in dozens of similar positions deemed socially and economically unfit for those in more fortunate circumstances.

Indeed, appalling working conditions existed for both male and female newcomers to America's industrial centers. Wright describes such conditions confronting young women in the 1880s in Boston: "It is interesting to note the 'life' experiences of a few who have been at

work for a number of years and have a history, and from them learn
what the future of working girls entirely dependent on their own labor
may be, if the conditions developed in regard to small pay, etc., should
continue." She continues, describing numerous case histories of young
working women, among which is the following:

> In a garret, four stories up, was found a machine operator on men's clothing who
> said she was married at the age of 20; her husband was consumptive but lived 16
> years after her marriage. During her married life she worked more or less, at home
> and in stores. She has two children, a boy of 11 and a girl of 5, but they do not now
> live with her; up to a short while since, the boy lived with her and went to school;
> her work failing, she could not pay his board in advance, and he was sent to live
> with relatives. At night, after working through the day, she makes clothes for her
> children and does her own sewing and washing; she has not had a new dress for
> three years, and she says it sometimes costs a good deal more than she earns to
> provide for herself and children, and that she has often had to go without her
> supper." (Wright 1889, cited in Feldstein and Costello 1974, 277)

But this "poor-but-honest" work offered a ray of hope for newcomers and their families in moving upward in American life. The historical record clearly shows the mistreatment and low pay that they received; yet their meager but growing savings enabled the newcomers to
commence the ever-so-slow process of mobility from the conditions of
poverty and misery. Some even managed to parlay this humble labor
into more lucrative endeavors. Mario Puzo humorously relates how
some in his family "made it" through legitimate jobs that presented
opportunities for mischief:

> There was one of our uncles who worked as an assistant chef in a famous Italian-
> style restaurant. Every day, six days a week, this uncle brought home, under his
> shirt, six eggs, a stick of butter, and a small bag of flour. By doing this for thirty
> years he was able to save enough money to buy a fifteen-thousand dollar house on
> Long Island and two smaller houses for his son and daughter. Another cousin,
> blessed with a college degree, worked as a chemist in a large manufacturing firm.
> By using the firm's raw materials and equipment, he concocted a superior floor
> wax which he sold door-to-door in his spare time. It was a great floor wax and with
> his low overhead, the price was right. My mother and her friends did not think this
> stealing. They thought of it as being thrifty.

> The wax-selling cousin eventually destroyed his reputation for thrift by buying a
> sailboat; this was roughly equivalent to the son of a Boston brahmin spending a
> hundred grand in a whorehouse. (Wheeler 1971, 40).

Labor in the unskilled and semiskilled occupations offered the new-comers a beginning from which they could maintain themselves and their families. Labor in these mean and difficult jobs became the "tool" that helped them gain entry to the American economy. If they occupied the lowest rung of the class ladder, at least they were on the ladder. Thus, ethnic labor became the basic foundation for the subse-quent mobility of the nation's newcomers, and since the vast bulk of incoming ethnic minorities were so employed, this route of upward mobility must be considered the most important.

The trade union movement greatly assisted these newcomers in uti-lizing their labor as a vehicle of upward mobility. The conditions of low pay, terrible working conditions, long working hours, inadequate health and social security benefits spurred the labor movement in the nineteenth and early twentieth centuries. Trade union leaders became the primary "vox populi," voicing the grievances and concerns of the newcomers, for they were instrumental in correcting the economic abuses under which newcomers lived and labored. With rare excep-tion, these union organizers, themselves unskilled and semiskilled la-borers, lived and worked among their impoverished brethren. The remaining routes of upward mobility carried little attraction for these trade unionists, and if they did participate in these routes (e.g., crime, politics) they did so as a way of enhancing their union roles. For them, crime and ward politics constituted means to bettering the working conditions for their union membership.

The numbers engaged in the other routes of small businesses, pro-fessions, clergy, entertainment, politics, and crime were small and depended either directly or indirectly on the prior presence of massive numbers of newcomers in the ranks of labor. The more ambitious members of the incoming ethnic minorities managed and profession-ally served, spiritually ministered, politically courted, and criminally preyed upon these newcomers. Unskilled labor comprised the critical artery supplying the economic sustenance to those utilizing the re-maining avenues of advancement. The overwhelming numbers of an ethnic minority employed as unskilled labor nurtured the scarce few pursuing other avenues of success, for without them these other routes of mobility would wither. In turn, they assisted the larger ethnic group in its upward trek.

Retail Small Businesses

This route attracted those newcomers seeking to better themselves in entrepreneurial careers. They became store owners, dry-goods sales-men, tailors, pawnbrokers, butchers, green grocers, bakers, diner own-ers, candy store proprietors, and operated dozens of similar small businesses devoted to serving the economic needs of their own ethnic group. Unsatisfied with the limited prospects of a future in a no-exit, low-skilled, or semiskilled job, they saved their pennies and nickels and eventually became "independent," setting up their own small businesses. Many, of course, did not survive economically in these businesses, but those who did earned respect for themselves and in many instances amassed small fortunes from these entrepreneurial en-deavors. Their vehicle out of the lower classes was the small retail shop. It enabled them to undergo the transition to the middle class, with its rewards of respectability and social position. In so journeying, these small-business proprietors became mediators, pursuing not only their own individual odysseys of upward mobility, but also assisting the bulk of the lower-income newcomers in their climb from the bot-tom rungs of the social ladder. Kenneth Kusmer (1986) has phrased this as follows: "In the nineteenth century, especially, there was a symbolic relationship between the ethnic working class and the more successful members of the community. Upward mobility occurred for ethnic businessmen, but within a context of reciprocal community obligations that contained the upwardly mobile" (Kusmer 1986, 45).

Many ethnic minorities epitomize this emphasis on mobility via the retail small business route, most notably Jews, Italians, Armenians, Greeks, Chinese, Japanese, Koreans, and West Indian blacks. Of these, perhaps the Chinese are the most noteworthy. During the latter part of the nineteenth century, Chinese immigrants worked largely in un-skilled labor positions, building railroads, laboring as miners, serving as domestics, and working in hand laundries. Yet slowly they with their wives and children moved into small retail businesses that ser-viced the needs, not only of fellow Chinese immigrants, but eventually of other groups as well. As Ivan Light states,

> For employment, Chinese had principally to look to domestic service, laundry work, restaurants, and small retail stores catering principally to other Chinese.

Whites rarely objected to Chinese in domestic service. They usually tolerated Chinese in the laundry trade, since this occupation was not one in which white males cared to engage. Chinese-owned restaurants were also tolerated. Serving cheap, appetizing meals, they were able, after 1896, to win the patronage of the white middle class. For the Chinese in the United States, obtaining a livelihood was a question of scraping the bottom of the barrel after the whites had helped themselves. (Light 1971, 7)

As opportunities presented themselves, the Chinese quickly took advantage of them and gradually moved into the middle-class American mainstream, particularly after World War II. In so doing, they left the confines of employment in Chinatowns and increasingly abandoned self-employment in retail business, preferring the more prestigious positions associated with white-collar professional classes.

The example of the Chinese has been duplicated many times over by other groups for the route of small business serves as a stepping stone to middle-class respectability for virtually all newcomer groups. In his study of recent Korean immigrants to the United States, Illsoo Kim (1981) clearly illustrates this point. Following the liberalization of immigration laws after 1965, thousands of Korean newcomers journeyed to America's cities, and frequently set up small greengrocery businesses. In New York City, as Kim notes,

Korean immigrants with an abundance of family labor but little capital have either pushed out or taken over the businesses of old Jewish and Italian shopkeepers, who are too old to compete with a new generation of relatively young and economically aggressive Koreans. (Kim 1984, 110)

He cites three structural factors which have enabled Koreans to pursue this route of small business success:

These businesses can be opened with little capital and managed without extensive knowledge of English; Koreans are willing and able to use an abundance of family labor; Koreans are willing to work long hours and thus compete favorably with larger supermarket chains. (Kim 1984, 110ff)

Thus, like the Chinese laundryman, the Jewish tailor, the Italian coal and ice man of past generations, Koreans, Caribbean blacks, Indians, and Vietnamese of contemporary America pursue entrepreneurial futures in retail outlets with as much ingenuity and skill as their predecessors.

Not all incoming groups are as successful in these small businesses.

African Americans have been noticeably underrepresented in small businesses. As Light has pointed out,

> the conspicuously missing figure is the black retail proprietor who does business in a black neighborhood and specializes in appliances, furniture, clothing, liquor or groceries. In fact this figure is missing because few black people operate such retail stores. In every large black neighborhood in the United States, white proprietors virtually monopolize retail trade. (Light 1972, 3)

Stolank and Friedman also offer similar reasons why certain ethnic groups are predominant in small business and others scarcely represented (Stolank and Friedman 1986).

The Professions

Still others pursued careers in the "learned" professions, and the "semi" professions. Many newcomers became doctors, dentists, lawyers, teachers, accountants, settlement-house workers, social workers, police, nurses, civil servants, reporters, editors, and funeral directors. They lived and worked in their own ethnic communities and, for the most part, spent their professional lives relating exclusively to that ethnic community.

They became parochial professionals, pursuing middle-class status from *within* their group rather than moving *beyond* the group into the unknown world of the dominant established middle class. Their sons and daughters would opt for middle-class professional futures but would do so by abandoning the ethnic neighborhood—the so-called ghetto— discarding much of the ethnic "baggage" of their parents' generation.

Like the clergy and the small business proprietors, these ethnic professionals constituted a mediating influence between the masses of their newcomer brethren and the dominant society. They interpreted the norms and values of the larger middle-class society and rendered them intelligible to the newcomer as they served in leadership roles in the myriad number of ethnic fraternal, social, political, and religious clubs and organizations; in turn, these professionals represented the interest and aspirations of the ethnic group to the larger society. Their status and prestige consequently stems from this crucial bridging of the two disparate cultures, and their mediating role greatly assisted not only their own personal mobility but the eventual mobility of the entire ethnic community.

Each incoming ethnic minority thus produced a handful of energetic men and women who entered professional careers. As Handlin notes, "A few professional men—doctors, lawyers, pharmacists, clergymen, and politicians—also catered to the needs of the people they understood and who trusted them. The children of the newest arrivals had no more desire to follow their parents' occupations than had earlier generations of Americans. In escaping from the immigrant callings to the professions, they found ties to their ancestral groups, supplemented by education and skills acquired in America, particularly advantageous" (Handlin 1962, 26).

Some moved directly to the prestigious professions of law, medicine, dentistry, social work, accounting, and so on via the mechanism of higher education. Others made the transition to the "semi" professions, concentrating on the civil service bureaucracies, becoming police and firefighters, newspaper reporters, and settlement house workers by means of formal education, though not necessarily college and post-graduate education. Together the "learned" and the "semi" professionals provided a solid core of the leadership in the ethnic community. When combined with the other routes of mobility, these professionals enabled the ethnic group to voice its concerns and aspirations effectively, helping implement the resultant changes in the larger social order.

Yet, unlike the style of other types of ethnic leadership, the style of the professional is somewhat stodgy and phlegmatic. As John Higham notes,

> the professional is distinguished not by passion . . . but rather by technical competence gained through advanced education. . . . On the whole, ethnic professionals seem to offer a relatively practical, accommodating style of leadership rather than a highly militant or ideological style. Enjoying widening success and esteem, they are little inclined to jeopardize their improving social status. (Higham 1980, 647)

Thus the ethnic professional's style and mode of leadership aids the newcomers in adjusting to their new social situation in America's urban industrial centers. The professional seeks slow, evolutionary, incremental reforms rather than radical, revolutionary changes.

This is characteristic even of those professions thought to be in the forefront of social change. Many think of the profession of social work as such a vehicle for radical social change, one that aims at uplifting the poor and elevating them to middle-class respectability. Indeed many young men and women enter graduate social work education with such intentions. Yet the real world of professional social work turns out to be far different, for the daily ethos of the profession is not conducive to substantive change in American society, but is more geared to what Frances Piven and Richard Cloward have aptly termed "regulating the poor" (Piven and Cloward 1971).

The heyday of radical movements within social work occurred in the 1960s with community action programs, the poverty programs, and the welfare rights movements. The community organization brand of social work had temporarily eclipsed the casework orientation, arguing that the cancer of poverty would be excised with the radical surgery of social change rather than with the band aid approach of individual counseling and psychotherapy. Such, though, did not occur, and social work has become static, seeking modest change rather than radical change. Social work is typical of the other professions as well, for none of them have, or probably could, radically alter the social milieu in which newcomers function. The ethnic professional career path thus attracts those interested in bettering themselves and the people whom they serve, seeking to make something of their lives, modestly endeavoring to meet the needs of those around them. Jack Agueros, a Puerto Rican writer and community organizer, discusses his early hopes of practicing medicine as a way of assisting others:

> I am an only child. My parents and I have always talked about my becoming a doctor. The law and politics were not highly regarded in my house. Lawyers, my mother would explain, had to defend people whether they were guilty or not, while politicians, my father would say, were all crooks. A doctor helped everybody, rich and poor, white and black. If I became a doctor, I could study hay fever and find a cure for it, my grandmother would say. Also, I could take care of my parents when they were old. I liked the idea of helping, and for nineteen years my sole ambition was to study medicine. (Agueros 1971, 91)

Each incoming ethnic minority has utilized the professions as one avenue of upward mobility. For example, the Irish chose finance and the civil services, particularly the fire and police departments; the Jews chose the "learned" professions of medicine, dentistry, and law. African Americans and other contemporary minorities are increasingly found in governmental areas where civil service status affords some protection from the discrimination found in other professional areas; Filipinos frequently are found in the nursing profession. Combined with the other routes of upward mobility, the professions provided a realistic avenue of movement from the bottom for those newcomers so inclined to use that route.

The choice of various professions by ethnic newcomers is probably due to actual realistic opportunities more than to the cultural traditions of that group. There is little in the background of the Irish in nineteenth-century Ireland that would have indicated their eventual success in urban politics in America. The success of Jews in the learned profession has more to do with opportunities in America than with the tradition of Talmudic learning. Slater, for example, questions the importance of Talmudic scholarship in the *shtetl* (the small Jewish hamlets scattered throughout Eastern Europe) as the key factor in the educational upward mobility of American Jews. She argues that commercial success preceded the large-scale movement of Jews into the professions: "The proclivity to professionalism appeared only after commercial success; therefore, it must be attributed to the co-existent secular rather than religious goals to which the humblest also felt entitled" (Slater 1969, 372).

Clergy

For those with similar luck or talent, other outlets for their abilities presented new opportunities. Many entered the clergy as priests, nuns, rabbis, preachers, and ministers so as to meet the spiritual and social needs of their ethnic brethren. This clerical route enabled these more ambitious members of incoming ethnic groups to raise their personal status while simultaneously striving to better the lot of their fellows within a context acceptable and legitimate to the dominant society. In working within their own ethnic group, clergy represented not only the newcomers' interests and concerns to the larger society, but greatly assisted their ethnic fellows in their socializaton to the norms of the dominant social ethos. Their social function frequently entailed working along with legitimate structures, assisting the assimilation of the newcomers while concurrently attempting to remedy those social conditions detrimental to the newcomers' welfare.

The importance of clerical leadership is best illustrated in the cases of Irish and black ethnic minorities. Each group looked to its "men of the cloth" for support, and endowed these clerics with enormous amounts of adulation and power, for they often provided the grass roots organization and talent so necessary for the newcomer groups' dealings with the larger, often hostile dominant society.

Irish Catholic priests immigrated to America together with their parishioners. The Irish bestowed on these priests considerable honor and respect, for frequently in Ireland the local priest was the only leader the peasants trusted. English penal laws denied Catholics formal education; priests, educated secretly in French seminaries, constituted the only truly educated group among Catholics. The priest filled the leadership vacuum created by English colonial policy and directed his parish not only in religious matters, but in political, social, and educational matters as well. His parishioners respected him and rarely challenged his viewpoint. He epitomized the struggle and aspirations of the Irish peasantry that had to deal with landlords and political overseers who often despised them.

Upon arrival in America, Irish Catholics quickly built churches and schools, and their clergy continued as their early spokesmen and "political" leaders. Bishops, frequently immigrants themselves, became the intermediaries between the masses of lower-class Irish and the Anglo-Saxon Protestant establishment of the nation.

One cannot overestimate the status of the priest in the lower-income Irish Catholic community. Parents often prayed that one of their sons be blessed with a vocation to the priesthood, and spared no expense in the insuring that boys so honored would be able to complete the rigorous training necessary. Having a son a priest was far more important to these parents than economic mobility. Just as commentators humorously speak about Jewish mothers who refer to "my son, the doctor" so also did Irish mothers speak of "my son, who I'm sure you know is a priest." Similar social honor accrued to Irish women who entered religious communities as nuns, dedicating their lives to God through work in teaching, and nursing. In such an environment many gifted, talented, and ambitious young men and women left their lower-income roots and became clerics and religious leaders. Certainly in the nineteenth century it was one of the few options available to the Irish seeking a better life, one in which they could meet the needs—spiritual and nonspiritual—of those fellow newcomers struggling in the Irish wards of the cities.

African Americans also endowed their religious leaders with enormous respect and authority. Like the Irish, they faced conditions of servitude and oppression that scarcely allowed for formal education, for in the antebellum South the only real black institution permitted to function openly was the church. The church, whether formal or informal, encompassed the hopes, dreams, needs, and sorrows of African Americans. Its ministers and preachers became the spokesmen of the community and for generations, provided, and still provide, for the spiritual, social, and political needs of their congregations. Most black political leadership historically has come from these local churches producing the Adam Clayton Powells, the Martin Luther Kings, the Andrew Youngs, the Jesse Jacksons, and so on. Historically these bright ambitious and talented young blacks joined the ministry and used it as a vehicle not only in providing for the spiritual needs of their constituencies, but also for guiding their congregations into the mainstream of American life.

For Irish Catholics and African Americans the clergy has played a pivotal role in assisting each group in its ethnic identity formation, in its sense of pride and self-worth, and in its initial attempts at dealing substantively with the dominant world. Upon those called to this religious life, the ethnic group lavished prestige, power, and respect. The Irish priest and nuns and the black preacher were people to be honored, for they encapsulated in their role the interests of the group itself. Proof of this can be found in the remarks of critics hostile to the influence of such religious leadership. Irish Catholics have frequently been ridiculed by their detractors as "priest ridden" and "subservient" to bishops and priests who dictatorially tell them what to think, how to vote, and so on; similarly African Americans have been accused of being too supportive of firebrand preachers and demagogues who do little to help them. Even eminent scholars have reiterated these criticisms. Handlin, for example, writes,

Hence the importance among the Negroes of clergymen of a general docile type. Hence too the opening for tragic demagoguery. The absence of responsible leadership in 1919 . . . permitted Marcus Garvey to lead them off in futile pursuit of a nationalist fantasy. . . . In the 1930s a similar vacuum made room for Father Divine's proffer of mystical relief from depression and prejudice. And the more recent parallel of Adam Powell showed how little progress has been made; not many who saw through his use of the color issue as a blind were willing to oppose him. (Handlin 1962, 113)

From the perspective of the ethnic minority, such criticisms confirm its belief that its religious leaders are effective; if they were not, why would the bitterness and hostility of their detractors be so evident? The clergy served as a viable route of upward mobility for many members of incoming minorities. In each group religious belief and practice served a critical need, helping newcomers deal with the new realities of American urban life. Here the religious leaders' presence was crucial for they bridged the gap between the familiar and the strange. They had greater prestige and power in some groups than in others. Jews, Italians, Puerto Ricans, and Orientals placed less emphasis on their religious representatives than did Irish, blacks, Poles, Haitians, and Greeks. Yet all of these groups valued their religious and ethical traditions, and to varying degrees honored those responsible for their continuance. In this context, Howe discusses the role of the rabbi in Jewish immigrant culture:

> Rabbis imported from Europe found it hard to adapt to the styles of American congregations and quickly had to confront a crisis of authority. Laymen in America, especially those who had grown wealthy and upon whom congregations depended, were likely to be more assertive—sometimes more vulgar than in Russia or Poland. For the rabbis, this often meant grief and humiliation. . . . The rabbi, unless he was a popular preacher, was considered a superfluous burden; he received only a small salary, or none at all, having to rely for a living on the emoluments of the rabbinical office. (Howe 1976, 194)

Entertainment

For still others legitimate opportunities existed within the sphere of professional entertainment whereby those so gifted pursued fame, fortune, and social respectability. Here their upward mobility prospects invariably were tied to their own individual talent and those so endowed climbed the social ladder in a manner approved by the larger American society. Indeed the appreciation of such unique talent and ability by the higher social groups propelled such individuals out of the lower classes to the more "respectable" classes.

The larger society rewarded those who pursued careers in athletic endeavors, music, writing, dance, and theater. It respected their unique talents and honored those successful in these endeavors displaying them as models, both to the members of the individual ethnic group itself and to the larger established society as well.

The possession of such unique talent, whether ability in a specific sport, or artistic ability in music, writing, dance, art, theater, provided the entertainer with a vehicle to circumvent the prejudice and discrimination directed towards his or her ethnic-minority. Handlin touches on this, noting that

> In the theatre, art, music and athletic worlds, talent was more or less absolute; and discrimination was much less effective than in other realms. This accounted for the high incidence among Negroes and Puerto Ricans to seek these pursuits as a way up; and it accounted also for the popularity and high status among them of prize fighters, musicians and the like, a popularity of which the incidence of references in magazines and newspapers is a striking index. (Handlin 1962, 72)

Each group produced those rare individuals who entertained the rest of the society, providing amusement and diversion. Hence professional boxers and basketball players entertain, just as do rock musicians, classical pianists, comedians, Broadway and Hollywood actors and actresses, ballet stars, best selling novelists, abstract painters, and dozens of other similar types. The larger American society and the ethnic minority group seek amusement from these entertainers, and American society provides ample leisure time, resources, and rewards necessary for such endeavors. Like the ancient Greeks and Romans, Americans love to play, and our social structure provides the settings for that desire. Like the ancients, Americans reward those who excel at their sport or art. Speaking of the prominence of such individuals in ancient Greece, Edith Hamilton noted that in Greece

> "glorious-limbed youth" . . . strove for an honor so coveted as hardly anything else in Greece. An olympic victor—triumphing generals would give place to him. . . . Splendor attended him, processions, sacrifices, banquets, songs the greatest poets were glad to write. . . . If we had no other knowledge of what the Greeks were like, if nothing were left of Greek art and literature, the fact that they were in love with play and played magnificently would be proof enough of how they lived and how they looked at life. Wretched people, toiling people, do not play. (Hamilton 1951, 169)

American society similarly endows its professional entertainers with phenomenal status, income, and fame. Many of these entertainers began their careers in the lower-income neighborhoods of America's cities, entertaining their newcomer brethren. As in the other routes of mobility, they also encountered considerable difficulties but eventually

overcame the obstacles. One need only recall the difficulties that African Americans, such as Jackie Robinson, encountered in entering
professional sports. Eventually discovering success, they quickly were
propelled into the large social arena beyond their ghettos. Irving Howe
discusses the manner in which Jewish entertainers moved into the
larger society beyond the Yiddish theater. In a footnote he cites Lenny
Bruce's criticism of earlier Jewish performers:

> Lenny Bruce would do a skit in the fifties about Jews getting into show business.
> The Jew, he said, had a "hip boss," the Egyptian in charge of the Pyramids, whom
> they were forever trying to charm. Tough as he was, the Egyptian finally suc-
> cumbed: "I mean," he said, "it's an *art* with them. Let's go watch a Jew be
> charming. Hey! Jew! Do that charming bit for us." Pretty soon "the Jew gets into
> show business . . . he's making the images" and charming the "gentiles." (Howe
> 1976, 565)

Nor were Jewish entertainers alone in facing such difficulties as they
moved into the larger society with their skills and talent; blacks faced
the same dilemma in the arts, in literature, in popular music, and in
sports. One might only remember the difficulty of Jackie Robinson in
baseball, James Baldwin in literature, and the host of black singers and
musicians who were under enormous pressure to produce music suit-
able to white society.

The talented thus begin their personal-mobility odysseys, aiming at
the American Dream. Speaking of the movement of such ambitious
young blacks into the entertainment industry, Kusmer writes:

> A community-based perspective on ethnic entrepreneurialism should also consider
> the importance of sports or entertainment figures and their promoters. . . . It is
> probably that among blacks especially, entertainment has been significant histor-
> ically as an outlet for entrepreneurial tendencies stifled by discrimination in other
> areas of endeavor. . . . One needed very little capital to set up a band, and the
> cabarets and nightclubs that blossomed in the post-World War I era provided plenty
> of employment for the jazzman and the blues singer. . . . Occupational statistics for
> northern cities show that, proportionally, there were at least two to three times as
> many black musicians as there were whites in the music business at that time.
> (Kusmer 1986, 50)

Yet a pecking order exists in the entertainment realm just as it does
in the dominant society. In every area of entertainment, the more
established groups occupy higher rungs on the ladder of status than do
the newcomers.

Sports clearly illustrate this principle. Professional boxing has served as a route of mobility for virtually all incoming groups and has been dominated in turn by Irish, Jewish, Italian, black, and Hispanic boxers (Weinberg and Arond 1952). When the Irish were predominantly lower class, professional prize fighters were overwhelmingly Irish, and Irish champions abounded (i.e., John L. Sullivan). Jews (i.e., Barney Ross), Italians (i.e., Rocky Marciano), blacks (i.e., Mohammed Ali), and Hispanics (i.e., Roberto Duran) repeated the process. Comparable examples can be found in other sports as well, particularly baseball, football, and basketball, though newcomers are largely absent from those sports in which they have little interest, minimal routine access, or ones that require a substantial economic commitment (e.g., tennis, polo, and golf).

Other avenues within the larger entertainment route attracted the talents of different groups. The Jews have been and still are prominent in the movie industry, having popularized that art form earlier in the century. Italians gained prominence in the realm of popular music, particularly in the 1940s and 1950s when they emerged from their lower-class position. Blacks are prominent in the current world of popular music, having moved through blues and jazz periods, to the rock-n-roll era of the 1950s, to the current rock scene. Hispanics also are active in the realm of popular music, though their influence and stature are restricted largely to the Hispanic community itself. If the lessons gained from previous ethnic minorities' experiences are accurate, Hispanics should emerge as a dominant force in the world of music in the foreseeable future.

Comparable examples and similar trends can be seen in the remaining forms of entertainment, including television programming, contemporary literature, dance ensembles, classical music, traditional and avant garde art, and so on. These entertainment forms suggest that those with the requisite talents choose the various options as a way of bettering themselves and maximizing their own goals of success in the eyes of others. Their respective ethnic groups are proud of their achievements, for they have successfully competed and performed in the dominant world, and have shown that often condescending world that the newcomers can "make it" on the dominant world's terms.

Semi-Legitimate Route—Ethnic Politics

The sixth route—ethnic politics—constitutes a transitional mode of upward mobility since it is neither fully legitimate nor totally illegitimate. Historically, ethnic politics has been closely allied to ethnic crime, and one cannot understand the ethnic political movements of the nineteenth and early twentieth centuries without observing the symbiotic relationship between these movements and the criminal organizations of that era (O'Kane 1969, 306). Herbert Asbury, in his work *The Gangs of New York*, illustrates this point:

> The political geniuses of Tammany Hall were quick to see the practical value of the gangsters, and to realize the advisability of providing them with meeting and hiding places, that their favor might be curried and their peculiar talents employed on election days to assure government of, by and for Tammany. . . . The underworld thus became an important factor in politics, and under the manipulation of the worthy statesmen the gangs of the Bowery and Five Points participated in a great series of riots which began with the spring election disturbances of 1834 and continued, with frequent outbreaks, for half a score of years. (Asbury 1929, 37)

Ethnic politics cannot be considered fully legitimate for other reasons as well for it often involved such disturbing features as the urban political machine, urban bosses, ward healers, and ethnic and religious bloc voting—attributes that in spite of their legality, disturbed the sensibilities of dominant groups. The close camaraderie between ethnic politicians and ethnic gangsters so apparent in the cities run by Tammany-style organizations further infuriated the established groups in American society that saw no real distinction between the two.

Yet the two groups are distinct, for even though the ethnic politician may have had connections with ethnic crime, his role per se is a legitimate one intimately connected to the American political process. Begrudgingly, the nation has come to accept the contributions of such famous bosses as Richard Croker, James Curley, Anton Cermak, Frank Hague, Carmine DeSapio, Adam Clayton Powell, and Richard Daley, all of whom helped assimilate their fellow ethnics into the political mainstream of American life. Yet the nation remains deeply ambivalent about their methods and tactics in pursuing legitimate political goals within the democratic context.

The main vehicle for ethnic political movements in the urban industrial locales in which the newcomers settled was the political machine, a uniquely American political invention. The machine is a political organization controlled by a "boss" seeking to monopolize political power and gain various economic and social advantages for those faithful to it. The primary purpose of this machine, lies in the fact "that it exists to secure and perpetuate power in the hands of a known organization" (Brogan 1960, 104). The organization had many names in different cities, but the most famous of these organizations was Tammany Hall (the New York County Democratic Party organization) that virtually ruled Manhattan for well over a century, and whose pattern of government established bosses and machines in city after city in the late nineteenth century.

The key person in the organization of the machine was the boss whose role involved maintaining the organization in power regardless of the issues or the ideologies of the movement. Historically, the "real role of Tammany was to 'organize' the newly enfranchised voters of what was now the largest city in the United States. A great and increasing part of that city's population was composed of recent immigrants, usually indifferent to American issues, having nothing to lose but their chains and little to sell but their votes" (Brogan 1960, 106).

The machine bosses did this rather well, organizing a remarkable system that catered to the needs of the newcomers, providing personalized service to them. If an Irish newcomer needed a bucket of coal, the boss and his machine provided it; if a Jewish newcomer needed help with the local public school, the boss saw to it; if an Italian family needed someone to intervene with the local police, the boss put in a good word with the police captain who also "worked" with the machine. Each incoming ethnic minority group had its problems and the political machines provided personalized solutions for these problems whether in the form of city jobs, turkeys for Thanksgiving, help with citizenship requests, intervention with large municipal bureaucracies, or assistance in keeping family members out of jail.

This was brought home to me in my youth. When I was a teenager in Brooklyn in the late 1950s, my family sought the help of the local political boss in a matter related to my grandmother's social security eligibility. She had immigrated from Ireland in 1901 and had never "paid into" the Social Security system. The family wondered if she would be entitled to benefits since my grandfather had worked in America for many years as a paver of the Brooklyn Bridge before his death in 1917 in Ireland. The bureaucracy of the Social Security System located in downtown Brooklyn proved to be incomprehensible to both my family and me.

At that point an Italian neighbor suggested that we go to the East New York Democratic Club and present our situation to the Club's leader (the Boss) who might be able to help. Since I had a high school education, I was selected to go and speak to him which I dutifully did.

He held office hours every Tuesday evening from 6 to 8 P.M. and would literally speak to everyone who came with a concern. There were a few people ahead of me on that night, and we each waited our turn on a wooden bench. When my turn came I nervously presented my grandmother's problem; he listened attentively and took notes. He was personable and polite, though he didn't think there was much that could be done since my grandfather died before the Social Security Act was passed in 1935, and that my grandmother never earned reportable income from the domestic work she had done earlier in her life. (As it turned out he was correct). He asked me to return and he would see what he could do. The following week I returned, and he explained the situation, indicating that he was sorry that the law didn't allow any benefits for my grandmother. I never forgot this service, and was flattered that he would spend his time on such a relatively minor problem. He went on to higher political office and became a prominent New York State judge; my family and I would support him for *any* office if we had the opportunity! As one might expect, the only thing he asked was: "Are you a registered Democrat?" Since I was, he then remarked "Don't forget to vote Democratic in November," which not only I, but my entire family did! It's for reasons such as these that the urban machine bosses were admired and voted into office campaign after campaign. The liberal reform groups never quite understood this.

In return for favors rendered, the machine and its Boss asked for only one thing—the newcomer's vote. To the newcomer, this was a small price to pay in return for men and an organization that helped them became Americanized and adapt to an urban environment, who spoke their language, understood their problems, and ran interference for them against the larger, condescending established society which resented them.

The machine ingrained itself in the lives of the newcomers and the entire hierarchical system of party bosses, district leaders, ward captains, and block captains provided social and economic security for them. Wave after wave of immigrants and migrants participated in this system, one originally perfected by the Irish and imaginatively duplicated by Jews, Italians, Czechs, Poles, and currently by African Americans and Hispanics. Reformers never cease announcing that the machine and bosses are dead, relics of a past era; yet bosses and machines constantly reappear in different forms, with different leadership styles, meeting the needs of new incoming minorities as well as perpetuating the political ambitions of their leaders.

For bright and ambitious young ethnic newcomers, this political world held promise. Historically, these young men could prosper in the machine organization without formal education, without great oratory skills, without a well-established family name or fortune. The only prerequisites were total loyalty to the organization, and the ability to deliver votes for the machine. One of the more famous bosses of the Tammany machine (circa 1900) was George Washington Plunkett who in his marvelous way spelled out how one could find a career in the party organization:

> There's thousands of young men in this city who will go to the polls for the first time next November. Among them will be many who have watched the careers of successful men in politics, and who are longin' to make names and fortunes for themselves at the same game. It is to these youths that I want to give advice. . . .
>
> Get a followin', if its only one man, and then go to the district leader and say: "I want to join the organization. I've got one man who'll follow me through thick and thin." The leader won't laugh at your one-man followin'. He'll shake your hand warmly, offer to propose you for membership in his club, take you down to the corner for a drink and ask you to call again. (Riordon 1963, 7, 10)

Bright ambitious newcomers heeded Plunkett's advice and began their political careers with the local machine. Through it they advanced beyond their humble origins and rose on the ladder of status. One of the most famous of these men, Al Smith, said, "I had a choice of hard labor at a small wage of ten dollars a week, or twelve at the most, in the kinds of jobs that were open to me, or easier work at a greater wage. I had a fondness for politics and I liked the excitement of public life. I had plenty of friends and I always took much satisfaction in being able to help them" (Brogan 1960, 112).

Thus, ethnic politics become yet another route to middle-class status and respectability. It served its Irish, Jewish, Polish, and Italian participants well, though these ethnic groups are increasingly absent in current local community-based political organizations, having moved to state and national prominence in state legislatures and in Congress. In their place have come the newer ethnic minorities who pioneer their own machines, offering status and power to bright ambitious African Americans, Puerto Ricans, Jamaicans, Haitians, and Cubans. Their goals are the same as those of Tammany Hall a century ago—to provide service to their newcomer brethren while perpetuating themselves in office. Such is the manner in which newcomers become part of the American political system.

Illegitimate Route—Ethnic Organized Crime

The seventh route of mobility—ethnic organized crime—is clearly illegitimate for it continues to be viewed as disreputable, immoral, illegal, and dangerous by the more established groups in American society. Whereas the larger society respected and even applauded those pursuing the other modes of mobility, it overwhelmingly condemned those engaged in ethnic crime. Its hostility has always been directed at lower-class crime whether it was organized or disorganized. The nation has remained remarkably unconcerned with white-collar crime that, by definition, excludes most lower-class minority newcomers.

Americans forget that many of our colonial ancestors came from England's prisons such as Newgate and Old Bailey, and travelled involuntarily to America as indentured servants. Davie reminds us of this heritage:

> Throughout the eighteenth century convicts were a never-failing source of supply for white servants. In this connection it has been suggested that American genealogists in search of missing data to complete their family tree would find a rich mine of unexplored material in the archives of Newgate and Old Bailey, the latter filling 110 volumes. (Davie 1936, 33)

American society has always been at odds with the criminal and all too often this criminal comes from the lower-class incoming minority group. A century ago these were the Irish racketeers and gamblers; in the 1920s these were the Jewish and Italian bootleggers and labor racketeers; today they are the black, Hispanic, and Asian drug dealers and vice promoters. As Daniel Bell has phrased it, crime is an "American way of life." (Bell 1953, 131).

Each incoming minority group has those men and women within it attracted to careers in organized crime. Most of them achieve only a fleeting degree of notoriety, soon to be forgotten by public and historian alike. Were it not for the work of Herbert Asbury (1928), we would hardly know of their existence. Asbury gives us an almost complete account of the dozens of gangs in the nineteenth and early twentieth centuries, and priceless vignettes about such "colorful" gangsters as Bill "the Butcher" Pool, "Yakey" Yake Brady, "Charlie the Cripple" Vitoffsky, "Banjo" Pete Emerson, "Red Rocks," Sadie "the Goat" Farrell, Ida "the Goose," "Cyclone Louie" Vach, "Eat 'Em Up" Jack McManus, "Slops" Connolly, "Googy" Corcoran, "Baboon" Connolly, as well as detailed information on the more famous gangsters of past eras. Those few who eventually succeed are both feared and admired by their own group and gain a certain amount of status both within and even outside their own ethnic group. Who among us has not heard of Al Capone, or Bugsy Siegel, or Bugs Moran, or Legs Diamond, or Machine Gun Kelly, or Dutch Schultz? In the decades to come American society undoubtedly will become aware of black, Hispanic, and Asian criminals, though to date few have emerged as important notorious figures in the public's mind. The passage of time will change that.

In a sort of distorted way, our society honors its organized criminals. Newspapers cover their "exploits," television specials portray their misdeeds, books are written about their lives. Films as popular as *The Godfather* and *The Untouchables* betray the public's ambivalent attitude towards gangsters, condemning their actions while honoring their memories. In earlier eras songs were sung about them, romanticizing their exploits and immortalizing their persons. Few would deny that the nation admires a Jesse James, while despising his killers, the Ford brothers.

Crime truly is an integral part of the American scene, and its most notorious practitioners accrue to themselves a degree of social honor, in addition to income and power. They become "legends in their own time" and models for the thousands of youths in ethnic neighborhoods who sought the gangster's success and easy, if somewhat dangerous, road to wealth and status in a society which demands success of its members.

The legendary status of the gangster was brought to my attention in 1963 when I spent a summer working in an orphanage in Lima, Peru.

This orphanage—Cuidad de Los Niños—housed approximately 250 boys, ages two to eighteen. In chatting with the older boys one day, I discovered that none of them knew who the president of the United States was, and few had any idea of where Spain or the United States were geographically located. Yet all knew who "Tuss Tony" was and they all knew about Brooklyn and its gangsters.

I was perplexed as to "Tuss Tony," and after repeated questioning, learned that they meant "Tough Tony" Anastasio, the leader of the Brooklyn Longshoremen's Association and the brother of Albert Anastasia, the alleged "enforcer" of Murder Incorporated. (Each spelled the surname differently). They spoke with admiration of Tough Tony and had learned about him and his family as a result of Lima's proximity to Callao, the main port in Peru. They were a bit saddened to learn that I did not know him and couldn't tell them more about him.

Interestingly, the Anastasia family represents much of this book's thesis of routes of upward mobility. The three brothers in the family chose different routes out of lower-income poverty in South Brooklyn's Italian-American section: one became a gangster, another a labor organizer, and the third a priest!

Yet for all its attraction, ethnic organized crime alone remains the pariah route of the various modes of upward mobility; true recognition of society rarely comes to its practitioners. The names of such famous gangsters as Al Capone, Meyer Lansky, and Dion O'Bannion, never appeared in the *Social Register*. Society accepts the laboring masses of newcomers, its small businessmen, its professionals, it clerics and religious leaders; it eventually accepts the ethnic politician. The ethnic organized criminal however remains a social outcast. In his brief career, he rarely receives the adulation and respect of the dominant society.

3

Ethnic Organized Crime: Historical Dimensions

Social observers tend to overlook the route of ethnic organized crime as an important vehicle of upward social mobility for many of America's incoming ethnic minorities. Since crime is disreputable, these observers largely ignore it, concentrating instead on the other more acceptable modes of movement. To them ethnic crime constitutes a mere footnote in the social history of specific ethnic groups, a phenomenon quickly to be noted, but not analyzed with any serious detail.

This is also true in relation to the middle- and upper-middle-class descendants of the earlier immigrants to our shores who deny that their forebearers involved themselves in crime to any appreciable degree. Many contemporary Americans ignore the fact that their respective ethnic group used organized crime as a mode of upward mobility. With an air of superiority, they lecture current minorities: "Why don't you blacks do it the way we did it in making something of ourselves in America, instead of terrorizing the rest of us?" "You Puerto Ricans will go nowhere in life if you continue to wallow in crime and vice"; "We Irish (or Chinese, or Italians, or Jews) worked hard and gained respect by our life styles when we came here—why don't you minorities do the same instead of living off welfare and spending half your lives in prison?" And so they freely offer their ethnocentric advice in a sanctimonious, condescending fashion.

Contemporary established Americans prefer instead a romanticized version of their particular ethnic group's history, complete with sterile, saccharine accounts of the rags-to-riches variety. These tales provide more fulfilling and comforting explanations of the move from the

51

bottom of America's class ladder, and enable those who have made it to distance themselves from those currently struggling to climb out of the bottom.

Yet even a cursory glance at American social history illustrates that violence, crime, and conflict played a more important part in the mobility of newcomers than the romanticists care to admit. The majority of Americans did not welcome the newcomers, and these established groups made known their collective opposition throughout the nineteenth, and twentieth centuries.

The ethnic organized criminal—the gangster—played an important role in this struggle, for he also desired the success promised by American society, seeking to achieve his goals of fame and riches through means deemed outrageous by the established society. He would achieve his aims of personal success and power by means of crime.

Female newcomers also desired the success offered by the society, but they are relatively scarce in the world of organized ethnic criminal gangs. Historically, women have been restricted to the areas of saloon keeping, fencing, prostitution, brothel proprietorship, small-time gambling operations, narcotics trafficking operations, and numbers rackets. Their criminal enterprises fell under the control and sponsorship of the larger all-male ethnic mobs and the females involved in these were few indeed. Among the Irish and the Jews in the nineteenth century, a number of women gained local notoriety: Roseanna Peers, "Battle Annie," "Sadie the Goat," and "Hell Cat Maggie," among the Irish; Marm Mandelbaum and her associates "Black" Lena Kleinschmidt, "Kid Glove" Rosie, Sadie Chink, Rosie Hertz, and Spanish Mary (Block 1977), among the Jews.

Notable Chinese and Italian female mobsters other than prostitutes or brothel owners are virtually nonexistent in the historical and sociological literature; black female criminals in the 1920s receive some notoriety, particularly in the Harlem numbers racket (e.g., "Madam Queen" Stephanie St. Clair). Hispanic female gangsters have received recent notoriety. Federal sources have identified a fifty-four-year-old Columbian, Eucaris Ceballos, known as Dona Tulia, the alleged "queen" of a New Jersey based cocaine syndicate. Her organization is reputed to be so wealthy that "its members weighed their money rather than counted it" (Rudolph 1987, 22). Dona Tulia has been sentenced to life imprisonment for her part in running a high-tech $600 million cocaine operation. (Gannon 1988, 33). The most famous women of American crime came from the rural areas of the country where social banditry flourished in the late nineteenth and early twentieth centuries (e.g., Bonnie Parker of *Bonnie and Clyde* fame, Ma Barker, and Belle Starr).

Current white outlaw motorcycle gangs have female members who are treated in an outrageous fashion. The President's Commission on Organized Crime notes: "Women are held to be less important than the gang itself and the gang member's motorcycle; and in some gangs, women are used to generate income through prostitution and topless dancing, as well as the transportation of drugs and weapons. Some gangs regard women hangers-on as 'club property,' available for the gratification of all members. Others are considered the 'property' of individual members." (President's Commission on Organized Crime, *Impact* 1986, 60–61.)

Apart from these notable exceptions, ethnic organized crime has been and continues to be a male-dominated pursuit among incoming ethnic minorities to our urban-industrial centers. In quick succession Irish, Jewish, Polish, Italian, black, Hispanic and Oriental young men have engaged in organized crime as a viable avenue to success in American life. As Albert Fried states in his analysis of Jewish criminals (circa 1900),

> It is no secret that Jewish criminals did what others did before them and have continued to do, that they all have used crime as another way of moving upward and onward in the American manner. First the Irish (and to a much lesser extent the Germans); then the Jews and Italians; and now presumably, the Blacks and the Hispanics and the Chinese too have successfully climbed the same "queer ladder." (Fried 1980, vxii; see also Bell 1953; Schlesinger 1969, xxv; Ianni 1974, 13–14).

The German and Scandinavian Newcomers

Not all the ethnic groups indulged in widespread organized crime. German immigrants, among the largest contingent of newcomers arriving in the mid-nineteenth century, had remarkably little involvement in crime. Largely similar to Anglo-Saxon Americans in cultural background and occupational skills, German newcomers avoided much of the prejudice that afflicted the Irish who arrived at approximately the same time in the 1840s and 1850s. As Handlin, in his discussion of recent Irish and German newcomers to Boston in the 1840s writes,

> While the chasm between Irish and native ideas deepened, cultural contacts favored the assimilations of other immigrants. . . . Germans were soon familiar in many phases of the city's activities. Admiring its school system and respecting Harvard, they sent their children to common schools as a matter of course. (Handlin 1979, 145)

Kathleen Conzen adds that, "Americans admired the skills, diligence, thrift, and family strength that seemed to make the Germans ideal candidates for Americanization" (Conzen 1980, 406). Their dispersal beyond the shores of the eastern seaboard to the smaller cities and farms of the Midwest similarly aided the German newcomers in avoiding the crushing poverty and the demographic concentration necessary to spawn large-scale collective social reactions such as crime. What little collective involvement in criminal activities they experienced related to defending themselves against nativist attacks during elections (e.g., Louisville in 1855, Baltimore in 1858) and combined nativist and Irish attacks nourished by anti-German prejudice (e.g., Hoboken, New Jersey in 1851). Germans consequently did not experience the need to advance on the status-mobility ladder by way of illegitimate criminal activities. The same can be said of the Scandanavian newcomers who followed a pattern similar to the Germans. Thus, Swedes, Finns, Danes, and Norwegians are likewise largely absent from the annals of the major mobs and criminal syndicates of the past 150 years.

The Irish Newcomers

But how did this phenomenon of ethnic organized crime begin? What are its origins? Certainly, American society had suffered the consequences of violence and crime long before the large scale immigrations of the 1800s. The incoming ethnic minorities thus did not invent organized crime, for it existed in embryonic form in both colonial America, and in the new Republic.

Yet the Irish newcomers of the mid-1800s pioneered new forms of existing organized crime and made it into what we now think of it. With their ubiquitous gangs, political protection, and tacit police approval, the Irish gangsters built criminal empires that provided "services" to urban politicians, gamblers, prostitution houseowners, saloonkeepers, and to corporations to break strikes and do other "odd jobs." Thus, the origins of organized crime in America lie not with the "Mafia" and Italian-Americans, as so many historically myopic commentators would believe, but with Irish Catholics who seized existing low-level criminal enterprises, imaginatively and ruthlessly expanding and organizing them. Their genius in crime is comparable to their genius in politics and in the Catholic church—they simply were superb organizers.

The catalyst for the rapid expansion of criminality involved the widespread urbanization and industrialization of America, for after the 1820s these two phenomena became fully enmeshed with each other. With the rapid growth of cities in both Europe and the United States, a myriad number of social problems arose that threatened the very foundations of the social order. The lower classes comprised the vast majority of these cities. They quickly became the "dangerous classes," and their behaviors genuinely terrified the more established elements in society. This was particularly true of crime, which in the eyes of the native Anglo-Saxon American seemed endemic in the new incoming immigrant groups of the early nineteenth century, particularly the Irish.

Irish Catholics represented the first major immigrant group that substantially differed in culture, life-style, and religion from the native Protestant-American groups. Their arrival in large numbers after 1840 rapidly transformed the cities of the eastern seaboard, so much so that by the 1860s they represented, if not an actual majority, then a substantial minority of the population of these cities.

In the lower-class wards of these cities, Irish newcomers quickly encountered the existing criminal element which was Anglo-Saxon and Protestant. In the 1820s and 1830s these native criminals intimidated the Irish immigrants and made no secret of their animosity to the Irish and their Catholicism. Thus began a generation of conflict between nativist gangs and Irish gangs, for the Irish soon learned that the organized gang became the vehicle, not only for warding off violent attacks from others, but for indulging in remunerative crime and gaining political advantage. In city after city, Irish gangs became fearsome realities in the 1840s, 1850s, and 1860s, engaging in predatory crime against victims overwhelmingly derived from the waves of Irish immigrants flocking to America's shores.

New York City became the focus of the scholarly interest in Irish gangs and much of the sociological and historical literature detailed the accounts of this city's gangs. The members of notorious Irish gangs of New York (e.g., The Dead Rabbits, Bowery Boys, Plug Uglies, Five Pointers, O'Connell Guards, Roache Guards, etc.) began their careers as youths engaged in brawling, thievery, and gambling and as adults joined with similar individuals to form these organizations. These gangs spent a great deal of time fighting with each other as well as fighting rival nativist gangs (e.g., American Guards). The animosity between two of these gangs, the Dead Rabbits and the Bowery Boys, always intense, reached epic proportions in 1857 when they fought each other. Virgil Peterson describes the battle as follows:

> Early on Sunday, July 5, 1857, the Dead Rabbits, armed with paving blocks and iron bars, swarmed into a Bowery clubhouse and tore it apart. The Bowery Boys rushed to the scene in force and the two gangs . . . joined battle. . . . A squad of Metropolitan Police attempted to march to the battle grounds but the two feuding gangs temporarily joined hands to fight off any police interference. As police retreated, the residents . . . pelted the officers with stones and brickbats from windows and rooftops. At one point came a lull in the fighting, during which screaming hussies from the Five Points district taunted the Dead Rabbits with charges of cowardice. The Dead Rabbits, spurred by the taunts, attacked again. At the height of the conflict, an estimated thousand rioters were involved in the bloody melee. Many of the men who fell wounded on a sidewalk or street were trampled upon. Two days of fighting passed, and the police remained helpless. . . . Finally, as a last resort, the police appealed to General Charles W. Sanford for help . . . (who) ordered three regiments of the militia to the troubled area. With the arrival of soldiers, the rioting ended. Casualties . . . included ten killed and eighty wounded. (Peterson 1983, 42)

Such battles between rival gangs occurred frequently in New York, Baltimore, Philadelphia, and Boston in this pre-Civil War period. Similar to contemporary violent youth gangs, these battles revolved around vengeance, honor, and territorial disputes. Yet the Irish gangsters advanced beyond these motives rapidly realizing the importance of political power and influence, for such political affiliations and connections provided the legal immunity so essential for their survival.

The politician, frequently the local machine boss, protected the gang, guaranteeing its freedom from arrest and harassment. In turn the gangsters and their gangs provided substantial financial "support" for the political bosses campaigns, and even more important, used "muscle" and violence in dissuading political rivals. In the 1856 mayorality election in New York City, the Bowery Boys backed the Know-

Nothing Party candidate while the Dead Rabbits and their allies backed Fernando Wood, the Democratic candidate. Extensive rioting between these two gangs occurred on Election Day, with the Dead Rabbits winning the battle and Wood the election.

Some of the earliest leaders of the political machines were, at the same time, the leaders of the most important gangs of this era (O'Kane 1969, 306). Mike Walsh, a gang leader of the Plug Uglies; John Morrissey, leader of a Five Points gangs; and Captain Isaiah Rynders, a leader of the Dead Rabbits—each held substantial power in the New York County Tammany Hall machine. Cloward and Ohlin comment on this symbiotic relationship between criminal and machine politician:

> The gangsters and racketeers contributed greatly to the coffers of political parties and were rewarded with immunity from prosecution for their various illegal activities. As the political power of the ethnic or nationality group increased, access to legitimate opportunities became enlarged and assimilation facilitated. . . . Blocked from legitimate access to wealth, the immigrant feels mounting pressures for the use of illegal alternatives. (Cloward and Ohlin 1960, 196)

By the 1850s, the Irish gangs closely involved themselves with the political organizations and the gangsters used their muscle to intimidate voters, stuff ballot boxes, harass political rivals, and serve the legal and illegal interests of their political mentors. The apex of Irish criminal organizations occurred during the Civil War, a time when Irish gangs and gang leaders controlled the important criminal endeavors in the larger eastern cities, supported by the protection of and collusion with, the urban political bosses and their machines, and the urban police forces which were disproportionately Irish. They yielded formidable power, for much of the violence in the New York City's Draft Riots of 1863 resulted from the combined force of the Irish gangs all of whom united in the collective rampage (McCague 1968; Banfield 1968; O'Kane 1979, 234).

By the latter part of the nineteenth century, Irish criminal organizations dominated crime in America's larger cities. With such criminal organizations there appeared a greater degree of coordination of criminal activities, and the pattern of street brawling and rioting so common in the pre-Civil War period began to subside. The economics of gambling and vice operations necessitated a rational, efficient coordination of political and criminal activities, and unorganized street violence hindered such endeavors. More could be accomplished by working quietly behind the scenes with politicians, judges, police, and legislatures than by attacking rival gang headquarters and disrupting the lives of ordinary citizens. This symbiotic relationship with machine politicians and police forces provided freedom of action to conduct the criminal activities of gambling, prostitution, vice, and other assorted crimes in a fairly orderly, efficient manner. Hugh Barlow sums this as follows:

> From loafing and brawling the New York gangs moved into extorting and the instrumental use of force. They soon discovered that money was easily made through the intimidation of brothel owners, gambling proprietors, and others in the business of providing illicit services. More money came, and with it power, when it was discovered that politicians and businessmen would pay for their muscle. Gangs were hired to break up picket lines, to intimidate voters, to stuff ballot boxes, and to protect establishments from harassment by other gangs, not to mention the authorities. By the 1850s the gangs were the muscle behind Tammany Hall, the Democratic headquarters and political heart of the city. With this new power, the gangs were able to open doors that formerly had been closed to their fellow Irish. The docks were under their control, and this meant work for Irishmen; city hall felt their power, and this meant city jobs for their fathers, brothers, and cousins. (Barlow 1978, 276–77)

The arrival of the twentieth century saw the decline and eventual fall of the Irish in organized crime. They had reigned supreme in crime for the previous fifty years, but circumstances now dictated that new groups, particularly Jews and Italians, would assert their roles in the criminal world. The decline of the Irish (as well as the Jews and Italians) in crime will be analyzed more fully in chapter 5; suffice it to say at this point that the upward mobility of the Irish in general, their desire to be middle class, the cessation of large-scale Irish immigration, the arrival of millions from the peasantries of Southern Europe and Jewish shtetls of Eastern Europe, the arrogance of Irish criminals, the decline of Irish political power in the urban machines—all these factors led to the loss of Irish power in crime. Prohibition in the 1920s constituted the coup de grace. Jews and Italians took greater advantage of the potentials of bootlegging than did Irish criminal chieftans, particularly in cities such as Chicago and New York; the Irish were not as forceful or ambitious as the chieftains of Jewish and Italian crime, and failed to see the long-term benefits derived from bootlegging and the implications of Prohibition for the growth of organized crime. As a consequence, most of those Irish remaining in crime were eliminated by newcomer competitors.

Hence, the Irish are virtually extinct in ethnic organized crime; their historical role in it is largely forgotten, and with it a colorful and frightening moment in the history of the Irish in America has passed. Vestiges of Irish organized crime still remain in a few cities. The Boston area, for example, continues to witness gang warfare among Irish gangs in Charleston and in Somerville. In Boston there are at least three Irish mobs: one controlled by Jimmy Bolger, another by Howard Winter, and the third by the McLaughlins. The membership of these gangs is not necessarily all-Irish, since a number of Italians belong to them (President's Commission on Organized Crime *Impact* 1986, 119). New York City has its Irish gang—the Westies—a pale remnant of the famous Hell's Kitchen gangs of Manhattan's West Side waterfront (The Gophers and the Hudson Dusters). Yet these are exceptions to the general rule.

In isolated situations, occasional Irish "lone wolves" try to reassert the long-lost hegemony of Irish criminal dominance. In Cleveland during the late 1970s, Danny Green, an Irish gang leader, attempted to take over the La Cosa Nostra Licavoli mob by murdering a number of its members. Green, a colorful character who drove a green Lincoln and wrote only in green ink, was finally assassinated after his LCN adversaries made eight attempts to kill him; on the ninth try, they succeeded by detonating a bomb in his car. So ended the resurgence of Irish criminal power in Cleveland.

In this period in the mid-1800s patterns of individual and group upward social mobility became established and individual Irish criminals made notorious reputations for themselves. Many started out as common street thugs victimizing fellow Irishmen. Their initial successes were at the expense of their newcomer neighbors in the lower-class Irish neighborhoods of the cities. Yet for those with intelligence and ambition, the more ordered world of organized crime was attractive. For these gangsters, organized crime provided a quick means of success in America. The rewards of income, power, and prestige within their own ethnic community were immense, as were the dangers of crime, for all too many criminals forfeited their lives in the violence that often surrounded their endeavors. Equally bright, ruthless, and ambitious criminals took their place attempting to achieve their version of the American Dream via crime.

Thus Irishmen such as John Morrissy, Honest John Kelly, Shanghai Kelly, Eat 'Em Up Jack McManus, Big Tim Sullivan, Peg Leg Lonergan, Danny Walsh, Denis Kearney, Dion O'Bannion, Mad Dog Coll, Legs Diamond and hundreds of others commenced their illustrious and infamous careers as street brawlers, gangleaders, gamblers, and bootleggers. Their fascinating individual biographies depict an era of Irish ethnic crime that has long since passed. They represented newcomers who yearned for what America promised—wealth, power, and social honor—but chose to achieve these goals through criminal means. Most never made it beyond the ghetto; those cited above were the more successful ones, but for many of these the end was tragic, for American society scarcely allows true success to be achieved by criminal means.

The Chinese Newcomers

As the Irish, German, and Scandanavian newcomers entered the United States in the mid-1800s in large numbers so also did the Chinese, settling primarily in California, but eventually in other cities such as New York City. San Francisco and New York contained the largest "Chinatowns" in the nation, and there Chinese newcomers lived in miserable conditions, confronted by the hostility of those around them, particularly the native Americans.

Like the Irish, the Chinese quickly developed criminal enterprises in their neighborhoods, concentrating on providing illegal services and commodities to their Chinese neighbors and the larger American community. Ambitious Chinese criminals belonged to tongs, associations which derived their income from opium, prostitution, smuggling, and gambling. These tongs competed with each other for status and power, and the frequent tong wars in San Francisco and New York mirrored the violence of the gangs of other ethnic minorities, for the tongs employed "highbinders," paid assassins who preyed upon each other as well as merchants and businessmen within the Chinese community. Light comments on these tongs:

The two largest fighting tongs were the Hip Sing and the On Leong. Highbinder tongs were trade guilds of Chinese gangsters. As such the tongs controlled gambling, opium, prostitution, extortion, and violence. Just as one could not open a laundry or restaurant without the approval of the relevant trade guild, so one could not traffic in prostitution, gambling, or opium without the consent and protection of a highbinder tong. (Light 1972, 94)

These feuding tongs controlled virtually all the crime in the Chinatowns. As the Irish before, and the Jews and Italians after, the leaders of these gangs spent much of their time trying to kill each other in what became known as tong wars. These tong wars started in San Francisco where Fung Jing Toy, or "Little Pete" dominated crime in the Chinese community, leading the Sum Yop Tong against the rival tong, Sue Yop. Following his assassination in 1897, his tong was almost eliminated by the highbinders of Sue Yop. American government officials appealed to the Emperor of China for assistance in stopping the carnage. His statesman, Li Hung Chang, solved the problem, stating, "The matter has been attended to. I have cast into prison all relatives of the Sue Yops in China, and have cabled to California that their heads will be chopped off if another Sum Yop is killed in San Francisco" (Asbury 1968, 196). Needless to say, the tong war ended.

In New York, in 1900, similar strife broke out among feuding tongs and their legendary chieftains. The greatest of these, Mock Duck, headed the Hip Sing Tong that successfully challenged the hegemony of the On Leong Tong, led by Tom Lee. The war that erupted occurred mainly in Chinatown, in an area referred to as the Bloody Angle. Carl Sifakis describes it as follows:

Mott Street became the stronghold of the On Leong Tong, while Pell Street belonged to the Hip Sing Tong. Doyers Street was a sort of no man's land with a certain sharp turn that journalists named the Bloody Angle. The police later estimated that more men were murdered there than at any other spot in New York City and most likely the entire U.S. . . . [A]rmed with a snickersnee, or hatchet, sharpened to a razor's edge, a *boo how doy*, or hatchet man, could strike before the victim had time to cry out, lay the weapon across his throat and flee through an arcade to safety. (Sifakis 1982, 82)

Another "typical" incident between the Hip Sing and On Leong tongs occurred one Chinese New Year's evening at the Chinese Theater on Doyers Street. A truce between the two tongs had been arranged in honor of the holiday, but during the performance, someone threw a package of lighted firecrackers into the audience. After the commotion had quieted, five On Leong highbinders were found dead, with bullets in their heads; the sound of the firecrackers concealed the gun shots of the Hip Sing assassins (Asbury 1970, 312; Sifakis 1982, 92).

The Chinese pattern resembles closely that of the Irish, Jews, and Italians. However, Chinese criminals rarely left the Chinatowns and did not expand their activities into the larger American community as did these other ethnic groups. The main reason why they did not is demographic, for the Chinese population concentrated itself in the enclaves of Chinatown and failed to become sufficiently large to produce criminal gangs or tongs that could successfully compete with those of the Irish, Jews, or Italians. These rival gangs were far too large to challenge; doing so would probably have been suicidal for the Chinese gangsters. The ambitious Chinese gangster thus had two choices: move out of the Chinese community and serve as "hit men" and underlings in other ethnic gangs, or stay in the Chinatown and gain the prestige, wealth, and power for oneself and one's tong. Historically, Chinese gangsters have chosen the latter.

The Newcomers of the Late Nineteenth Century— The Jews and the Italians

As the Irish began to wane in criminal power, new ethnic groups immigrated to America and, like the Irish before them, settled in dire poverty in the lower-class ghettos of the urban centers. By the 1900s these lower classes disproportionately comprised millions of Jews, Italians, Poles, Greeks, Romanians, Ruthenians, and so on, who emigrated from Eastern and Southern Europe. Their dreams and ambitions scarcely differed from those of their Irish, German, and Scandanavian predecessors—to make something of themselves, to grow rich and respectable in the land of opportunity. The realities were quite different for they also found that they were not welcome, either by the dominant native Anglo-Saxon groups or by the Irish.

This hostility prevented normal access to reputable jobs and respectable careers and served as a catalyst for the generation of criminal careers within the newcomer community. Young ambitious newcomers questioned how they could make it in America working in a sweatshop or digging ditches. They saw a world which closed its doors to them, and they vowed that they would make it by whatever means at their disposal. For many, this meant a life of crime, with all its glitter and excitement.

Many Jewish newcomers from Eastern Europe, diverse as they were in terms of cultural backgrounds and degrees of religious orthodoxy, actively sought criminal careers and life-styles, to the displeasure of the larger Jewish ethnic group and to the families of individual Jewish gangsters. The ways of the Old World, particularly those of Eastern Europe with its orthodox religious practices and shtetl mentality, repelled these young Jewish criminals who viewed them as remnants of a past they wished to forget. One must take America on its own terms, and for these youth crime offered the ticket to all that America promised.

Within the Jewish ghetto, the gangster undoubtedly regarded himself as a success, exemplified by his demeanor and life-style. Writing about prostitution in the Jewish Lower East Side of New York (circa 1900), Fried quotes the memoir of Marcus Ravage—*An American in the Making*—in his discussion of young Jewish pimps, or "cadets": ". . . a young gentleman with piercing, relentless eyes, faultlessly attired in modish clothes, high collar, and patent leather boots who painted me a dark picture of the fate of the fool who thought he could succeed in America with the antiquated notions he had brought with him from the old country. That young gentleman had come to terms with America" (Fried 1980, 14).

The same held true for the Italian newcomers who arrived in America in massive numbers shortly after Jewish immigrants. They also yearned for the success promised by America, but, like their Jewish predecessors, the poverty of their lower-class neighborhoods in the larger industrial cities prevented its realization. Significant numbers of Italian newcomers thus chose to pursue careers in crime, preying upon fellow Italians, engaging in extortion, theft, kidnapping, and murder.

Charles "Lucky" Luciano serves as an example of this type. In discussing Luciano's early life at the turn of the century, Nelli writes,

Luciano took a job as shipping boy in a hat factory, but one week of work and a $7.00 paycheck convinced him that he wanted something more from life: This type of work was for—in his words "crumbs." A "crumb," according to Luciano, was someone who "works and saves, and lays his money aside; who indulges in no extravagance." Luciano wanted "money to spend, beautiful women to enjoy, silk underclothes and places to go in style." (Nelli 1976, 106)

And so young criminals pursued the escape routes of crime that seductively offered them all that America promised. The benefits of living an honest, God-fearing, respectable life were vague and nondescript; the promise of success was so much more exciting in the criminal's ghetto community where he daily encountered successful prostitutes, racketeers, gamblers, and extortionists. He chose to pursue crime, with all of its risks and rewards.

But many other newcomers in the Jewish and Italian communities thought similarly, and just as paths to success are limited in the legitimate conventional realm, so are they also in the ethnic criminal realm. Often ruthless competition ensued. Successful gangsters eliminated (or at the very least neutralized) their competitors, mostly members of their own ethnic group. Those surviving these battles learned that cooperation as well as conflict were important virtues and oftentimes succeeded in organizing large criminal gangs that looked beyond the Jewish and Italian neighborhoods for fresh lucrative opportunities.

From the beginning of their careers in America, Jewish, and Italian criminals were relegated by the Irish gangsters to the lower echelons of criminal enterprise, such as street prostitution, loan sharking, petty crime, and low-level gambling. The Irish kept the richer plums of crime (i.e., higher level gambling and prostitution, commercial extortion, racketeering, etc.) for themselves. Likewise, the newcomer Jewish and Italian criminals confined themselves almost exclusively to their own neighborhoods where few opportunities for large-scale criminal economic success existed. Essentially they adhered to Old World customs and traditions wherein they distrusted and feared outsiders, particularly the Irish who resented the Jews and Italians. Unable to speak English and function comfortably outside their neighborhoods, the early Jewish and Italian criminals preyed upon their own brethren.

In discussing this neighborhood "confinement," Ianni quotes one of his Italian-American respondents who comments on early Italian criminal activity in New York City: "Can you imagine my father going uptown to commit a robbery or a mugging? He would have to take an interpreter with him to read the street signs and say "stick 'em up" for him. The only time he committed a crime outside Mulberry Street (Lower East Side of New York City) was when he went over to the Irish section to steal some milk so my mother could heat it up and put it in my kid brother's ear to stop an earache" (Ianni 1972, 50). By the 1900s, however, the Irish could no longer maintain their dominance over these predominantly Jewish or Italian neighborhoods. Lower Manhattan serves as a useful example.

Historically, Irish gangs dominated that area. The famous gangs of the Five Points and Bowery sections had been the nurseries of organized crime, and until the 1880s Irish residents inhabited these areas. After 1880, the area changed its demographic profile, and Jews and Italians gradually displaced the Irish who had moved to "finer" neighborhoods. Thus the Jews resided in the eastern section of the neighborhood (the Lower East Side), the Italians in the western part (Little Italy). The criminals of each group originally had joined the old Irish gangs; eventually, they took over these gangs, transposing them into Jewish mobs and Italian mobs.

Jewish gangsters headed by Monk Eastman, who Asbury labeled the "prince of thugs . . . as brave a thug who ever shot an enemy in the back, or blackjacked a voter at the polls" controlled the Lower East Side, forming a gang known as the Eastmans (Asbury 1970, 272, 274). The Italians took over the old Five Points gang under the leadership of Paolo Vaccarelli who chose to be called by an Irish name, Paul Kelly, since he felt it gave him more clout in both the criminal world and the political realm where the Irish still reigned unchallenged. Each of these gangs had members of different ethnic groups within it, but the Eastmans were predominantly Jewish, and the Five Pointers predominantly Italian. Each relied for its political protection and police protection on Tammany Hall, still a bastion of Irish power. Thus the ethnic rivalries and animosities of all three groups coexisted with the equally important need for each group to accommodate its rivals.

The growth of the Jewish gangs commenced with frequent internecine warfare within Jewish neighborhoods, neighborhoods as heterogeneous and culturally diverse as the mobsters themselves. Jewish gangsters pitted themselves against each other for the control of gangs, for control of gambling and prostitution houses, and for the control of virtually any lucrative criminal venture in the neighborhood. Murders and assassinations were common, with dozens of gangsters vying for leadership status. After Monk Eastman was jailed in 1904 for shooting a Pinkerton detective, Max "Kid Twist" Zwieback took over the Eastmans after killing another gangster rival, Richie Fitzpatrick (a pseudonym). Kid Twist in turn was gunned down in 1908 and Big Jack Zelig controlled the gangs of the Lower East Side, only to be killed in 1912 by Red Phil Davidson, Gyp the Blood Horowitz, and Lefty Louie Rosenberg. Leadership of the Jewish gangs now went to "Dopey Benny" Fein who differed from most of his predecessors because he involved himself in the increasing conflict between management and labor. In this sense Fein pioneered the industrial and labor protection rackets, a new era of criminal endeavor that would witness the rise and fall of dozens of Jewish gangsters in the 1920s and 1930s. Fried discusses this transition:

> The neighborhood had been experiencing a radical economic transformation. Sweatshops were giving way to factories. The garment industry was learning to meet the demands of a national market. Production grew by leaps and bounds, as did the number of workers and the amount of capital invested. Meanwhile, the workers . . . were becoming increasingly restive . . . many employers . . . hired strong armers (guerillas or "schlammers" or "bolagulas") as never before to terrorize the rank and file and above all punish the [union] leaders as only professionals knew how. Under the exigent circumstances, the unions had little choice but go to the same source, hiring gangsters in turn as protection for their organizers and strikers. (Fried 1980, 33)

Thus in the pre-1914 period, the Jewish gangs had grown rapidly and had moved from low-level petty crime of the immigrant days to highly organized crimes of industrial racketeering. The street brawler style of the Monk Eastman types gave way to the ruthless rational style of Fein and his more illustrious successors who were poised to make the transitions beyond the Jewish neighborhoods with the industrial rackets, the bookmaking, and policy racket and, perhaps the most lucrative of all—bootlegging. The end of World War I signaled this extension of Jewish ethnic organized crime to the "big time."

The Italian Newcomers

But the Jewish gangsters were not alone, for Italians had been undergoing an equally violent transition from lower-level street crime to highly rational organized crime. The time frame for Italians overlaps that of the Jews, but Italians lag at least two decades behind the Jews; they immigrated to America slightly later than the Jews and were not as urbanized as the Jews who had the advantage of town-shtetl backgrounds.

Italian crime, like Irish, Chinese, and Jewish crime, began in the lower-class neighborhoods inhabited by recent immigrants. Their criminal acts mainly involved predatory crimes such as the shakedown of store owners and fruit peddlers, extortion and kidnapping, small-time gambling, protection rackets, and vice operations. Typically, such crimes illustrated minimal organization, involving small gangs of criminals, and receiving little attention beyond the Italian neighborhoods. Unlike Jewish gangs largely centralized in New York City, Italian gangs existed not only in eastern cities, such as New York, Boston, and Philadelphia, but also in locations such as San Francisco, Detroit, Cleveland, Chicago, and New Orleans. Eastern European Jews were overwhelmingly concentrated in these eastern cities and the Jewish gangsters reflected this demographic reality. Italians, on the other hand, evidenced a more widely dispersed pattern of immigration, and their criminals followed suit.

During the 1890s in New Orleans, Italian crime received initial national attention due to the murder of an Irish police chief, David Hennessy. Though never officially solved, the murder related to the feud between the Provenzanos and the Matranga factions, and provoked an international incident between Italy and the United States since six Italian nationals were lynched in retaliation for the chief's murder. This incident also popularized the idea of a secret *mafia* at work. According to Nelli, "The New Orleans press reported on December 9, 1892, that the 'dreaded *mafia*' had struck again, and in subsequent years, robberies, vendettas, extortion attempts, and murders in the Italian colony were publicized in New Orleans' papers" (Nelli 1976, 66). In his interesting discussion on the derivation of the term "mafia" in Italian-American crime, Nelli reports that leading Italian editors in Boston and New York debated the term's origin in 1908, and suggests that it was used as a term to differentiate Italian-American criminals from Sicilian Black Hand criminals. Others believe that the term mafia may have been used probably by some Italian desperado who had heard of the exploits of the Spanish society of that name and considered the combination of words to be high-sounding and terror-inspiring (Nelli 1980, 71).

Much of Italian crime centered on New York and Chicago, the two cities with extensive Italian populations. In New York, one of the more famous Italian gangs, the Black Hand, thrived under the leadership of Ignazio Lupo, "Lupo the Wolf" who terrorized both criminal and innocent Italians alike. Asbury described him thus:

> The most celebrated of the Italian gangs was that captained by . . . Lupo the Wolf, who was one of the most desperate and blood-thirsty criminals this country has ever seen, and his followers who were just as ferocious. They were greatly feared by their simple countrymen, for not only were they amazingly proficient in the use of the bomb, revolver and stiletto, but were reputed to be able to cast an evil eye, and to possess other magical powers. Whenever an honest Italian so much as heard the name of Lupo the Wolf, he felt impelled to cross himself, and to extend his crossed fingers to ward off spells which the evil man might throw about him. Frantic men who had been marked for slaughter or robbery frequently appealed to their priests to protect them against Lupo's magic, but the holy men had scant success. (Asbury 1970, 267–68)

But the tactics and approaches of gangsters such as Lupo were primitive, and like those of similar Irish and Jewish gangsters, soon fell into disfavor among the more ambitious Americanized Italian criminals, for they invited unwelcome official police and political scrutiny. The use of extortion via Black Hand letters to victims became less and less prominent, particularly after well-known Italian gangsters had themselves been victims of these extortion notes. After Diamond Jim Colosimo, the major Italian gangster in Chicago in the early 1900s, received such a Black Hand extortion note, he employed Johnny Torrio (Al Capone's mentor) who tracked down the three extortionists and ordered them murdered. He likewise made sure that their subsequent fate was well publicized. That ended extortion letters to Colosimo (Nelli 1980, 85).

In the period immediately preceding World War I, Italian crime moved beyond Black Hand activities and gangsters such as Johnny Torrio, Frank Costello, the Genna Brothers, Frankie Yale, Al Capone, Diamond Jim Colosimo, Ciro Terranova, Tony D'Andrea, John Lazia, Lucky Luciano, Joe "the Boss" Masseria, Albert Anastasia, and hundreds of others sought to expand their activities to the larger world beyond the Little Italys in their respective cities. Like their Irish and

Jewish counterparts, they saw the opportunities that existed outside the ethnic neighborhood that they already controlled. By the end of World War I, these Italian gangsters and their organizations were poised, ready to expand their syndicates and deal as equals with the Irish and Jewish racketeers who also sought to augment their criminal activities. Jewish and Italian gangs consolidated their power within their own ethnic areas and began their encroachment into areas and activities long dominated by the Irish mobs.

The Prohibition Era

Prohibition proved to be the turning point in ethnic organized crime for with it Jews and Italians ascended the ethnic ladder of organized crime while the Irish fell from grace. The proscription of the manufacture, transportation, and sale of alcoholic beverages, the Eighteenth Amendment outlawed a substance highly desired by large segments of the American public, particularly those residing in the larger cities. Virtually overnight, Prohibition supplied to the gangster a new, lucrative field of operations, and the young, ambitious Jewish and Italian criminals responded to this golden opportunity. America now entered the bootlegging era, perhaps the most violent period of ethnic crime. Irish, Polish, Jewish, and Italians criminals pitted themselves against each other, with temporary alliances, shifting coalitions, and ethnic solidarity and betrayals characterizing this period of near anarchy in the world of organized crime. Yet this new era also offered immense opportunities to Jewish and Italian groups to cooperate with each other in encroaching on the territories of the Irish gangs, which many willingly did.

Many of the Americanized Jewish and Italian gangsters knew each other, grew up in the same neighborhoods, and understood each other's cultures. "Lucky" Luciano worked closely with Jews as a child and prided himself in cementing an Italian-Jewish criminal alliance, in "speaking a language that Waxey Gordon and Longy Zwillman 'Bugs' [Siegel] and 'Meyer' [Lansky] and Dutch Schultz and Louis 'Lepke' Buchalter could understand and reciprocate" (Fried 1980, 120–21). The Irish criminal organizations, particularly those in Chicago and New York resented such attempts to compete with them but the twilight of Irish criminal power had arrived. The Irish gangs no longer had the monopoly on either violence or political protection. Times were changing for them; new Irish recruits into criminal gangs proved harder to find since opportunities in legitimate endeavors now were available to them. Consequently, Irish criminal leadership became isolated from the daily realities of Irish-American life that no longer nurtured the criminal, and no longer bestowed adulation on him. The Irish were increasingly in touch with middle-class propriety and Irish gangsters constituted an embarrassment to the ethnic group as a whole.

The old Irish neighborhoods had changed from those of a generation earlier and the geographic mobility of the Irish from their traditional wards of the cities to better neighborhoods signaled the fundamental changes that were in process. The "lace curtain" Irish were replacing the "shanty Irish." The machine politicians foresaw this long before the gangsters did, and the Irish bosses quickly courted the ethnic newcomers in their districts and provided them with the same services that had successfully maintained the machine in power for so long. As early as the 1890s, "Big Tim" Sullivan of Tammany Hall befriended and cultivated not only newcomer Jews and Italians but their criminals as well. In Chicago, the famous Irish ward bosses Hinky Dink Kenna and Bathhouse John Coughlin did similarly, successfully enmeshing the criminal and political worlds, integrating Italians, Jews, and Poles into the machine while preserving their own power.

But the Irish gangsters were remarkedly shortsighted. The older Irish criminal recognized reality and "retired" from crime, leaving their enterprises to ambitious Jews and Italians. The younger Irish chieftains were not so malleable and consequently had to be removed forcefully from power (e.g., Dion O'Bannion, Legs Diamond, Vincent "Mad Dog" Coll, etc.). Dion O'Bannion illustrates this ethnic criminal transition; he was truly one of the most colorful and frightening of the Chicago mobsters who rose to power during Prohibition.

He commenced his criminal career as a slugger in the newspaper circulation wars in 1912 between McCormick's *Chicago Tribune* and Hearst's *American*. Subsequently, he formed the North Side Gang, composed primarily of Irish gangsters, but with significant Polish support (Hymie Weiss [nee Wajeiekowski] and Bugs Moran), and Jewish support, (Nails Morton and Frankie Gusenberg); Schemer Druci was the only Italian in his gang, for O'Bannion detested Italians, and the Italian mobs of Chicago detested him. Samuel "Nails" Morton, the top Jewish gangster in O'Bannion's gang, liked horseback riding. In 1924 a horse kicked him to death in a riding accident. In revenge O'Bannion, Bugs Moran, Hymie Weiss, and Two Gun Alterie kidnapped the horse and executed it gangland style on the spot where Morton was killed.

O'Bannion's arch rivals, the Italian gangsters, allied to the Torrio-Capone gang, and the Genna gang began the encroachment on the North Siders in the early 1920s. Johnny Torrio and Al "Scarface" Capone had moved to Chicago from New York and quickly organized and neutralized other Italian criminals, particularly the Terrible Gennas. Torrio and Capone's mob fought the Irish of the South Side under the O'Donnells who in turn were warring with another predominantly Irish gang, the Saltis-McErlane mob. O'Bannion in turn launched his North Siders against Torrio and Capone by raiding the speakeasies, hijacking their beer trucks, killing their gangsters. The battle lines now drawn, a large scale conflict ensued with truces quickly made and broken, alliances between different gangs and gangsters cemented and just as rapidly destroyed, for O'Bannion and the Italians truly despised each other. O'Bannion was finally assassinated in 1924 in his florist shop, across the street from Holy Name Cathedral where years earlier he had been an altar boy! The alleged killers were either the "Terrible" Gennas or the Capone associates, Johnny Scalise, Frank Yale, or Albert Anselmi.

Hymie Weiss took over the North Siders and met the same fate as O'Bannion in 1926. Another Pole, Bugs Moran assumed leadership but the famous St. Valentine's Massacre of 1929 sealed the fate of the Irish-Polish mob in Chicago, though Moran escaped the massacre. The most famous "hit" in American criminal history had been masterminded by Capone, allegedly through his hit man, James DeMora (alias, Machine Gun Jack McGurn). DeMora hated the Genna brothers who killed his father, and he eventually murdered six members of the Genna Gang. In each of their hands he placed a nickel to show that they were mere nickel-and-dimers, beneath contempt. When he was gunned down in 1936, the police found a nickel pressed in his hand (Sifakis 1982, 457).

Hence, the St. Valentine's Day killings symbolized the demise of the Irish in organized crime in Chicago, as it did also for the Poles and Jews. Italians under Al Capone had ascended to leadership, and for the most part the remaining Irish, Polish, and Jewish gangsters quickly joined dominant Italian factions becoming their gunmen and hired killers. At a 1930 Atlantic City conference of criminals from the East Coast and the Midwest, the only Irish gang represented was the Saltis-McErlane mob. The major gangsters at this meeting included Joe Saltis (a Polish gangster), Frank McErlane, Al Capone, Frank Nitti, Johnny Rio, Boo Boo Huff, Sam Lazar, Charlie Schwartz, Dutch Schultz, Nucky Johnson, Lepke Buchalter, Larry Fay, Frank Erikson, Lou Rothkopf, Moe Dalitz, Joe Bernstein, King Solomon, Nig Rosen, John Lazia, Lucky Luciano, Bugsy Siegel, Joe Adonis, Meyer Lansky, Frank Costello, and Longy Zwillman. The meeting had been called by Johnny Torrio to assist the larger forces in organized crime in "reigning in" Capone who had become too much of a celebrity, drawing public attention and government investigators to mob activities. The ethnic representation of the conference participants was largely Jewish and Italian, with the Irish playing a relatively minor role (Abadinsky 1981, 85–86). By 1930, Italian gangsters controlled crime in Chicago, having moved into other areas beyond bootlegging (e.g., extortion of dry cleaners, laundries, beauty parlors, construction, fisheries, and garages (Abadinsky 1981, 84).

In New York a similar dethroning of Irish mobsters occurred. As second-generation Jews and Italian criminals advanced in the rackets and bootlegging, they encountered recalcitrant Irish gangsters with whom they quickly came to blows. But unlike their experience in Chicago, the New York Irish were largely eliminated by Jews and Italians.

In Brooklyn, Irish gangsters still controlled large segments of organized crime and bitterly resented the Italians who were moving in on their territories in the 1920s. Rather than work with Italian newcomers, the Irish mocked their Italian competitors and considered themselves superior to them. Confrontations resulted and in the mid-1920s the White Hand Irish mob under Richard "Peg Leg" Lonegan was eliminated by Capone who had returned for a visit to Brooklyn. John Kobler describes the event:

Ever since Capone could remember, Irish gangsters had controlled Brooklyn dock labor. . . . But lately Italian gangsters had been challenging the Irish monopoly, and the White Handers had responded by killing a few of them.

Lonegan's presence in the Adonis Social Club, traditionally an Italian dive, was an added provocation, and he aggravated it by loudly referring to the regular custom- ers as "dagos" and "ginzos." He chased away some Irish girls who walked in on the arms of Italian escorts, shouting after them, "come back with white men!" (Kobler 1971, 167–68)

When Capone and his bodyguards arrived at the club, the lights went out and Lonegan and two other White Handers were murdered. The event served notice to the Irish that their hegemony in Brooklyn crime was over.

Another major figure in this takeover of the Irish interests was Arthur Flegenheimer, known as Dutch Schultz, a brilliant and ruthless Jewish mobster who quickly saw the lucrative potential, not only in bootlegging, but in the policy racket—the numbers game. Schultz, in his rise to power in bootlegging in the Bronx dealt harshly with op- position to his movement into Irish domains. His biographer, Paul Sann, describes how the Dutchman handled two Irish bootleggers, John and Joe Rock:

As in any enterprise nourished by the profit motive, of course, the two chums [Schultz and Joey Noe] did run into some spoilsports. . . . John and Joe Rock who had established a foothold in the Bronx. . . . John Rock stepped aside with a decent show of early resistance, but Joe, made of sterner Irish stuff, refused to withdraw from the beer business. He paid a very high price: He was kidnapped one night, beaten, hung by the thumbs on a meat hook and then blindfolded with a strip of gauze, which, as the story goes, had been dipped into a mixture containing the drippings from a gonorrhea infection. Whatever the potion was, Joe Rock came out of it a blind man—and even at that there was a story that the family had to ante up $35,000 to get back what was left of him. (Sann 1971, 112)

Schultz moved just as viciously into the independent black numbers rackets in Harlem and quickly took control of their operations, even- tually dominating this form of gambling in New York City. His main opposition came from two Irish mobsters—Legs Diamond, and Mad Dog Coll—who fought each other as much as they fought Schultz. Many writers mistakenly refer to "Legs" Diamond as a Jewish gang- ster. His background was Irish Catholic, and at times he used an alias name—Jack Noland. He grew up in Philadelphia, attended St. Anne's Church, married an Irish wife (Alice) and was refused a Catholic burial in Calvary Cemetery in Oueens, New York City.

The confusion over Diamond's ethnicity probably results from his association with Arnold Rothstein and Little Augie Orgen, Jewish gangsters for whom he had worked. Legs had learned his criminal trade under Orgen who had been assassinated in 1927. Asbury notes that the inscription on his coffin read: "Jacob Orgen, Age 25 Years." Since he was born in 1894, Asbury continues, remarks, "His real age was thirty-three. But it had been eight years since he had assumed leadership of his gang, and on that day his father had proclaimed him dead" (Asbury 1970, 373). Eventually Diamond moved into labor racketeering with Louis "Lepke" Buchalter and Gurrah Shapiro—the famous Lepke and Gurrah duo. Following this internship, Diamond made his name in bootlegging and gambling, murdering a series of gangster rivals. As his businesses became more successful, Diamond found Schultz moving in on them, and full scale warfare broke out between their two gangs, with Schultz emerging the victor after assassins killed Legs in Albany in 1931. (An interesting, partly fictional account of Diamond's life is found in William Kennedy's book *Legs*.)

Another Irishman, Vincent "Mad Dog" Coll, equally as vicious as either Diamond or Schultz, started out with his brother Peter working for Schultz as enforcers. They then turned independent, challenging not only Schultz's operation, but those of every other major gangster in New York. Schultz bitterly resented the Colls' betrayal and had Peter gunned down as revenge, thus commencing a vicious war between the Mad Dog and the Dutchman from which Schultz eventually emerged the winner when Coll was murdered in a phone booth in 1932.

With the murders of Diamond, the Colls, and Peg Leg Lonegan, the Irish mobsters quickly faded from the organized criminal scene in New York, just as they had previously departed in Chicago. The same transitions of power to Jews and Italians occurred in other cities as well with the Irish gangster consigned to history. In their day they had been *too* successful and consequently were not as adroit in seeking new markets, and pioneering new rackets. Content in their criminal pursuit, they became vulnerable to those lower-status ethnic gangs of Jews and Italians obsessed with achieving criminal success. Prohibition proved to be the transition point, and Jews and Italians quickly capitalized on the large-scale organizational efforts needed to control bootlegging. The Irish did likewise but by the late 1920s were "burnt-out" and lacked the sufficient manpower, determination, and drive to compete with Jews and Italians.

The vacuum created by the decline of the Irish in organized crime propelled Jews and Italians into leadership positions, each group establishing its own dominance over its respective territories and peculiar criminal ventures. As Prohibition ended, Jews (e.g., Arnold Rothstein, Louis "Lepke" Buchalter, Jacob "Gurrah" Shapiro, Dutch Schultz, Bugsy Siegel, Meyer Lansky, Longy Zwillman, Moe Dalitz, etc.) and Italians (e.g., Lucky Luciano, Vito Genovese, Frank Costello, Thomas "Three-Fingers Brown" Luchese, Al Capone, Carlo Gambino, Albert Anastasia, etc.) virtually controlled organized crime in America. Pioneering new forms of criminal activity and revitalizing other types (labor racketeering, numbers, gambling, prostitution, narcotics, loan sharking) Jews and Italian gangsters more often than not continued to cooperate with each other, for the internecine gang wars of the bootlegging era clearly showed open warfare to be destructive and counterproductive.

Like the Irish before them, the Jews eventually fell from criminal power, ousted by Italian gangs and by state and federal prosecutors. The decline began in 1928 with the murder of Arnold "Czar of the Underworld" Rothstein by unknown assailants, the ouster of Abe Bernstein's Purple Gang in Detroit by Joe Zerelli, and the assassination of Dutch Schultz in 1935 by the Lucky Luciano and Lepke Buchalter gunman, Charlie Workman. It continued in the 1940s with the imprisonment of Gurrah Shapiro and the legal execution of Lepke Buchalter, the exposure of Murder Inc., the murder or suicide of Abe "Kid Twist" Reles, and the assassination of Bugsy Siegel; in the 1950s Longy Zwillman, heir to Dutch Schultz's empire, committed suicide under questionable circumstances.

By the 1960s and 1970s only a few prominent Jews remained (e.g., Moe Dalitz, Meyer Lansky, etc.) though even they had shifted their talents to quasi-legitimate endeavors such as legalized casino gambling in the Caribbean and Las Vegas. Indeed many such individuals had moved into legitimate business simply because they had ample capital to do so, having gained these resources from less reputable dealings. Whether they had infiltrated legitimate business, or had simply used criminally gained capital to launch respectable business careers in hotels, resorts, and entertainment is debatable and probably can't be answered, for America is often loath to question the source of respectable enterprise capital. By the 1980s, all the prominent leaders of Jewish organized crime were gone.

As Jews as an ethnic group "made it" in the conventional realms, achieving middle- and upper-middle class positioning, the involvement of Jewish gangsters in organized crime quickly faded, and organized crime as a major route of upward mobility was jettisoned. They simply no longer needed it. Like their Irish mentors and enemies a generation earlier, Jews found more socially acceptable routes to income, power, and prestige and individual Jewish criminals moved into white-collar crime where they became indistinguishable from the other groups pursuing this form of criminal activity. Where once there was admiration for the Jewish gangster, now there remained only disdain, for the criminal image of the mobster does not sit well with the realities of middle-class Jewish life and conventional respectability. The Jewish gangster was consigned to history, an interesting and fascinating paragraph in the upward mobility odyssey of Jewish newcomers and their descendants. The last of the Jewish gangsters, Meyer Lansky, who died of natural causes in 1983, epitomizes this transition from success to ostracism. As Fried states,

> even if Lansky is as awesome as he is reputed to be, he is by now scarcely more than a lonely isolated old man on the criminal landscape of America. He bears the mark of Cain and knows no peace. Government investigators (and sometimes reporters too) watch and trail him without letup. Nor is he welcome anywhere else on earth. In 1970 he sought asylum in Israel under the Law of Return, which gives every Jew a right to settle in the Promised land. . . . Did Lansky intend to retire in Israel in good faith? Or was he planning to use Israel as a cover for his worldwide operations? Obviously, the Israeli government urged on by the United States, assumed the latter. Since no other country would have him, he went back to Miami Beach to face—and ultimately survive—a sea of troubles. (Fried 1980, 281–82)

Italians clearly reaped the spoils of organized crime as the Irish and Jews waned in criminal power and influence. Though historically allied with Jewish gangsters since the Prohibition era, Italians increasingly took over all the major rackets by the late 1950s. In the 1960s and 1970s, the public viewed organized crime and Italian "mafiosi" as identical entities and congressional committees, law enforcement agencies, and the mass media did everything possible to reinforce this stereotype.

Thus, Carlo Gambino, Vito Genovese, Crazy Joe Gallo and the Gallo mob, Joe "Bananas" Bonnano, Frank "The Banker" Costello, Sam "Momo" Giancana, Willie Moretti, Joe Valachi, Raymond Patriarca, Santo Trafficante, Vinnie Teresa, Joe Profaci, Carlos Marcello, Carmine Galante, Paul Castellano, and dozens of other reputed gangsters fascinated the public with their feuds and enterprises. They were the heirs of the syndicates pioneered by the Jewish and Italian gangs of the post-bootlegging era, and indebted to the organizational geniuses of those gang leaders, particularly Dutch Schultz, Al Capone, Lepke Buchalter, Frank Costello, and the trio Lucky Luciano, Meyer Lansky, and Bugsy Siegel. These individuals systematized organized crime and placed it on firm entrepreneurial foundation, expanding it into new uncharted domains.

The earlier syndicates exploited new areas of endeavor, moving beyond gambling, vice, and bootlegging, to labor racketeering, casino operations, and the most lucrative of all—narcotics. Drug traffic, initially engaged in by virtually all of the Italian and Jewish mobs in the 1930s, reached its full potential in the post-World War II era and provided a new, unlimited source of revenue for the Italian gangsters of recent times. Yet the public, as well as some of the Italian groups, feel that drugs are a dirty business, and the trafficking in them has brought the animosity of the public upon the heads of the gangs indulging in the narcotics trade. Where once the public tolerated the speakeasies and brothels and gambling houses of former eras, it now condemns drug traffic and the "dope pushers." They are the pariahs of the 1990s.

As Italian criminals made it to the apex of organized crime, they have had to deal with the public's condemnation of their narcotics enterprises. Seeking the approval of society for having made something of themselves via crime, they find only disdain. Rarely does the public honor the gangster of today, as it did some of those of the Prohibition era when the prestige of the gangster reached phenomenal proportions. With respect to one such gangster, Al Capone, his biographer, tells us that in 1930 Chicago's Medill School of Journalism students voted Capone as one of that year's ten "outstanding personages of the world." At an Indiana racetrack, thousands cheered him and at a college football game in Evanston, a local troop of Boy Scouts cried "Yea, Al" (Kobler 1971, 307). Big Al's prestige was further heightened when in the midst of the Depression, he fed thousands daily in his Chicago soup kitchens (Abadinsky 1981, 84).

The death of Dion O'Bannion in 1924 similarly attracted enormous public attention; at least 19,000 mourners, most of them curious onlookers, viewed his funeral. The mile-long cortege included twenty-six cars for flowers, three bands, and a police escort (Kobler 1971, 130). Gone are the days when gang bosses could openly boast about their crimes, as Capone did when he said, "All I ever did was sell beer and whiskey to our best people. All I ever did was to supply a demand that was pretty popular" (quoted in Browning and Gerassi 1980, 330).

Today's syndicate heads rarely appear in public, unless it is to appear in court to defend themselves against an ever-increasing number of federal indictments under the RICO statute (Racketeer Influenced and Corrupt Organizations), never grant interviews, and literally hide themselves from photographers and television reporters. Gambling and policy businesses are condoned; vice operations are somewhat hidden and condoned, as is a certain amount of labor racketeering. Even murder is condoned, providing the mobsters eliminate each other and do not injure the noncriminal public; the public even takes a certain delight in its voyeuristic interest in discovering which mobster rubbed out a rival and for what reason, be it a power struggle or a betrayal of personal loyalty. Films such as *The Godfather* and *The Untouchables* fascinate Americans; those films romanticize the Vito Corleones and the Scarfaces in their "wars" with society. Yet the public's tacit approval of crime does not extend to the "dirty business" of narcotics which touches the middle class, unlike the other enterprises. When drugs stayed in the ghettos, the public could not care less; once they made the transition to middle-class abuse, the full wrath of public opinion descended on the drug "pushers" and their alleged mentors and financiers, the Italian syndicate heads. Much-desired adulation and social honor never come to these "crime family" chiefs however much they yearn for such respect from the dominant world. Their success is hollow, and they seek alternative, respectable modes of mobility for their sons and daughters.

4

The Decline of the Italians and the Rise of the New Ethnic Criminals

Stages in Criminal Mobility

The analysis of the behavior of ethnic criminals and their criminal organizations indicates that each ethnic group passes through six stages in its rise and fall from power. These stages present a reasonable interpretation of Irish, Jewish, and Italian crime; whether they will assist in explaining African American, Hispanic, Asian, and other ethnic minority organized crime in America remains to be seen but we would be foolish to discount the historical record in speculating about the future of ethnic crime. The six stages are as follows:

Stage 1—Individual Criminality

This stage represents the phase in which lower-income minority individuals engage in predatory crime independent of an organization. Relative "loners," they perform criminal acts against their fellow ethnics in a haphazard, opportunistic fashion. They are the common street criminals who fill our jails and about whose crimes we read in our daily newspapers. They may join with other criminals on an erratic basis but these unions are short-lived, ever-changing, and with minimal organization. The organization of these units is minimal. Those engaging in this type of crime rarely move beyond it. They spend major portions of their lives in prison, generally lacking the intelligence, personalities, and organizational skills necessary to "move up" in the criminal world.

Stage 2—Intra-Ethnic Gang Rivalry

This stage represents the phase where the criminal moves beyond the predatory nonorganized crime of his neighborhood by joining with like-minded fellow ethnics who see that a tight organization—a gang—can achieve far more income and power than could be gained through individual criminality. This organized criminal gang evolves either as an offshoot of a previous teenage gang, or prison friendships. It is comprised of ambitious individuals who seek a better life in crime than was previously available to them.

Yet other similar gangs exist in their neighborhoods competing against each other, seeking the same scarce goals of income and power. Since there is no legal way of adjudicating the differences between these factions, violence and murder often result. Violence then becomes the hallmark of such gangs as they consolidate power, take over territories, and so on. In this intraethnic competition the gangsters seek to eliminate their fellow ethnic rivals, who are likewise seeking to eliminate them. Prominent Irish gangsters began their notorious careers by eliminating other Irishmen; so also did Jews and Italians; Chinese, African Americans, Puerto Ricans, Soviet Jews, Colombians, and Jamaicans will do so also.

Stage 3—Inter-Ethnic Gang Rivalry

This stage represents the phase where the rivals in the conflict between competing ethnic gangs in the community consolidate their organizations and move on to challenge the criminal organizations of other ethnic groups, most of whom are also newcomers. Their ambitions and aspirations have moved beyond the ghettoes, their appetites whetted for the spoils and booty of the larger society. Yet here they encounter equally ambitious and ruthless competition from the other ethnic groups which intensifies the volume of violence. Thus in the 1920s O'Bannion's Northsiders fought the Italians under both Capone and the Gennas; in the 1930s the Legs Diamonds and the Vincent Colls fought the Dutch Schultzes; Schultz's mob fought with Luciano's organization.

Stage 4—Organized Criminal Accommodations

This stage represents the phase where the successful mobs of each competing ethnic group, recognizing that they can't eliminate each other, seek to accommodate each other. The previous interethnic violence constitutes a stalemate that is unhealthy for the "business" of each gang. Rather than continue the senseless assassination of each gang's members, the gangs work out a temporary truce that replaces interethnic rivalry with interethnic accommodation. These truces may be short-lived, as those between the Irish and Italian mobs in Chicago or relatively permanent, as those between various Jewish and Italian syndicate organizations. The model of accommodation is the fruitful union in the 1920s and 1930s of Italians under Lucky Luciano with the Jews under Bugsy Siegel and Meyer Lansky.

Stage 5—Ethnic Gang Criminal Supremacy

This stage represents the phase where full-scale violence between ethnic gangs reemerges, either because the accommodation breaks down, as in the case of Irish gangs and their rivals, or because one of the ethnic gangs becomes so dominant that it can persuade its rivals either to retire or be eliminated. In either, case one ethnic organization emerges supreme by eliminating its "partner." This usually occurs when an ethnic mob declines in stature and influence, leaving itself vulnerable to its stronger, ambitious rivals. Just as the sick fish is devoured by the healthier fish, so were the Irish gangs devoured by the Jews and Italians; the Jewish gangs by the Italians, and if historical trends continue, Italian gangs by their current ethnic newcomer rivals. The outcome is the supremacy of one ethnic organization in crime that dominates all others either through intimidation or through alliances.

Stage 6—Decline and Fall of the Ethnic Gang

This stage represents the phase where the once-dominant criminal gang begins to wane in power and influence. Beset with recruitment difficulties, negative public opinion, increased judicial scrutiny and prosecution, decreased ambitions, and so on, the gang cannot successfully compete with the new ethnics. The frontiers of their empires no longer hold back the incursions of these new "barbarians." As a result many of the chieftains simply retire; some are assimilated into the newcomers' gangs. Others infiltrate new businesses, often those in white-collar organizations, pursuing new forms of sophisticated crime relatively safe from newcomer competition; still others become totally legitimate, developing businesses scarcely different from those of the conventional society. If their new behavior is criminal, it is indistinguishable from the endemic white-collar crime so characteristic of so-called legitimate society.

The end of the ethnic group in the top echelons of criminal power has arrived, and other groups ascend to succeed them. The process repeats itself, assuring us that ethnic organized crime continues in its own vigorous fashion.

The Decline of Italian Criminal Power

These six stages enable us to analyze the current transition within ethnic criminal hegemony in the United States. Italian gangsters now reign in the twilight of their criminal power. Like their Irish and Jewish predecessors, their decline is as increasingly evident as it is inevitable. Their obvious success in organized crime and their concentration at the upper levels of criminal syndicates belie the fact that African American, Hispanic, and Asian newcomers are encroaching on the Italian criminal realms. The days of the Italians in crime are numbered. These new ethnic minorities lust for what their Irish, Jewish, and Italian exemplars accomplished in organizing crime as a quick viable route to the success offered by American society, yearning for the power, income, and privilege accompanying such success.

The decline of Italians in crime stems from this phenomenal success. They command the top positions in the rackets in virtually all of the nation's larger metropolitan areas, yet are failing to replenish their ranks with fellow Italians. The staffing of the myriad subordinate criminal positions necessary to run a successful enterprise creates the natural conditions and opportunities for the ascendancy of ambitious black, Hispanic, and Asian newcomers.

In 1985 the FBI reported that Cleveland's "Mafia" had been depleted of its Italian organizers. A *New York Times* article reported that:

Only a few leaders of Cleveland's Mafia are left to run what once was one of the most powerful organized crime units in the nation . . . what remained of the local Mafia "family" was run by the owner of a Cleveland vending machine company. . . . One reputed Mafia leader, John T. Scalish, once sat on the commission that allocated territories and settled disputes among Mafia families across the nation. His death from natural causes in 1976 touched off a gang war in which family members and rival figures were killed . . . and many others were sent to prison. (*New York Times* 16 January 1985, 35)

The article goes on to report that the remaining heads of the organization received life sentences in 1983. So much for the Cleveland enterprise pioneered by Moe Dalitz and Frank Milano in the 1920s!

As the Irish and Jews before them, Italians have largely been assimilated into the American middle-class mainstream, and organized crime no longer constitutes a primary upward mobility outlet for their young, ambitious members. In his study of one Italian-American crime family, the "Lupullos," Francis Ianni found that fourth-generation Italians have little desire to follow the criminal careers of their older kinfolk in the family. Instead, they are pursuing careers as lawyers, dentists, teachers, and businessmen. He writes,

I discovered that each succeeding generation of the family had been moving quietly but certainly out of crime. I had managed to trace the family history back seventy-years through four generations and could see that from the second generation on, fewer and fewer sons had gone into criminal careers. Now, in the fourth generation, only four of the twenty-seven males were involved in organized crime. (Ianni 1974, 11)

The children and grandchildren of these prominent Italian gangsters seek legitimate routes to respectability and are genuinely embarrassed by the association with criminal elements. Even the criminals themselves seek legitimate futures for their family members, for true respectability in American society rarely stems from a life associated with crime and gangsterism. So-called "mafiosi" are a declining breed unable to sustain their organizations with younger family members, or recruit significantly large numbers of young Italians either here in America or from Italy.

Annelise Graebner-Anderson researched an Italian crime family, the Benguerras (a pseudonym), indicating their problems in recruiting:

One of the reasons the Benguerra family may be having difficulty recruiting is that the life of a member of an Italian-American organized criminal group is less attractive, relative to alternatives, that it once was. Many children of members of organized crime families, including the Benguerra and Lupollo families choose legitimate careers, and what information is available suggests that their member-fathers are proud of them and do not wish them to become members.

She continues:

The Benguerra family may consider it necessary to restrict recruiting to members of its own ethnic minority in order to maintain its capacity for governing. The problem is that young Italian-Americans . . . are often third-or-fourth-generation Americans with American values and culture . . . unwilling to give primary loyalty to the hierarchy of an organized crime family and acknowledge its quasi-governmental authority as legitimate indefinitely. (Graebner-Anderson 1979, 48)

Ianni also notes this bleak future for Italian ethnic crime:

The outlook for the Italian crime families is not promising. Ethnic succession in organized crime will force them out. . . . An era of Italian crime seems to be passing in large measure because of the changing nature of the Italian community which resides in American culture and its inclusion in the society. To that extent, the pattern of Italian crime seems to be following that of previous ethnic groups. (Ianni 1972, 194)

Italian criminals also lack the sustenance and support from the larger Italian-American community that they once enjoyed. The Little Italys of our major cities are aging, dying communities, unable to sustain the rich cultural traditions of the past. Mainly inhabited by those abandoned in the exodus to middle-class suburbia, these neighborhoods mainly serve as tourist areas for those seeking good restaurants, street festivals and feasts, and the nostalgia of a bygone age. New incoming minorities and young upper-middle class professionals increasingly reside in these neighborhoods filling the vacuum created by the exodus of Italian youth to more affluent areas. A walk through New York's Little Italy would reveal that much of the geographical area of what once had been an all Italian section is now largely Chinese, and as Chinatown grows, Little Italy withers.

In the past, the Italian gangster epitomized the folk hero to the larger Italian-American community. The Capones, Lucianos, Costellos, Gambinos commanded the attention of the larger community and dealt with America on their own terms. To Italian newcomers, the gangster showed that the larger American society had to reckon with the Italian community, and newspaper accounts of men like Capone socializing with established politicians, judges, and businessmen reinforced this pride in "Italians who had done well." They were the "Davids" battling the American "Goliaths."

Today this adulation has given way to embarrassment. Many middle-class Italians resent the influence of the Italian gangster and do not mourn his decline. Increasingly a number of Italian-American state and federal prosecutors have initiated "search and destroy" actions against the Italian mobs and syndicates, scarcely rendering any quarter to the gangster. Respectable Italians are affronted by the societal stereotype that suggests that all Italians are criminals and they seek to eradicate this prejudice. Often this implies that the Italian mobster's influence and reputation within the ethnic community must be quietly excised. Increasingly the gangster becomes a pariah in his own ethnic community, someone perhaps to be feared, but also shunned. His image has changed from that of a noble chieftain, such as Vito Corleone in *The Godfather*, to the tired imbecile mobster in books and films such as *The Gang That Couldn't Shoot Straight* and *Prizzi's Honor*.

In the 1980s, the RICO Act (Racketeer Influenced and Corrupt Organizations) signaled the death knell for most of the Italian-American syndicates in the nation's crime centers (e.g., Kansas City, Philadelphia, Boston, Newark, and Chicago) wherein indictments and long prison terms against leading "mafiosi" crippled their operations. The Scarfos of Philadelphia, the Patriarcas of New England, the Bonannos, Genovese, and Gambino factions in New York—all have been decimated by RICO prosecutions. Even those alleged criminals who survive such prosecutions (e.g., John Gotti) find that Federal prosecutors are waiting in the wings with a never-ending list of new indictments that make it difficult if not impossible for crime family leaders to conduct their usual businesses (Raab 1990, E6). The title of Raab's news article captures the mob's plight: "A Battered and Ailing Mafia is Losing Its Grip on America" (Raab 1990, 1).

The recent prosecutions of scores of Italian organized criminals throughout the country has weakened their criminal syndicates. Even the vaunted secrecy—the code of *omerta*, of silence—has been broken by numerous Italian gangsters (e.g., Joe Valachi, Vincent Teresa, Jimmy

"The Weasel" Fratiano, etc.), which suggests that the former power of Italian mobs to control even their own members has been compromised: " 'The government of the mob, the ability to make secret agreements and set up spheres of influence has been weakened' says Thomas L. Sheer, head of the Federal Bureau of Investigation's New York Office. 'We are even starting to hear some members say 'Hey, maybe this thing of ours is over' " (Kerr, "Chinese Now Dominate New York Heroin Trade," *New York Times* 9 August 1987, 30).

History repeats itself. The similarity between the Irish mobsters of the early 1920s and today's Italian gang leaders is striking. Like the Irish, current Italian syndicate leaders are unsure of their power and influence, seeing their base of power within the larger Italian community slowly eroding. The Irish gangsters of that former era similarly isolated themselves, persisting in outmoded forms of criminal activity, ignoring the realities of the new bootlegging and labor racketeering eras. They thought of themselves as noble tribunes guarding the empire's frontiers against the incursions of the Jewish and Italian barbarians bent on destroying all they had built. Yet the Jews and Italians forcibly crashed the frontiers, "convincing" many of the Irish gangsters to either retire or fill subsidiary roles in their organizations; for the determined "rogue elephants" who resisted, (the Dion O'Bannions, the Vincent Colls, and the Legs Diamonds) assassination settled the issue.

Today's Italian mobsters similarly see new barbarians at the gates of their criminal enterprises. Tired and weary, their hearts are no longer in their work as had been true in past eras. They have "made it" to the apex of crime and consequently many lack the driving ambition to pioneer new avenues, building fresh empires and monopolies. Instead they increasingly fight a rear-guard action against the blacks, the Hispanics and the Asians, hoping to hold on to the territories and enterprises once commanded with impunity. Ianni quotes one of the Italian leaders of a Brooklyn crime family about his reactions to increasing African American crime:

> Things here in Brooklyn aren't good for us now. This neighborhood right here used to be all Italian and the people looked up to us because we kept things quiet here. We tried fighting them for a while but there is no way to win. Lindsay and the other politicians are scared of them and they will give them anything they want to get their votes. A couple of years ago it really got bad and there was a lot of knifing

and fighting between colored gangs and some of the Italian boys. Mayor Lindsay had to get somebody to Joey Gallo who ran things in the neighborhood, and tell him it was a bad thing and would he help stop it. But Joey didn't need Lindsay to tell him anything. Joey was always crazy but he was smart, too. When he was in Green Haven [prison] he saw that the blacks were going to take over on the street in Brooklyn so he began making contact with them even then. . . . They're going to keep taking over but if you watch the way they run things in Harlem now you know it's not going to be the same. A lot of times they refuse to pay off, even to their own people. In the thirty years we were in East Harlem we always paid off, even when we knew we were being taken. Now nobody knows what is going to happen, but what the Hell, those guys want to make a little, too. We're moving out and they're moving in. I guess it's their turn now. (Ianni 1974, 12–13)

To maintain their dominance in organized crime Italian gangsters must extend themselves further into new and innovative forms of criminal activity. As Peter Lupsha points out, some are doing so:

The Italian-American groups, while withdrawing from street and direct front-line operations, remain as leading members in the orchestration of organized crime enterprises in the United States . . . it appears that traditional Italian-American organized crime members have not left the business, but simply moved to upper management positions. With capital and efficient associates, fewer people can carry out these director functions while there is ethnic succession in certain functions and enterprises and on the street. (Lupsha 1981, 5)

Yet the traditional forms of organized crime (i.e., narcotics, gambling, numbers, and extortion) increasingly move beyond their control. No longer is it possible for individual Italian criminals to enter black, Asian, and Hispanic neighborhoods demanding the spoils of crime. Indeed, as Reuter observes, the Italian mobs have not contested the challenges to their power in these neighborhoods (Reuter 1983, 136). To do so would largely be suicidal since the newcomer criminals are not about to play a subsidiary, second-rate role in these rackets as they once did. Like an empire in decline, the Italian mobs must increase the threat of violence in these minority areas if they are to be successful. Yet the demographic realities preclude such a show of force, for the new Italian recruits to the traditional Italian mobs are simply not there in depth. Like imperial Rome, these mobs must rely on mercenary forces to "govern" the "colonies"; as with imperial Rome, the time is ripe for the mercenary newcomer mobsters to claim these territories for themselves, ousting the Italian criminals from their areas, refusing to pay the tribute traditionally extracted from them.

Those Italians seeking to remain in organized crime consequently will drift elsewhere—to new unchartered areas of criminal activity, to white-collar corporate, and computer crime. Some will involve themselves with the "new" Mafia which has emerged in Italy, centered in Palermo. This new breed of mobster differs from the old mafiosi who were interested in power and respect; the newcomers are much more materialistic in their goals, and nouveau riche in their behavior (Arlacchi 1986). Some have attempted to reach an accommodation with the newcomers. In Philadelphia they have been involved in drug dealings with that city's "Black Mafia." In the New York City area, some Italian gangsters have worked closely with blacks in importing heroin, with Colombians in the cocaine trade, with Soviet Jews in excise tax schemes, and credit card fraud. This is done in the form of "bankrolling" the new ethnic criminals, thus allowing the Italian gangsters to "keep their hands clean" as they preserve their criminal niche. As Lupsha argues, "Italian groups are not giving up control, they are simply engaging in wider use of non-Italian criminal associates, entering new and more complex criminal matrices, and licensing the new ethnics to operate the more traditional, more risky, and lower profit organized crime markets" (Lupsha 1981, 19).

Other Italian criminals will simply retire from organized crime to die peacefully in their own beds, finding solace in their memories of the old days when they piped the tune and everyone else danced to their melody (Reuter 1983, 133). Still others will forcibly resist their ouster from power and privilege and, more than likely, will die violently in the struggle for power. If they choose to fight the newcomers, probably they are doomed, destined to be eliminated like the Irish and the Jews. In sensing this "last hurrah," paper-tiger quality of the Italian mobsters, the newcomers position themselves and plan for the day in the not-so-distant future when they will be the lords of the underworld supplying the tabooed substances and services demanded by the public. As Reuter states, "the Mafia may be a paper tiger" (Reuter 1983, xi).

Whether these Italian mobs retire from traditional organized crime, franchise it to new groups, or forcibly resist the newcomers, may thus be immaterial. More important is the strength and determination of the African American, Hispanic, and Oriental newcomers who will be setting their agenda, and charting the future course of organized crime in the United States.

Thus the historical succession of ethnic minorities in organized crime constitutes one of its most notable features, with no ethnic group retaining its supremacy in crime indefinitely. Ethnic groups dominant in organized crime are eventually replaced by lower-echelon ethnic competitors. A new incoming ethnic minority group struggles to gain a foothold in the criminal world. In time, it rises to the top, consolidating its new-found power and influence. Its criminal leaders bask in the glory and notoriety bestowed upon them by their ethnic brethren. They are public figures and to the larger middle-class world, public enemies—forces to be either courted or condemned. Yet this stability and attention are short-lived for this ethnic group, rarely lasting more than one or two generations. Other lower-positioned ethnic groups envy this group's prerogatives, desiring these same attitudes of criminal power. Eventually they dethrone the original ethnic group and establish their own hegemony in the world of organized crime. A cycle is thus created wherein today's "bagmen" and "gorillas" and "hitmen" are tomorrow's chieftains and syndicate heads.

The Rise of Ethnic Newcomers

Into this breach created by the growing exodus of Italians from organized crime step the newcomers—the ambitious, resourceful criminals from many of the new ethnic minorities. Blacks, (American and Caribbean), Hispanics (Cuban, Mexican, Puerto Rican, Colombian, Bolivian, Venezuelan), and Asians (Chinese, Japanese, Vietnamese, Filipino, and Korean) comprise the largest segments of these new ethnic minorities although smaller segments are also operative (e.g., Soviet Jews, Nigerians, Ghanians). They have been "waiting their turn" on the ethnic queue, anticipating the moment when they will rise on the ladder of success.

Many of these minorities are new to the urban-industrial life of America. The key to understanding which groups make it, both in the normal world and the criminal realm, is the length of time that an ethnic group has been exposed to urban-industrial values and lifestyles. Those ethnic groups that have had the longest exposure to America's cities (e.g., Irish, Jews, and Italians) are placed higher in the status order and historically have commanded the higher positions in organized crime. The pecking order is clear: the Irish came early to America's cities and occupied positions until their dethronement by the

Jews who came later. The Jews in turn were displaced by the later arriving and less urbanized Italians who subsequently have monopolized organized crime for the past forty years. Italian criminals in turn are about to be displaced by the minority newcomers—African Americans, Hispanics, Asians, and other ethnic newcomers.

African Americans, Hispanics, Asians, and Other Ethnic Newcomers

Behind the Italians came a substantial number of ethnic minorities, most of whom have had only minimal exposure to America's urban-industrial life-styles. American blacks comprise the largest number of these newcomers to the nation's cities, commencing their mass exodus from the rural South in the 1920s. Settling in the industrial centers of the Northeast, Midwest, and West Coast, their in-migration to these urban centers peaked in the 1950s and 1960s. Residing longer in America than most ethnic groups, African Americans are relatively new to urban life-styles and values. Other blacks, primarily West Indians from Jamaica, Trinidad, the Bahamas, and Barbados also immigrated to America's cities, particularly in the post-1965 years. Haitians arrived in substantial numbers in the early 1980s.

Hispanics also began their trek to America's cities at the same time. Mexicans left their homeland and the rural areas of the Southwest, arriving in the cities of the Pacific Coast and the Midwest in the post-1910 era, but overwhelmingly more so during the past twenty-five years. Puerto Ricans began their exodus from the island to the mainland in the post-1945 period with large-scale emigration to the cities, particularly New York, in the 1950s and 1960s. Cubans, many of whom had exposure to cosmopolitan life-styles and middle-class values in Cuba, flocked to American urban centers in the 1960s, and again in the 1980s (the Mariel influx). Added to these were substantial numbers of Central and South Americans coming from virtually every nation in those regions in the 1970s and 1980s, particularly Colombia.

Asian immigrants arrived at America's shores largely after the change in immigration legislation in 1965 (Hart-Cellar Act) which liberalized immigration levels for all groups. Substantial numbers of Chinese, Filipinos, Koreans, Indians, Cambodians, Vietnamese, and Japanese, many of whom had previous middle-class professional life-styles in their homelands, arrived in the 1970s and 1980s. They settled primarily in the cities of the Pacific Coast, particularly Los Angeles and San Francisco, as well as those on the eastern seaboard, most notably New York City.

How these various groups will fare in the criminal enterprises of the future is open to question, for realistically there is no accurate way of predicting which of these groups will inherit the mantle of power now claimed by Italians. Police intelligence rarely projects future trends in ethnic leadership in organized crime. Instead, it often reacts to what has happened, seriously considering new ethnic criminal groups only after they have become entrenched. It was only in the 1960s that J. Edgar Hoover, the Director of the Federal Bureau of Investigation, even acknowledged that organized crime exists in the United States. Justin Dintino, the head of the New Jersey State Police, noted this lack of awareness of the existence and momentum of new organized crime groups, particularly African American, Asian, and Hispanic:

> I've stated publicly that I firmly believe there's organized groups out there more powerful than the LCN [La Cosa Nostra], both numerically and in money and viciousness. Colombian cartels, they got it all over the LCN and forget about them just being in Colombia. They're here. . . . I think that the Mafia or the LCN have put a tag on Italian-Americans that's unjustified and because of these sleazebags, a lot of people have to take a lot of heat. . . . We've got to get off our butts. We've got to start looking at these other groups or we're going to have the same problems we had with the LCN—even worse. (Larini 1988, 1, 24)

Which of the New Ethnic Mobs Will "Make It"?

If history tells us anything about ethnic succession in organized crime, it suggests that those newcomer groups that are demographically large and that have urban-industrial backgrounds will do better in crime than those groups lacking these prerequisites. This scenario favors African Americans and Mexicans, as well as Cubans and Chinese.

African Americans and Mexicans, two of the largest of all current ethnic minorities, are not concentrated or restricted to a handful of geographical locations and their presence in urban-industrial centers for over a generation, in some cases two generations, has socialized them to urban life-styles. Their sheer demographic size provides a reservoir of potential individuals willing to pursue careers in organized crime. Coast-to-coast networks of criminal syndicates and contacts are thus possible for each group while the same is very difficult for the smaller ethnic minorities that simply do not possess the manpower sufficient to staff and control vast criminal enterprises.

Furthermore, some of the smaller ethnic gangs restrict themselves primarily to one type of illegal enterprise. Colombian gangs in the United States for example, have concentrated on cocaine production, transportation, and distribution. In the highly volatile world of narcotics fad and fashion, such may be an unwise business decision, for if American consumers should tire of cocaine and opt for some other drug, the Colombian drug dealers will have suddenly lost their highly lucrative market. Similar dilemmas confront Jamaican crack and marijuana dealers who likewise specialize in only a few types of drugs and who will be unable to expand their markets nationwide if consumer interest suddenly shifts.

Portents of such shifting tastes have appeared in the late 1980s when the Federal Drug Enforcement Administration spokesmen indicated that methamphetamine ("crank," "ice," "speed") would rapidly compete with crack and possible replace it as the drug of choice among drug users. Speed is relatively cheap to produce, and does not depend on foreign sources of supply as do cocaine and heroin. Domestically produced, it can be injected, snorted, smoked, or mixed in beverages. (Gross 1988, 1) By 1990, however, this threat had not materialized and only the future will tell whether "ice," the smokeable form of methamphetamine, will become the addict's drug of choice (Pennell 1990, 13).

Unless these demographically weaker ethnic gangs can cash in on these shifting consumer interests, they will be isolated in a fiercely competitive drug world with products and services no longer in demand. Their chances of competing in new products (e.g., speed, and amphetamines) are slim, since they have no monopoly over the production of the raw materials as they had with drugs such as cocaine which is grown in areas outside the United States, such as Colombia and Peru.

What power the numerically weaker ethnic groups possess can only be put to maximum criminal use in supplying other ethnic gangs with drugs (e.g., Colombian cocaine trafficking in Florida, New York, and

Chicago) or by exerting criminal influence in localized areas (e.g., Jamaican crime in parts of New York City; Soviet Jewish counterfeiting gangs in Brooklyn; Nigerian and Ghanian credit card fraud in New York City; Portuguese rackets in areas of Newark, New Jersey, and New Bedford, Massachusetts; Greek mob activities in Philadelphia; Vietnamese gangs in California, Texas, Louisiana, and Alabama; Cambodian gangs in California; Japanese Yakuza gangs in Hawaii and California; and Korean enterprises in sections of Los Angeles).

Rosner shows how Soviet Jewish criminals bring their criminal skills with them as they immigrate to the United States using these skills to "beat the system" here just as they did in Russia (Rosner 1986). They follow in the footsteps of previous immigrant groups who did likewise (i.e., Chinese triads, Italian mafia, etc.) One group known as the "Potato Bag Gang" began its operations in the time-honored manner of preying upon recent Soviet Jewish immigrants. Posing as sailors these Odessa gangsters offered to sell gold rubles to the immigrants at a cheap price. Gullible victims paid thousands of dollars for what they believed were sacks of the rubles but which turned out to be sacks of potatoes (*The New York Times*, 4 June 1989, 1, 38). Federal sources indicate that Russian newcomer crime is relatively centralized in New York City's Brighton Beach, but has expanded to other cities such as Philadelphia and Los Angeles and involves con games, extortion, insurance fraud, counterfeiting, tax fraud, arson, burglary, and murder. In New York, the Russian gangs operate under the nominal protection of various mafia-style Italian gangs (President's Commission on Organized Crime, *Impact* 1986, 24).

Even in these localized areas, many of these smaller operations in theory, if not in practice, fall under the nominal control of larger ethnic criminal gangs that provide political protection, relative safety from competitors, judicial settlement of inter-group rivalries, and so on. Philadelphia, for example, has a "Greek" mob allied to the larger Italian syndicate headed by Angelo Bruno who was assassinated in 1980. In the aftermath of Bruno's killing, a full-scale war broke out for control of the Philadelphia and Atlantic City rackets, resulting in the assassinations of a number of reputed Greek mobsters (e.g., Chelsais Bouras, Harry Peetros) (*The New York Times*, 31 May 1981, 23).

Soviet Jewish newcomers provide such an example. Residing primarily in the Brighton Beach section of Brooklyn, New York, their background is certainly one of urbanization/industrialization from Russia. Interestingly, they have concentrated more on the white-collar aspects of organized crime (e.g., counterfeiting, excise tax fraud, credit card fraud, and welfare scams). In these endeavors some Soviet Jewish criminals work closely with Italian criminals who bankroll these operations and protect them. In the New York City area, according to Robert Creighton, the former principal investigator of the New York State Organized Crime Task Force and current chief investigator for the Suffolk, New York District Attorney's Office, they have allied themselves with the Colombo mob under "Sonny" Franzese and his son Mike, organizing tax evasion schemes with local oil companies. Though powerful and important in the Jewish sections of New York City crime, they have established criminal enterprises in Los Angeles, San Francisco, Chicago, Boston, Miami, and Dallas. The probabilities of Soviet Jews becoming major forces in future organized crime throughout the United States is somewhat remote, given the relatively small number of immigrants from that group. This could change radically if massive emigration of Jews from Russia were to occur.

Thus, just as the Polish rackets during the Prohibition era allied themselves under larger Irish and Italian domination, so also will the smaller ethnic newcomer groups of the present. By their very demographic size, African Americans and Mexican criminal gangs can largely dictate to smaller-sized competitors the terms of operation and cooperation, and can impose their will through violence on those gangs unwilling to submit to their hegemony.

Whether or not this occurs is hypothetical; to date Mexicans have not yet moved beyond localized organized crime and blacks are further advanced in establishing such networks but still evince a parochial attitude toward large-scale organized crime. Yet both Mexicans and blacks have the sine qua non for success—large numbers of young ambitious men and women who see crime as a viable avenue to all they want from American life.

Blacks though have begun to develop autonomous criminal syndicates in areas, such as New York City and Detroit. Independent narcotics operations have been created outside of the jurisdiction of Italian gangsters and function with varying degrees of success under American black or Jamaican dominance. Robert Kelly notes this development in New York City:

It is believed that gambling profits and those derived from other enterprises such as loansharking and fencing in stolen goods, were the capitalization instruments for their autonomous drug ventures. Eventually, the Black drug rings developed their own international sources of supply, importing methods, processing, and distribution outlets. As with their white counter-parts, the huge profits earned in narcotics were allegedly funneled into legitimate businesses in the ghettoes and Black communities of the Metropolitan New York region. (Kelly 1987, 28–29)

Kelly further remarks that some of these African American narcotics syndicates (i.e., those controlled by LeRoy "Nicky" Barnes, Frank Matthews, and Charles Lucas) spread far beyond the ghettoes and became very sophisticated in their operations (Kelly 1987, 29).

Detroit provides a similar example, witnessing the mercurial rise and fall of the Chambers Brothers (Billy, Larry, Otis, and Willie) who cornered the crack market in that city in the late 1980s. Their sophisticated operations employed approximately 500 workers and grossed up to $3 million a day in sales. It even recruited its own "employees" from Marianna, Arkansas, the town from which the brothers migrated to seek fame and fortune in Detroit. Marianna's police chief, Mark Birchler, remarked, "The Chambers brothers came down here with fancy cars and fancy clothes and girlfriends and drugs and jewelry and offered these kids life-style they couldn't get in Marianna" (Wilkerson 1988, 1, 42).

Cuban criminals also demonstrate the potential for large-scale successes within organized crime. Though numerically modest, Cubans illustrate attributes crucial to success in organized crime, possessing middle-class organizational skills derived from their prior occupational networks and from the extensive organized crime networks that thrived in Cuba prior to Fidel Castro's revolution in 1959. They gained this criminal expertise working as underlings in the Havana casino rackets pioneered and controlled by Jews (e.g., Lansky) and Italians (e.g., Luciano and Costello) and after 1959 brought to the mainland these networks and criminal organizational skills. The subsequent forced exodus of common street criminals from Cuba in the early 1980s—the Marielitos—added the sufficient "firepower" to expand Cuban narcotics and gambling operations well beyond the "Little Havanas" of the cities of Florida and the Gulf Coast to those of the Northeast and Midwest.

Chinese newcomers likewise demonstrate enormous potential for succeeding in organized crime primarily because of their increased demographic size as well as their historical, well-developed tongs and criminal syndicates within their own communities in the larger cities. All that is needed is the move beyond the ghetto which, until recently, Chinese mobsters have been reluctant to make. Their parochialism represented their response to the historically widespread hatred and fear of Orientals, particularly on the West Coast. Currently, anti-Oriental sentiment has been muted and as Chinese and other Asian-background individuals continue to move into the world beyond their communities, their criminal gangs will do likewise.

J. Chuan Chu, a vice president of a major American corporation, stated, "If you have the ability and can adapt to the American way of speaking, dressing, and doing things, then it doesn't matter any more if you are Chinese" (*New York Times* 1970, 1). The article continues "the majority of Chinese and Japanese Americans, whose humble parents had to iron the laundry and garden the lawns of white Americans, no longer find any artificial barriers to becoming doctors, lawyers, architects, and professors" (1ff.). Such also can be said about the movement of Asians into organized crime as they interact and compete with the more established criminal groups.

Furthermore, their access to the narcotics producing areas of Southeast Asia provides a distinctive advantage to Chinese criminals moving into and controlling large segments of drug trafficking (Bresler 1980, 67). Funded by this access to a highly desired "product," and by the substantial number of lower-income immigrants from highly cosmopolitan centers such as Hong Kong, Bangkok, and Singapore, the Chinese gangsters have begun to make their move into the larger arena of American crime. Butterfield notes this new extensive immigration of Chinese to the United States: "From 1970–80, according to the Census Bureau, the number of Chinese in the United States jumped 85 percent to 806,027 from 435,062. In 1984 alone, nearly 50,000 ethnic Chinese from China, Hong Kong and Taiwan settled in the United States making them the second largest group of legal immigrants after Mexicans" (Butterfield 1985, 42).

Chinese crime has established a foothold in the larger sphere of American organized crime, peddling superior quality "China White" heroin at discount prices. One such individual, Johnny Kon (born Kon

Yu-Leung), was arrested in New York City in 1988 for conspiring to import a half-ton of heroin into the United States from Asia. He was also suspected of importing sizable amounts of heroin that had been seized in New York, Seattle, and Chicago after it had entered the United States from Bolivia and Panama (Levin and Krajicek 1988, 7). Another heroine importer Kok Leung Woo was arrested in 1989 for allegedly concealing 820 pounds of the drug (street value $1 billion) inside of rubber tires. His operations reportedly extended over half a dozen cities throughout the world (*Time* 6 March 1989, 33). Nor are the Chinese alone in their criminal endeavors, for the Japanese have transported some Yakuza groups to Hawaii and the California areas. The Yakuza have a long tradition of organized crime in Japan and have elaborate organization and customs (Haberman 1985). One observer notes the unusual rituals practiced by Yakuza members:

> Yakuza groups are large with elaborate organization into "families" that are subdivided into still smaller units. One group, the Yamaguchi-gumi, is thought to have 13,000 members. . . . The Japanese organized crime groups are best known for two ritual practices: tatooing their bodies and self-mutilation practices (cutting off a small finger at the first joint for failing to successfully comply with the instructions of a superior. (Kelly 1987, 35)

Yakuza crime is largely confined to the Japanese-American neighborhoods on the West Coast, but some observers fear that they will extend their trade beyond the ethnic enclave (Kaplan and Dubro 1987, 268–69).

Drugs and Liquor—The Parallels with Prohibition

The current situation in organized crime is remarkably analogous to that of the Prohibition era, a time when the Irish fell from criminal power, unable to deal effectively with their new Jewish and Italian rivals in mastering the manufacture and sale of a desired but illegal substance—alcohol. Bootlegging provided the impetus for the phenomenal expansion of organized crime, furnishing it with new markets in a society with an insatiable appetite for the outlawed "demon rum." Perhaps Capone was prophetic when he said "You can't cure thirst by law" (Kobler 1971, 306). Prohibition doomed the Irish and "made" the Jews and Italians.

Pax Caponeana

Yet the violence of the Prohibition era ended not because of the legalization of alcohol but only after the emergence of centralized control on the part of the mobs themselves.

In Chicago this control was instituted in 1929, four years before Prohibition's repeal. The landmark event was the St. Valentine's Day Massacre, wherein Chicago witnessed the final ascendancy of Al Capone over his Irish, Polish, and Italian criminal competitors. A few years earlier he had eliminated most of these rivals—Dion O'Bannion, the O'Donnells, the Genna Brothers, Hymie Weiss; on February 14 of 1929, Capone disposed of the remnants of Bugs Moran's Polish-Irish Northsiders. Capone now reigned supreme and ushered in a *Pax Caponeana*, a strictly enforced criminal peace in Chicago.

In New York, this centralized criminal control occurred much later, years after Prohibition's demise, with the ascendancy of Lucky Luciano and Meyer Lansky in the late 1930s and early 1940s. In a Capone-like scenario Luciano and Lansky's rivals were slowly eliminated. By the 1950s most, if not all, of the prominent Irish and Jewish gangsters were dead; Arnold Rothstein, Legs Diamond, Vincent Coll, Dutch Schultz, Peg Leg Lonnigan, Bugsy Seigel. The post-World War II era witnessed the consolidation of the Italian control over organized crime aided by the remnants of the once powerful Jewish gangs.

As a consequence of this violence, a *Pax Caponeana* emerged in virtually all our major cities—a peace enforced primarily, but not exclusively, by Italian mobsters. The result was the emergence of regulated and normalized criminal conduct. Occasional mob "rub outs" still took place, but these remained relatively rare compared to the violence of the 1920s and 1930s. Street crime receded, organized crime went about its usual business and the public slept soundly in their beds at night. Street criminals and urban riff-raff were neutralized by local mafiosi whose invincible image of toughness kept the lid on predatory street crime.

Yet times have changed. As Italian mobsters wane in organized crime, they face a situation not unlike that encountered by the Irish in the 1920s. Currently their criminal endeavors face serious trouble, encumbered by numerous difficulties beyond their total control. Their fields of "expertise" have not kept pace with the social and political changes of recent years. Their interests in labor racketeering have been stymied by the overall decline in the labor movement throughout the nation; their interests in prostitution have been hurt by the liberalization of sexual mores as well as the decrease in the incidence of prostitution itself; their interests in gambling have been affected by the growing legalization of lotteries, and off-track betting; their interests in pornography, loan-sharking, and extortion remain lucrative yet do not offer promise as fields of enormous future profits. Only drugs and narcotics offer such a bonanza, and the new ethnic minorities are rapidly pushing the Italian mobs out of this area.

And so, by the 1980s this *Pax Caponeana* began to unravel. Today's mafia is no longer the threat it once was. The ever-growing Italian-American middle class no longer admires nor nurtures the mafiosi who are often old, infirm, and unable to replenish their ranks. Today's Italian middle class sees its children and grandchildren emulating doctors and lawyers rather than the gangsters that some Italian Americans had earlier taken as models. These once formidable "dons" and "capos" now spend their days either in federal prisons or in court contesting federal prosecutors. Their vaunted hegemony over poor neighborhoods has passed to other groups who now control the supply of the forbidden narcotic fruits—Jamaican marijuana posses, Columbian cocaine hidalgos, Chinese heroin triads, Dominican crack crews. Mafia mobs are no match for these new, vicious ethnic upstarts.

Just as Imperial Rome in the fourth and fifth centuries A.D. withdrew her legions from the fringes of her empire because of the incursion of the barbarians, so do the old mafiosi retreat from minority neighborhoods. They take with them their *Pax Caponeana* leaving these areas to the anarchy and violence that result as the new barbarian warlords vie for the mantle of power.

Drugs and narcotics are to the 1990s what liquor was to the 1920s—tabooed substances, highly desired by many Americans. They offer their users euphoric highs, release from tensions and stress, and the chance to engage in something exciting, rebellious, and criminal. Their very illegality guarantees an extremely lucrative situation for organized crime offering a market likely to continue and expand, for there is no realistic political movement to legitimate their manufacture, sale, and use as had been so with alcohol in the Prohibition era. Politicians also may find drugs potentially attractive: their sale and protection provide a possible source of campaign funds; they provide a method of making the underclass less of a problem since drug income fuels the underground economy of virtually all our impoverished inner-city neighborhoods even as it robs them.

Prohibition lasted but thirteen years until the Twenty-First Amendment rescinded it in 1933. Widespread drug use has been apparent for the past thirty years and its end is nowhere in sight. On the contrary, the use of certain drugs, such as marijuana, cocaine, crack, and speed by segments of the middle class implies that new potential markets are available and the new ethnic criminals are more than eager to exploit these opportunities risking everything, including their lives, to get a chance to "make it big" in America.

The results of this transition from Italian mobs to black, Hispanic, and Asian mobs are apparent everywhere. No one ethnic group is in charge. We witness the never-ending nightmare of carnage in the cities. In the poorest areas, the once stabilizing force of family, church, school, community, and even neighborhood gang, have disintegrated. The alienated youths in these areas join with similarly disaffected peers—often mere acquaintances—as they roam in wolf packs in "wilding" sprees seeking their prey. Bereft of stable criminal role models, they do the despicable deeds we see on the nightly news. Beholden only to themselves rather than to an organization, they lust for power and status, viewing competitors as deadly rivals.

Warlords appear, gain local notoriety, and are quickly gunned down; new leaders appear and a new cycle of internecine violence begins with drug dealers competing for prominence in a criminal realm without any clear codes of behavior. Today's drug pushers and steerers are tomorrow's drug czars. An Al Capone or a Lucky Luciano has not yet emerged to impose a peace. Instead each ethnic minority battles within itself for a share of the spoils. Black drug dealers kill other black dealers; so also do Puerto Rican, Colombian, Chinese, Mexican, Jamaican dealers turn against their ethnic peers. It's almost as though the O'Bannions were still fighting the O'Donnells, the Capones still feuding with the Gennas, the Dutch Schultzs with the Lanskys. The beer wars have been replaced by the drug wars.

City after city has reported increases in drug-related homicides in the late 1980s. Miami, for example, reported that 24 percent of its murders were related to narcotics and that 72 percent of these murder victims did *not* have drugs in their bodies at the time of their murder implying that these deaths were "business-related" crimes. In 1986, 50 percent of all those murdered in Manhattan died in drug-related situations. Drug-related homicides and the feuding between rival gangs for control of drug markets have become a notable feature of all our large metropolitan centers.

The Upward Mobility of the New Ethnic Gangs

The more resourceful new ethnic criminals of our current narcotics era have abandoned the first stage of individual criminal mobility: the remaining four stages of mobility in crime await those who successfully survive their odysseys.

These few new ethnics have "made it" beyond the world of common street crime, graduating from burglary, mugging, thievery, assault, rape, murder, and so on, entering the more rational world of organized gang activity. Their tactics and felonious deeds may be the same as before, but the gang channels them toward its established ends that invariably further the power, prestige, and income of the gang and its members. Thus murders are committed in order to realize the gang's goals of increasing profits, controlling renegade members, protecting existing territories and markets, and terrorizing competitors. The crimes of ethnic newcomers become organized crimes governed by rational patterns and motives.

Having moved beyond common nonorganized street crime, these gangsters enter the realm of intraethnic gang rivalry where they contend, often violently, with similar newcomers from their own ethnic group for the spoils of narcotics trafficking. Their primary aim rests in consolidating their own power and the power of their gang. This entails the elimination and neutralization of fellow ethnic competitors. A casual reading of newspaper accounts of drug-related homicides reveals this daily intraethnic conflict where the violence often appears incomprehensible to both police and public alike. Competitors are executed in bizarre ways and oftentimes family members and innocent bystanders are similarly murdered. Yet this viciousness is a planned terror calculated to intimidate ethnic rivals into submission. It serves notice to the local community and competing criminals within the neighborhood that no opposition will be accepted.

The more cunning and brutal the gang, the better its chances of success, for no quarter is rendered in these local massacres. Their leaders gain prominence and status and are feared by both criminals and the public. The early beginnings of Capone, Schultz, Diamond, Genovese, and O'Bannion revealed their proclivity for the use of terror in eliminating rivals and establishing hegemony within their own ethnic groups. In their pursuit of power, current ethnic gangsters clearly match the vicious violence of their predecessors of past eras. Howard Blum reports on a South Bronx drug war between three Puerto Rican gangs that resulted in twenty-seven murders over a two-year period. Two such homicides illustrate the heinous nature of these executions; Blum reports these as follows:

> Two days after Valdo's murder, the bodies of Gumersindo Torres and Oscar Ocasio were discovered by children playing in a deserted lot across from a public school in Hunts Point. More specifically, the two corpses were found in three separate La Flor De Mayo Moving Company cartons; the bodies had been dismembered.

> Both men had been taken by members of the Teenager gang to a dim, windowless basement room on 149th Street. While Oscar Ocasio was handcuffed to a wooden chair, Gumersindo Torres, who had already been shot, was held spread-eagle on a Ping-Pong table. A single bulb hung from a chord directly above his head.

> A man present in the room who later became a police witness remembered that there was a loud click immediately followed by the rapid, whirring drone of an electric saw. The buzz of the saw was lost in a fury of screams. When they finished with Gumersindo Torres, Oscar Ocasio was dragged to the Ping-Pong table. The Medical Examiner's office later theorized that he died of a heart attack either before or soon after they began cutting into his body. He was, literally, scared to death. The basement room was soaked with so much blood that the next day the murderers returned with a blow torch to cleanse the walls and cement floor. (Blum 21 December 1978, B8)

The solutions of all twenty-seven homicides and the convictions of the killers scarcely dented the drug traffic for new ambitious Hispanics quickly moved in and took over the territory. The only thing that continued to change were the names of the victims (Blum 22 December 1978, B4).

Black inner-city neighborhoods witness similar drug-related violence, frequently involving control of the ever-expanding crack market. A derivative of cocaine, crack presents newcomer criminals—particularly African Americans—with a golden opportunity for advancement in the underworld and the stampede of black gangsters seeking such stature has resulted in hundreds of killings. In New York City the degree of violence reaches bizarre proportions. In 1989 a twelve-year-old boy was kidnapped on his way to school and held for ransom by abductors seeking $500,000 from the boy's brother—a reputed middle-level crack dealer. A day later, the kidnappers cut off the boy's right index finger and mailed it with an audio tape that recorded the victims frantic pleas to his mother. The ransom of $350,000 offered by the family was never accepted. A month later the boy's brother was murdered execution-style; a few weeks later the twelve-year old's body was discovered by police who theorized that the entire incident was related to the crack trade (McKinley 6 January 1990, L27).

Chicago provides further illustrations of drug-related violence. The Blackstone Rangers, an adolescent street gang in the 1960s and 1970s, has evolved into an adult gang, El Rukns, with loose ties to Black Muslims and which is, according to the F.B.I., "a violent criminal organization involved in narcotics trafficking and other illegal enterprises" (Harris 1987, 9–10). In 1987, most of its leadership, including its founder, Jeff Fort, were convicted in federal court of conspiring to commit terrorist acts on behalf of the Libyan government, and in 1991 its remaining leadership faced narcotics, racketeering, and murder charges (Terry 1991, 18).

Jamaican criminals have organized narcotic networks in at least fifteen major American cities. The resultant internecine warfare among Jamaicans, and between them and American-born blacks, has been responsible for 300 to 400 murders in the late 1980s. George Volsky cites James Brown, special agent of the Miami district of the Federal Bureau of Alcohol, Tobacco, and Firearms, who states that Jamaican mobs—"posses"—have been identified in New York, Philadelphia, Hartford, Boston, Toronto, Washington, Miami, Fort Lauderdale, Cleveland, Chicago, Kansas City, Dallas, Houston, Denver, and Los Angeles (Volsky 1987, 17). In December 1987, a shootout at a Brooklyn social club between rival Jamaican posses left two dead and more than a dozen injured. The best organized and most prominent of these posses is the Shower Posse based primarily in New York and Miami; other posses include the Dog Posse, the Tel Aviv Posse, the Spangler

Posse, the Dunkirk Posse, the Water House Posse, and the Banton Posse. The main business of these posses is narcotics trafficking, particularly crack trafficking ("AFT" 1987, 3).

Many of these Jamaican gangsters are associated with the Rastafarian religious cult and have been enormously successful particularly in Brooklyn. Other newcomer criminal gangs pattern their criminal lifestyles after these Rastas and, in a case of imitation being the sincerest form of flattery, newcomer criminals from Panama have mimicked Rastafarian hair locks and dress as a way of breaking into their drug operations.

In Detroit, black gangs, such as the Pony Down and the Young Boys Inc., have evolved from opportunistic violent street gangs to sophisticated criminal enterprises. Drug dealing is their main business and their membership increasingly attracts middle-class youths as well as the traditional lower-class members. They operate in secrecy, with a small tightly knit core of leaders whose style mimics that of corporate entrepreneurs more than the traditional style of urban street warriors (Taylor 1990). Their modus operandi suggests that black organized crime is patterning itself after its historical predecessors from the Irish, Jewish, and Italian underworld.

Another section of Brooklyn—Brownsville—illustrates the chronic warfare among American-born and Caribbean-born black gangsters for control of the crack trade. In the late 1980s at least three rival black gangs fought each other for control of this neighborhood. At least eleven murders in a two-year period have been associated with one of these mobs—the Wild Bunch—allegedly headed by Donny Smallwood. Rosenbaum detailed Smallwood's rise to power in a series of *New York Times* articles (February 15, 1987 and November 15, 1987), describing his feuds with "Halfback" James Baker (murdered in 1986) and "Pretty Rob." Whether men like Smallwood can maintain their power over gangs like the Wild Bunch and compete successfully against rival mobs, remains to be seen. Their modes of operation, however, are remarkably similar to those of the Irish, Jews, and Italians of former eras for a leader like Smallwood "didn't hide his existence in the shadows but boldly made himself a public figure in the community, a provider of parties, dispenser of largesse, something like a Tammany Ward boss, or an old-fashioned mafia don: a folk hero" (Rosenbaum 1987, 46).

In another New York City neighborhood, the South Jamaican section of Queens, alleged black criminals, such as "Pop" Freeman, Lorenzo "Fat Cat" Nichols, and Howard "Pappy" Mason have "inherited" the narcotics trade previously operated by the Mafia chieftan, Vito Genovese. Nichols eventually organized the many Black competing drug gangs by dividing the territory of that section of Queens among the previously warring factions. McAlary describes this truce as follows:

Fat Cat was next in line. He figured what with so much profit to be made, there was no sense dying in a drug war. So Nichols called a meeting with other dealers in the area, including the Corley brothers, Claude Skinner, Kenneth "Supreme" McGriff, Gerald "Prince" Miller, Tommy "Tony Mantana" Mickens, and Robert "Cornbread" Gray. After a night of partying in Fat Cat's clubhouse, a grocery store at the corner of 106th Avenue and 150th Street, the area was split up.

The Corley brothers were given control of the Forties Houses, The Supreme Team got the Baisley Houses. Tony Mantana got Laurelton and Hollis. Prince and Skinner were made enforcers. Cornbread remained hidden, handling distribution. And everyone answered to Fat Cat. (McAlary 1990, 28)

This operation ran reasonably well until Fat Cat's enforcer, "Pappy" Mason assassinated a New York City police officer, Edward Byrne, in response to an encounter with another police officer who had "dis'ed" (disrespected) him in public. The results of this assassination were disastrous for the entire drug empire of Fat Cat since the entire wrath of the city descended upon his operations. Even the associates of Pappy and Fat Cat were startled and infuriated at such an act which is a clear violation of even the drug dealers' code. One such associate remarked, "Man, I don't know why "Bebo" [Mason] did that. . . . What "Bebo" did was fucked up. He messed up everything for everybody. Now nobody will make no money" (McAlary 1990, 224). Other African American drug dealers quickly occupied the vacuum created by the demise of Fat Cat's operations.

Colombian gangs are also active in the cocaine traffic; an estimated 75 percent of cocaine consumed annually in the United States is imported from Colombia, supplied by sophisticated gangs that control its importation and processing. The President's Commission on Organized Crime notes that

at least 20 Colombian drug trafficking rings control America's cocaine supply.

Their members and workers handle every phase of production and trafficking, including manufacture, transportation, distribution, finance, and security. Thus a single ring typically includes investors, lawyers, bankers, chemists, logistics experts, wholesalers and retailers, exporters, and enforcers. . . . Colombian traffickers are ruthless in the pursuit of profit, and routinely use violence to protect their criminal enterprises. Their hired assassins kill not only informants and sometimes innocent bystanders. (President's Commission on Organized Crime, *Impact* 1986, 117–18)

The Colombian gangs often reflect the regional origins of the Colombian newcomers. The so-called Medellin cartel and the Cali cartel derive their names from the two principal cities in Colombia where the cocaine production and distribution are centered. Likewise, the ruthless violence between these two factions has become an everyday occurrence in Miami and New York where each competes for criminal dominance.

Chinese immigrants form one of the largest segment of Asian newcomers. Historically, Chinese immigrants came from China's Canton province. Current Chinese newcomers come from Hong Kong, Taiwan, Vietnam, Malaysia, and Indonesia, as well as from other sections of China such as Fujian province. Challenging the Cantonese dominance of Chinatown life, these newcomers have formed new gangs that have grown into criminal organizations that control gambling, drug marketing, and that extort money from Chinese merchants. These organizations provide a vehicle that will move Asian gangsters not only into the mainstream of American organized crime but into the larger, respectable American mainstream as well.

San Francisco's Chinatown has spawned the Wah Ching gang under the alleged leadership of Vincent Jew. Another gang, United Bamboo, operates in a number of cities; a number of its members have been prosecuted for the 1984 murder of Henry Liu, a San Francisco writer who authored a critical biography of the President of Taiwan, Chiang Ching-kuo. The Los Angeles area has its Four Seas Gang, a powerful criminal gang linked to similar organizations in Taiwan. New York's Chinatown has witnessed the rise of numerous new gangs challenging the traditional hegemony of the Hip Sings, the On Leongs, and the Tong Ons. These new organizations often use teenage youth as enforcers against rivals and as extortionists of Chinese businessmen.

Like their black and Hispanic counterparts, they are heavily involved in drug traffic seeking ways to dominate this business within the Chinese community as well as serve as suppliers of "China White" heroin to other gangs and syndicates outside the community.

Other Chinese gangs work closely with the traditional tongs. The Ghost Shadows engages in narcotics trafficking, gambling, loansharking, and extortion and has close ties to the On Leong Tong in New York City. The Tong's president Eddie Chan (Chan Tse-Chin) has been identified as a major leader of the Ghost Shadows (President's Commission on Organized Crime, *Imapct* 1986, 87; Curry 1990, 35). The other major tong in New York, the Hip Sing Tong under the its leader "Uncle Benny" Ong (Fei Lo Chat) sponsors the Flying Dragons that engages in considerable drug-related crime. Chapters of these gangs operate in Chicago, Boston, San Francisco, and Los Angeles.

As has been true of other ethnic gangs past and present, frequent internecine warfare occurs within and among these Chinese gangs. The struggle for control of the Ghost Shadows is reflected in the following description of the feud between rival leaders:

> At one time the gang was led by Nicky Louie, whose influence in the groups was such that he attempted to wrest control from Eddie Chan. Loyalists from Ghost Shadow groups in Boston and Chicago sided with the Louie faction in the gang war that resulted when Chan ordered the murder of his rival. Eventually Louie and his coterie fled to Chicago. Eight assassins from the Chan faction of the New York Ghost Shadows were dispatched to Chicago; a car they used was eventually traced back to the rental account of *On Leong Tong* officials in Chicago; Louie was critically wounded in an ambush at *On Leong* headquarters in Chicago; he survived but his driver was killed. (President's Commission on Organized Crime, *Impact* 1986, 88)

In a negotiated settlement, Nicky Louie retired from his criminal endeavors and Eddie Chan maintained his position as leader of the On Leong and its Ghost Shadow gang.

Other Asian gangs also vie for power in the traditional Chinatowns of the nation's largest cities. In New York, open warfare exists between the traditional Chinese gangs, and the new Vietnamese gangs seeking to encroach on their terrain. One such Vietnamese gang, Born to Kill, is made of recent Vietnamese immigrants who seek to extort and rob Chinese merchants and restaurants throughout the New York area (Lorch 1990, 20). In retaliation, three of its members were assassinated, presumably by Chinese gang members, illustrating the age-old rivalry between contending ethnic newcomers seeking a toehold in America's underworld.

Other Vietnamese gangs roam the nation's highways preying upon Vietnamese immigrants and refugees living in California, Texas, and Pennsylvania, invading their homes, robbing and brutalizing their victims. Mydans describe their modus operandi: "They travel to distant cities and then pick a target by linking up with local contacts, often friends from refugee camps where they spent part of their childhood, or by ripping the page with the name Nguyen from the local telephone book. . . . When they invade, they spend one to four hours in a home, climb back into their cars and move on" (Mydans 1991, A11).

Similar examples of new emerging criminal organizations could be taken from hundreds of neighborhoods throughout the nation. The patterns remain the same with rivals killing each other, consolidating power, expanding their criminal enterprises. Much of this would go unreported, except for the enterprising work of a few dedicated journalists, prosecutors, and police investigators. The names of the new gang chieftains are relatively unknown outside their domains and are scarcely remembered after these mobsters have been eliminated. It's only when someone with the stature of a Dion O'Bannion, a Dutch Schultz, or a Carlo Gambino emerges that the society takes note. Their underlings rarely achieve the notoriety and status that they so desperately crave.

As America approaches the next millenium, it will witness and record the successes and failures of these new ethnic mobs. Violence and bloodletting will continue; mob czars will emerge, reign, and disappear, replaced by new contenders. African Americans, Hispanics, Asians, and other ethnic newcomers will battle each other in escalating open warfare. Temporary alliances will be made and broken. Politicians, judges, and police will continue to be corrupted as the public maintains its insatiable demand for drugs, gambling, and vice. Prosecutors and press will announce the death of the Italian Mafia only to find new, equally powerful mafias reigning in its place. The cycle of ethnic crime will continue as organized crime supplies the public's demand providing an invaluable opportunity for many newcomers seeking to fulfill the American Dream.

A new *Pax Caponeana* has yet to emerge, but as American social history tells us, undoubtedly one will as the new Capones—Asian, African American, Hispanic—assert their power and will over the chaos. Like the *Pax Caponeana* of yesterday, it will be a peace not necessarily of our choosing but one which will impose control in our cities. As it does, the Italian mobs will be consigned to the footnotes of history, following their Irish, Jewish, and Polish predecessors. Center stage will be occupied by the new wiseguys and godfathers—African American, Hispanics, and Asians.

5

Individual and Group Mobility in Crime

Few ethnic newcomers moved beyond their lower-class origins either geographically or socially. The largest segment lived their lives within the ethnic neighborhood working in unskilled and semiskilled jobs. In this ethnic enclave—"the old neighborhood"—they socialized, married, raised families, retired, and eventually died. Nurtured by their clubs, religious associations, and ever-present friends and kin, these newcomers lived poor but relatively contented lives however harsh and burdensome their existence appears to middle-class observers.

But such an existence carried little appeal to those ambitious newcomers desperately craving what American success offered. These few became the shop owners; the ethnic professionals; the priests, rabbis, and ministers; the athletes and entertainers; the ethnic politicians; and the ethnic criminals. Each of these disparate roles offered a route of opportunity to a "better life," and the ambitious few within every ethnic minority group quickly seized the opportunity.

The lives of individual newcomers reflected these choices, for their innate talent and intelligence would wither if confined to lower-class, no-exit jobs in factories and sweatshops. These resourceful few chose something better and far more risky: one would become a clothing store owner; another, a doctor; another, a preacher; another, a dancer or night club singer; another would enter politics; and still another would choose to become a gangster.

The Newcomer's Free Choice

Why one person chooses a legitimate path, another an illegitimate one is beyond the scope of this analysis and beyond the realm of current social science explanation. Common sense tells us that the

111

individual's personal volition—his or her own free will—plays a major part in this decision. Why does one person become a bus driver, another a mechanic? Why does one person choose to reside in a hotel, another in a house, another in an apartment? Why does one person like liver and onions, while another cannot bear the thought of eating such an entrée?

Just as the social sciences can give only limited answers to these questions, so also are the social sciences limited in explaining why one newcomer became a business proprietor rather than a thief, a priest, or a politician. Scientific inquiry can provide us with many of the predisposing factors that help explain one choice rather than another; it cannot deal convincingly with the personal free choice that every person makes in deciding whether to pursue legitimate or illegitimate avenues of opportunity. At some point in his life, Al Capone chose a criminal life-style rather than a conventional one; unlike thousands of others of similar social background who are totally unknown to us since they chose to be "butchers, bakers, and candle stick makers" rather than bootleggers and gangsters. Social and environmental determinism scarcely help us in explaining these choices.

In all probability many successful newcomers were not quite sure why they chose one route rather than another. Obviously, individual talents and personalities of newcomers played critical roles but so also did the familial and environmental backgrounds in which they matured, as well as did luck and the chance variations that they encountered.

James Cagney serves as an example. Perhaps one of the most admired Hollywood stars, Cagney had a number of possible routes out of the poverty of his Irish-Catholic Yorkville neighborhood in New York. Possessing ability as a dancer, singer, street brawler, and amateur boxer, he could have chosen entertainment or crime as possible careers. He also spoke fluent Yiddish! Undoubtedly Cagney could have pursued a successful career in ethnic politics: his personality and outgoing nature would easily attract a wide spectrum of voters of different nationalities. All these routes were open to Cagney. His conscious and free choice of show business is more or less fortuitous; he loved to dance and when a dancing opportunity presented itself in the vaudeville show *Every Sailor*, Cagney literally "jumped" at it. The rest is history. In his autobiography he tells us why conventional employment held no appeal:

> The *Every Sailor* act died a natural death in time, and because I know Mom didn't
> really want me in something as uncertain as show business, I got a job at a
> brokerage house in Broad Street as a runner. I picked up comparison slips, went to
> the other firms that had made the deal with us, and awaited verification that a sale
> had been made of the stock. Back then to my office. If that sounds dull, I am here
> to tell you it was dull, and I hated it with a great intensity. (Cagney 1976, 27–28)

Crime was also a possible career but Cagney emphatically attributes
his rejection of this route to his mother:

> A question people have asked me . . . is why the Cagney boys didn't get involved
> with guns and crime the way my old Sing Sing pals did. The answer is simple: there
> wasn't a chance. We had a mother to answer to. If any of us got out of line, she
> just belted us and belted us emphatically. We loved her profoundly, and our driving
> force was to do what she wanted because we knew how much it meant to her.
> (Cagney 1976, 25)

Each ethnic group has its Cagneys and their biographies undoubtedly illustrate similar decisions in life, with meaningful family members and fortuitous circumstances channeling the inherent talents and
ambitious of these successful few. The routes which they chose to
move beyond their lower-class origins are secondary. What remains
primary is their own volition, their driving ambition to make something of themselves, to "make it" in the larger society, to climb the
ladder of success.

Anticipatory Socialization

The social and psychological mechanism through which they accomplished this upward mobility beyond their lower-income newcomer origins is referred to by social scientists as anticipatory socialization. This concept implies that individuals adopt as a reference point
a group to which they aspire and socialize themselves toward this
group's perceived norms, values, and beliefs *before* they actually attain membership in it (Merton and Kitt 1950; O'Kane 1970; O'Kane et
al. 1977). They anticipate their future status as middle-class members
and, as adolescents, they socialize themselves for this expected status.
As Robert Merton has pointed out, much of this socialization and
preparation is informal and unwitting, and adolescents respond to the
behavioral cues in their environment in such a manner that they orient
themselves to future statuses not yet achieved (Merton 1957, 385). He
writes:

It serves to prepare the individual for future statuses in his status-sequence. An explicit, deliberate and often formal part of this process is of course what is meant by education and training. But much of such preparation is *implicit*, *unwitting*, and *informal*, and it is particularly to this that the notion of anticipatory socialization directs our attention. . . . The individual responds to the cues in behavioral situations, more or less unwittingly draws implications from these for future role behavior and thus becomes oriented towards a status he does not yet occupy. Typically, he does not expressly codify the values and role requirements he is learning. (Merton 1957, 385)

The child's parents play a crucial role for the initial impetus for this upward mobility comes from them. Objectively, newcomer parents are lower-class in terms of their jobs, incomes, and formal education yet through their attitudes, aspirations, and behavior, they motivate their children towards a better life, a middle-class life that will give these children everything that the parents lacked. From their families, newcomer children learn to differentiate themselves from the other lower-income newcomers. They are different, "better" than the others, destined for a better life than that provided in the newcomer ghetto. They want to make something of themselves in the middle-class world and, as a consequence, the lower-income neighborhood and its values are perceived as burdens and appendages which hinder their aspirations. Hence they reject the status quo nature of lower-class life and seek a new life that in many essential aspects is the antithesis of the world and culture into which they were born and reared.

Formal Schooling

Those seeking a future in the worlds of the professions, business, or the clergy found formal education an important socializing factor in their lives. The school presented to these ambitious strivers role-models after whom they could pattern their lives. Kenneth Langton offers supportive evidence in his study of the political socialization of Jamaican adolescents. He writes:

homogeneous class schools reinforce the norms of the lower classes, while maintaining the political cleavage between them and the middle and the upper classes. With the exception of economic attitudes, heterogeneous schools resocialize working-class students in the direction of higher class political values. (Langton 1969, 171)

Teachers and administrators in lower-income schools offered these strivers standards to emulate, goals with which they could identify, and patterns of thinking and behavior commensurate with the class to which these young men and women aspired—the middle-class. They oriented these striving young men and women toward a world very different from that of their lower-income culture. They took an interest in these strivers, singling them out of the amorphous mass of lower-class students, providing them with special attention, encouraging them, mentoring them. A glance at the autobiographies of businessmen, clergy, and professionals from newcomer origins clearly reveals the positive impact of such teachers and other school personnel on the lives of the upwardly mobile.

These "bright and resourceful" newcomers would "make it" for formal education became the medium that propelled them into the various legitimate routes of upward mobility. Unlike the overwhelming majority of their newcomer peers, these strivers typically did well in school, reacting positively to the encouragement of their families and their teachers, ignoring the criticisms and disdain of those peers who had no desire to move beyond their origins. Schooling became the focal point of their early lives, providing them with the literacy skills and intellectual values necessary for their future middle-class careers and status.

However, the concern and passion for formal education that these ethnic strivers exhibited were not shared by the majority of their newcomer peers who viewed schooling as irrelevant to their future goals. For them, schooling was an irritant, an imposition not to be taken too seriously. They viewed teachers and administrators as "foreigners" who didn't understand the needs and wants of newcomers. Though respected, their life-style and values remained alien both to those newcomers who chose to lead conventional lower-class lives within their ethnic community, and to the remainder who would pursue futures that didn't require much schooling, i.e., sports, show business, urban politics, and organized crime. Formal education appealed only to those desiring those future careers dependent upon it; for the others, it remained superfluous, particularly in the world of certain professional sports. In their analysis of ethnic mobility in professional boxing, S. Weinberg and Henry Arond quote a promoter who offers his assessment of college-educated boxers:

They say that too much education softens a man and that is why the college graduates are not good fighters. They fight emotionally on the gridiron and they fight bravely and well in our wars, but their contributions in our rings have been insignificant. The ring has been described as the refuge of the under-privileged. . . . An education is an escape, and that is what they are saying when they shake their heads—those who know the fight game—as you mention the name of a college fighter. Once the bell rings, they want their fighters to have no retreat, and a fighter with an education is a fighter who does not have to fight to live and he knows it. (Weinberg and Arond 1952, 462)

Ethnic politicians and ward bosses also regard suspiciously those educated types seeking positions within their political organizations. Viewed as out of touch with the realities of urban political life, those with formal education beyond what was "normal" for newcomers were encouraged to seek futures other than politics. In the early 1900s Tammany Hall's ward boss George Washington Plunkett phrased this suspicion as follows:

go to him [district leader] and say: "I took first prize at college in Aristotle; I can recite all Shakespeare frontwards and backwards; there ain't nothin' in science that ain't as familiar to me as blockades on the elevated roads and I'm the real thing in the way of silver-tongued orators." What will he answer? He'll probably say: "I guess you are not to blame for your misfortunes, but we have no use for you here." (Riordan 1963, 10)

Education—the Pseudo-Solution to Newcomers' Problems

Ironically many commentators view education as the sole answer to the plight of lower-income youth: "If only they would get an education their lives would be happy and fruitful." In the 1950s, the social critics blamed the educational failure of lower-income youth on the children themselves: they were culturally deprived, reared in multi-problem families, and so on. In the 1970s, they blamed the failures on the "system"—the repressive, racist schools that did not allow children to learn. But the source of the failure lies beyond the children and the schools. Let us view the current situation from the vantage point of a hypothetical young Hispanic—José.

José knows that his world is one where high rates of young-adult unemployment are epidemic. In spite of the public service advertisements, he also knows that completing high school will not help him appreciably in finding a good job, for such jobs are in scarce supply for lower-income youth whether or not they possess high school diplomas. Too many of those around him have high school diplomas, are unemployed, and are economically poor. If José could cite U.S. Census Bureau statistics, he would tell you that 57 percent of all poor adults have completed high school (Hunger Action Forum 1990, 3).

Realistically, what difference does it make if he reads well, if he completes high school? The sad truth is that it means little, for American society currently cannot absorb a growing number of lower-income youth into respectable stable jobs. Simply put, educational attainment is irrelevant to José. Only a small minority of lower-income youth will "make it" via the educational route, and he knows that he does not belong to that group of upwardly mobile strivers. Furthermore, he doesn't want genuine upward mobility of the types now available, for this would entail abandonment of everything dear to him—his family, his friends, his neighborhood, and his values.

Consequently, José "fails." Yet he does not consider himself a failure, for all those close to him have undergone a similar odyssey—his older brothers and sisters, his parents, his friends—and he does not view them as failures. Furthermore, they do not expect him to do well in school. His older brother pumps gas at the local service station—surely not a middle-class idea of success. Yet his brother has a family, earns a modest wage and is well-regarded by his relatives and friends. In lower-class terms he is successful and both he and José know it.

Why shouldn't José identify with his older brother and seek to emulate his way of life? In reality he does and gets by in life without the benefits of formal education. What we regard as failure is viewed by José as the normal direction of one's life. In his own way he is pursuing his version of the American Dream, just as we pursue ours.

Blaming José's values or blaming the school is somewhat myopic for the root of the dilemma lies outside the realm of education. Yet the tinkering with both the schools and their pupils continues while the more fruitful analysis of the larger social situation remains largely untouched.

This is particularly true of young ethnic criminals who remain suspicious of education and uneasy with fellow ethnics. They believe that schooling exists for "suckers," those who don't place much value on loyalty in their neighborhoods and its traditions. When these ethnic strivers successfully complete their education, they move away from the old neighborhood to a "better" one and look down on the people with whom they grew up. They become "hoity-toity," thinking themselves better than others. They abandon, or at least deemphasize, those things dear to ethnic gangsters—the machismo orientation, family, friends, the values of the neighborhood, and so on. To the future gangster, education implies that he must burn these cultural bridges behind him—too high a price to pay for the nondescript rewards of a dull middle-class life.

Lure of the Streets

For this newcomer, the lure and excitement of the street are far more enticing than the tedium and monotony of the local school. On the street, he sees the successful criminals who have "made it" in the community—gamblers, numbers operators, pimps and prostitutes, drug dealers, thieves, and racketeers. They flash their success for all to see, traveling in fancy cars, wearing expensive exciting clothing, appearing poised and confident, and rarely without lots of cash. They command respect and usually get it. They are generous to friends and tough on their enemies. They frequently befriend the youth of the area, giving them money for candy, encouraging them to pursue careers similar to theirs, showing them that immediate wealth is indeed possible. They rapidly become role models for many lower-class ethnic newcomers who idolize them and mimic their life-style to the dismay of those in the community seeking to orient these youth to respectable middle-class behavior.

The 1939 film *Angels With Dirty Faces* vividly illustrates this struggle for the hearts of lower-class youth. The protagonists are the Irish gangster Rocky Sullivan (James Cagney) and the priest Father Jerry Connolly (Pat O'Brien). Father Jerry wants the local teenage gang to pursue healthy middle-class life-styles wherein sobriety, good manners, fair play, clean-cut appearance, and so on are encouraged. The adolescents, however, seek to emulate Rocky who dresses well, acts tough, treats them to money, clothes, and excitement. Though the film ends by the gang following the priest after Rocky dies in the electric chair in Sing Sing, one cannot help but feel that the middle-class role models are too few and too weak to counteract the previous attachments to criminal life-styles. In real life the Rockys win more often than do the Father Jerrys.

From a very young age, lower-class youths find in crime an attractive and desirable outlet for their ambitions and talents. Writing about the typical gangster in the 1920s and 1930s, Kenneth Allsop noted that as a youth he had

> seen what was rated as success in the society he had been thrust into—the Cadillac, the big bank-roll, the elegant apartment. How could he acquire that kind of recognizable status? He was almost always a boy of outstanding initiative, imagination, ability; he was the kind of boy, under different conditions, would have been a captain of industry or a key political figure of his time. But he hadn't the opportunity of going to Yale becoming a banker or broker; there was no passage for him to a law degree from Harvard. There was, however, a relatively easy way of acquiring these goods that he was incessantly told were available to him as an American citizen, and without which he had begun to feel he could not properly count himself as an American citizen. He could become a gangster. (Allsop 1961, 236)

Crime is an exciting, thrilling game where criminals pit their skills and personalities against the "world out there." The excitement makes it all worthwhile and each small success confirms the youth's belief that it is the only future worth pursuing. They are not pushed into crime; instead they rush headlong into it, lusting for the thrills and opportunities that come with it. Surrounded by a culture that remains suspicious of the larger dominant culture of middle-class America, seeing that for many in their community crime *does* pay, these youths start to engage in criminal activities. "Barefoot" Rafer Dooley, a Chicago gangster during the Prohibition era phrased this as follows:

> They say crime don't pay. You tell that to the real hierarchy of crime and they'll laugh theirselves into nervous hysteria. It don't pay only if you're apprehended. The saying is a misnomer used to dissuade youthful offenders from progressing into criminology. If the venture succeeds, like when me and my constituents were distributing liquor on the North Side, it pays fine, very fine indeed. (Kobler 1973, 335)

Undoubtedly, current successful mobsters involved in narcotics trafficking would reiterate Dooley's assessment of the value of crime.

Early Criminal Socialization

These activities often begin as games which have a quasi-criminal aspect to them. Clifford Shaw noted these games over fifty years ago observing that many lower-income boys in Chicago engaged in the "cap game." He writes about one such youth:

> When we were shoplifting, we always made a game of it. For example, we might gamble on who could steal the most caps in a day, or who could steal in the presence of a detective and then get away. This was the best part of the game. I would go into a store to steal a cap, by trying one on when the clerk was not watching, walk out of the store, leaving the old cap. With the new cap on my head I would go into another store, do the same thing as in the other store, getting a new hat and leaving the one I had taken from the other place. I might do this all day. . . . It was the fun I wanted, not the hat. I kept this up for months and then began to sell the things to a man on the West Side. It was at this time that I began to steal for gain. (Shaw 1933, 3; cited in Cloward and Ohlin 1960, 164)

From Shaw's description it is apparent that the primary object of the game was the excitement it created in the boys playing it. The theft aspect was secondary. Similar exciting games existed in my childhood neighborhood in the Bedford-Stuyvesant section of Brooklyn. One such game involved my friends and me "beating the fare," that is entering the subway without paying the fare. Three different variations of this game existed; climbing onto the roof of the stairs leading to the "el" (elevated train) platform, thus bypassing the ticket window; crawling on all fours around the ticket agent's booth beneath the view of the agent; running boldly through the turnstile area just as the train entered the station before the agent had any inkling of what was happening.

As with Shaw's cap game, the object of our game involved the fear and excitement in seeing how far we could get before being caught; actual theft of subway service was of minimal concern. Oftentimes we were caught but the penalties were minor, invariably consisting of a tongue-lashing by the agent or transit police and the subsequent payment of the subway fare—in those days (the 1950s), ten cents!

Though most lower-class youth engage in games similar to these, few actually continue in a life of crime. For the most part, these criminal activities are abandoned as these youths approach adulthood. They represent the rebelliousness of adolescence, a passing phase in the journey from childhood to adulthood.

For a small minority of adolescents however, criminal activity does not cease with the arrival of adult status. These few escalate their crimes, consciously deciding to pursue criminal life-styles. The world of crime fascinates them. As Jack Katz has noted, the excitement of crime seduces them (Katz 1988). They enjoy "hanging out" with gangsters as they notice others bending to the gangsters' wishes. Their associations with these criminals intoxicate them; they clamor for admission into the gangs of older admired criminals. Nicholas Pileggi captures this as he writes about the early life of his "wiseguy" informant, Henry Hill, who speaks of his fascination with mafia-style organized crime in Brooklyn in the 1950s, vividly depicted in the 1990 film *Goodfellas*:

> From the first day I walked into the cabstand, I knew I had found my home—especially after they found out that I was half Sicilian. . . . I wasn't just another kid from the neighborhood helping around the stand. I was suddenly in their houses. I was in their refrigerators. . . . They gave me everything I wanted.

> Even before going to work at the cabstand, I was fascinated by the place. I used to watch them from my window, and I dreamed of being like them. At the age of twelve my ambition was to be a gangster. To be a wiseguy. To be a wiseguy was better than being President of the United States. It meant power among people who had no power. To be a wiseguy was to own the world. I dreamed about being a wiseguy the way other kids dreamed about being doctors or movie stars or firemen or ballplayers. (Pileggi 1985, 19)

Adolescent Criminal Socialization

A new world opens to these youth who wholeheartedly embrace criminal activities. Whether they are incorporated into the more organized criminal gangs (i.e., mafia-type mobs) or into loosely federated gangs (i.e, black narcotics gangs) is of secondary importance; the primary factor motivating these youth is the opening of a new world where they see success, status, and power before them. No one coerces them to pursue this life-style. They consciously and eagerly desire it, working for it the same way a middle-class youth pursues a career in medicine, law, or business. The mobs never need to post "Help Wanted" signs for these ambitious newcomers.

In their teenage years, these fledgling mobsters engage in more serious crimes that provide them with money, clothing, cars, and status within their circle of friends. Devoid of educational skills and often either unemployed or marginally employed, they crave the "goods" of American society that they daily see paraded in front of them in mass-media advertising. From their perspective, crime provides the only means of obtaining these goods. In his descriptions of the teenage gangs—"wolf packs"—that stalk New York's Times Square seeking to rob middle-class "Vics" (victims), Michael Daly captures this craving and life-style:

> On the first Friday in April, eighteen-year old Mark Ross of Brooklyn heard a familiar voice call up to his second-floor bedroom window. Mark peered down and saw a friend named Alan waving nine 100 dollar bills. Alan said he had "taxed" a man of $946 on 39th Street in Manhattan. Mark said he would have to reconsider a recent vow to give up crime.
>
> Alan say, "Yo, Mark, these is hundreds," Mark remembers. "I say, I got to get some money, too." (Daly 1985, 24)

What do they do with the money they steal? Daly tells us:

> During the ride to Manhattan, the teenagers talk about Alan's $946 score. If they, too, could "catch a stack," Alex planned to buy a Guess? denim-and-leather suit. Kelly hoped to get a suede outfit and sky-blue Puma sneakers. Mark had a yen for a blue leather coat and matching suede shoes. . . . A robber who returns home with a big score becomes . . . "a project celebrity." Almost all the money usually goes towards getting fresh [new clothes]. Many robbers seem to live for the moment they first step out wearing a Guess? suit or flashing pair of monogrammed gold teeth. "When you get extra, extra out-of-the-ordinary fresh, people be watching you," Mark says. "You feel like above the rest, and you get girls," Kelly says. "You might not have a penny in you pockets, but the clothes be nice," Alex says. (Daly 1985, 29–30)

Daly's description aptly captures the status motivations of the robbers he interviewed, motivations that are scarcely different from those of Irish, Jewish, and Italian young criminals of times past. The style, language, and modus operandi of current ethnic newcomer criminals may be different from those of bygone eras but the factors motivating their crimes remain the same. They want what all Americans want: income, material possession, a sense of importance in the eyes of their friends and families. Their methods of obtaining these things are, of course, condemned by the larger society but that condemnation scarcely concerns the adolescent gangster.

The successful adolescent gangs both in the past, as with the Irish, Jews, and Italians as well as present ones with African Americans,

Hispanics, Asians, socialize their members in the criminal life-style, tutoring them in the skills and techniques of crime as well as the mental and social attitudes of the criminal. Edwin Sutherland pointed out in 1937 that criminal behavior is learned behavior and the learning takes place in the close intimate structure of the gang. Differential association, as Sutherland termed it, distinguishes the criminal from the non-criminal: birds of a feather flock together (Sutherland 1972, 206 ff.).

Like their counterparts pursuing other roads to success, the adolescent criminal's behavior is partially explained by the process of anticipatory socialization. They also seek a better world for themselves and, as criminals, they choose as role models successful gangsters and mimic and emulate, not only what they perceive as their actions, but their thinking patterns, mannerisms, value orientations as well.

Early in their adolescence they begin this socialization process which is both conscious and unconscious. Just as the teenage gang in the film *Angels With Dirty Faces* idolize and copy Rocky Sullivan's behavior and values, so also do contemporary adolescent gangsters emulate their heroes. The combination of differential association and the process of anticipatory socialization create a fertile ground for the development and maturation of young criminals who, like their mentors, will strive to make something of themselves—"be somebody"—in the world of crime.

For many of these adolescent newcomers, this desire to "be somebody" quickly deteriorates into vicious, predatory acts of violence that are often heinous and frightening to police and criminal alike. These adolescents quickly short circuit their quest for success, for they are "going nowhere" in crime. Their crimes frequently appear psychotic and almost defy rational explanation. For example, in the Williamsburg section of Brooklyn, a very high crime area to which I frequently bring my criminology classes, these adolescent crimes are readily apparent. The detectives of that neighborhood's 90th Police Precinct describe to my students an appalling litany of youth homicides. Sergeant Jack Hughes detailed how one sixteen-year-old boy shot another for his Puma sneakers, placing the body in the first floor apartment of an abandoned building where other youths and adults, over the next few hours, robbed the corpse of everything except its underwear. Detective Rich Conforti spoke about the fifteen-year-old boy who shot a seventeen-year-old youth because he wanted his designer sunglasses.

Detectives Paul Weidenbaum and Al Cachie recounted their homicide investigation where youths kill others for thrills, for alleged insults, for retaliation for violations of gang "turf," for drug deals gone sour, and so on. All of the police spokesmen in the 90th Precinct are dismayed over the low value of human life and the constant assaults of people on each other. Sergeant Hughes stunned the students on one such trip when he remarked, "the value of human life in the Nine-O today is $1.26"—the amount over which one youth killed another in an incident in 1984.

The wanton, frightening violence in the 90th Precinct continues to shock not only my students and me, but police also. On one trip to that area, Sergeant Hughes introduced my class to Ramon (pseudonym) a victim of crime a few months earlier. Ramon explained that he and his wife were returning from a Christmas holiday party at 1:00 A.M. when, in an apparent robbery attempt, a fourteen-year-old Hispanic boy approached him, said nothing, and shot him, the bullet lodging in his spinal column. The assailant fled but was apprehended a few days later, and released on bail. While awaiting the trial, the assailant's girlfriend assaulted Ramon's pregnant wife, stabbing her three times, warning her not to testify against her boyfriend. Ramon was partially paralyzed with his wounds and lost his job as a skilled factory worker since he couldn't perform his normal work. His disability benefits had also expired, as had his unemployment benefits. Subsisting on welfare, he asked all of us if this were fair, if law and justice were served by this series of events. None of us could either answer him or look him in the eye. A few weeks later his assailant received a six months jail sentence.

Such violence in the 90th Precinct has provoked retaliatory actions by the Hasidic Jewish community which resides in the southern part of the precinct. For years the Hasidin had been cruelly victimized by crimes similar to Ramon's. Police measures and the criminal justice system were powerless to prevent such crimes. In the late 1970s, the Hasidic community formed "protective associations" that patrolled their section. Their measures have frequently been described as vigilante in scope, and alleged criminals apprehended in their neighborhood have been dealt with harshly: arms broken, skulls fractured, and so on. Though police do not condone such measures, they note that the Hasidic section of the 90th Precinct is remarkably safe.

Sergeant Hughes remarked, "the Hasidic section is an area on the move. There's negligible poverty, solid community spirit, constant renovation of homes and apartments. The Hasids are an exclusive group, not about to put up with crime from their neighbors in the Hispanic part of the Nine-O. To see how safe it is, all you have to do is notice the number of women wheeling baby carriages in the streets — you don't see that in many sections of Brooklyn."

Adolescent assailants such as the ones described in the 90th Precinct and in other high crime areas, rarely "make it" in organized crime, for their personalities are unstable, their behavior sporadic, impulsive, and unpredictable, their loyalty to gang and fellow criminals suspect. If they survive the ghetto they usually become the common criminals who fill our prisons. Bereft of status and protection even within the world of crime, they go "nowhere" in crime. Only a few will ever make it to the realm of successful organized crime.

For other adolescents wishing to "be somebody," the road to criminal success does not end so abruptly, for they behave in a more rational, predictable fashion. By late adolescence this ethnic criminal is relatively secure in a criminal life-style. Until that point crime had been an exciting, relatively safe avocation. Rarely had he been arrested or jailed even though his crimes may be numerous for the larger society wishes to give him the benefit of a doubt, a chance to "go straight" before reaching adulthood. To the adolescent gangster however this leniency reinforces his life-style for from his perspective crime does pay and is rarely punished. He thinks, "Well, I'm eighteen years old and have committed over 300 crimes since I was twelve years old. I've been arrested four times for these acts and have spent no time in jail since the judges gave me suspended sentences, put me on probation, sent me to talk to social workers. That's not bad; the proceeds of these crimes are well worth the minimum risk of jail time."

Claude Brown contrasts the 1980s style of African-American male adolescents in Harlem with that of his generation of the 1940s and 1950s. Money and clothing are key ingredients in their quest for status, of "being somebody":

> The motivations, dreams and aspirations of today's young men are essentially the same as those of the teenagers of their parents' generation — with a few dramatic differences. They are persistently violent. They appear driven by, or almost obsessed with, a desperate need for pocket money that they cannot possibly obtain

legally. They possess an uncompromising need to be able to "rock" (wear) a different pair of designer jeans at least twice a week, or even a different pair of ordinary pants twice a week. As one 16-year-old Harlem teenager said: "Man, it's a bring-down to have to wear the same pants, the same shirt, to school three or four times a week when everybody else is showin' fly [coming to school dressed to the nines]. This is somethin' Moms can't understand. You don't have to have a pair of Nikes, a pair of Ponys, a pair of Pumas and a pair of Adidas, but it's embarrassin' not have a pair of one of 'em."

Nobody is more cruel or more ruthless in his relationships with his peers than the poor child. He has so few possessions of any material value that he cannot afford the additional insult that being deprived of these very commonplace symbols of "being somebody" inflicts upon him. ("Everybody wants to be a somebody; if just a little somebody," this same teenager said. "Nobody but a fool wants to be a nobody, or somebody who don't count, right?") Conceivably, this paradoxical American creature called manchild—pathetic and simultaneously terrifying—is an extreme human manifestation of brand-name madness in a society severely afflicted with materialism. (Brown 1984, 30)

The combination of society's leniency and the adolescent gangster's haughtiness convince neophyte criminals that crime is a worthwhile endeavor, far superior in earning power to anything available to them in conventional life. Adolescent males wonder why they should work at minimum wage in a mindless, monotonous job as a stock clerk when they can average more than $150 a day pushing narcotics. Adolescent females ask why they should work for $3.75 an hour in a fast-food restaurant when they can earn $200 a day in "the life," prostituting. Given these economic realities of lower-income newcomer life in an urban neighborhood, it is startling that so few actually become engaged in a life of crime.

Prison Experiences

Yet jail time does come for these newcomers and their stay in prison opens a new world of big-time crime to the more ambitious, intelligent inmates. Few are rehabilitated in the prison system. The vast majority do their "time," anxious to return to the streets to "perfect" their crimes, anticipating bigger "scores" than previously. In prison, they meet a wide range of fellow ethnics who assist them, showing them how they erred, how they got caught, teaching them new tricks of the trade, and encouraging them in pursuing "bigger" crime. In prison also, as Peter Letkemann points out, adolescent criminal careers takes on a more structured form. Prison helps these adolescents realize that they cannot afford the haphazard life-style they once pursued, that they have to organize their criminal activities in such a way as to avoid future prison sentences (Letkemann 1973, 129). In prison they form new social units that become the nucleus of the post-prison newcomer organized gang. This is particularly true of black and Hispanic criminals whose prison friendships form the core of this post-prison organized criminal mob. Ianni writes, "throughout the various networks that we observed, we found that prisons and the prison experience are the most important locus for establishing the social relationships that form the basis for partnership in organized crime, both among blacks and among Puerto Ricans" (Ianni 1974, 158).

For all-too-many current minority youth, prison is simply a necessary, expected rite of passage between childhood and adulthood. It symbolizes one's acceptance in adult criminal culture, and confirms the newly chosen life-style of crime. It carries no stigma. Continuing his analysis of youth in New York's Harlem, Brown writes,

> Prison, and doing "bits" (time), has strangely ambivalent, perhaps even pervertedly romanticized appeal to poor black teen-agers. It is viewed as an inevitability, or least a probability, accompanied by nothing more than the mild apprehension or anxiety that attends, for instance, a bar mitzvah, joining the Marines or any other manhood initiation ritual in any normal society. One goes into the Marines as a young boy and comes out a "real man." It is the same with going into the "joint," as prison is called. . . .
>
> Reformatory and prison bits are still an accepted, often anticipated and virtually inevitable phase of the growing-up process for young black men in this country. They have no fear of jail; most of their friends are there. They are told by the returning, unsung, heroic P.O.W.s of the unending ghetto war of survival that even the state joints are now country clubs. (Brown 1984, 44)

In an increasing number of federal and state prisons, new "mafias" have been spawned. These differ from the Italian mobs of former years and have come about because of the rising interethnic violence in these prisons. White, black and Hispanic prisoners openly resent each other and assaults and murders are all too common. For protection, prisoners have banded together creating new ethnic gangs that not only protect their members but also engage in drug distribution, loan sharking, and extortion of other prisoners. Whites belong to white gangs, Hispanics to Hispanic gangs, blacks to black gangs. These gangs become family to their members, nurturing them, protecting them, disciplining them, and providing them with a sense of importance and power within the prison.

In numerous states, white gangs, often derived from outlaw motorcycle gangs, have became major factors in state prisons. Gangs, such as the Hell's Angels, Pagans, Outlaws, and Banditos, not only are operative nationally, but continue their crimes in prison. The same is true of blacks and Hispanics who have formed their gangs which have different names in different states. In the California prisons, African-American gangs such as the Black Guerrilla Family and the Crips (named because of their reputed reputation of crippling their victims) have emerged; so also have Hispanic gangs, such as, the Mexican Mafia, and La Nuestra Familia. Texas prisons have witnessed another Hispanic gang, the Texas Syndicate. In a number of state prisons, particularly those in Illinois and New York, white gangs operate largely under the title of the Aryan Brotherhood, or the Nation (Lindsey 1985; President's Commission on Organized Crime, *Impact*, 1986, 58 ff.).

The existence and operations of these various prison gangs has been documented in the 1986 President's Commission on Organized Crime Report:

> Many prison gangs have a "blood-in-blood-out" policy, meaning that an inmate may become a member only after killing or assaulting another prisoner or staffer and that his blood will be spilled before he is allowed to quit the gang. Members released from prison remain in the gang, often providing support and enforcement for the organization inside.

> Gangs have grown inside California prisons since the 1950s, and have spread throughout the U.S.; 28 states and the Federal prison system report the existence of prison gangs. Members may constitute as much as three percent of the prison population. The Department of Justice has identified 114 different gangs, not all of which are formally organized. Several gangs, however, are sophisticated, self-perpetuating, and involved in illegal acts for power and profit with operations outside the prison.

> A close examination of the 114 identified gangs yielded five that appear to meet the criteria of an organized crime group: the Mexican Mafia, La Nuestra Familia, the Aryan Brotherhood, the Black Guerrilla Family, and the Texas Syndicate. All five operate in more than one State. In all five either murder or the drawing of blood are prerequisites for membership. (President's Commission on Organized Crime, *Impact*, 1986, 74–75)

They develop a tight, ongoing organizational structure, with a small number of prisoners serving as the leaders of the gang. The more rational, ambitious, and violent of these leaders serve as catalysts for the foundation of new organized mobs after they have left prison. Hardened by their prison experience, lusting for new criminal conquests and continued status, these leaders form gangs composed of friends from prison. They know and trust each other, and have demonstrated their loyalty to "the family" in prison. Now they are ready to "take on" higher-level dope dealing and marketing. They have matured beyond the level of individual predatory crime, with its endless cycle of arrest and imprisonment. They have "hit the big time."

Legal and Political Immunity from Arrest

But the "big time" proves problematic for current newcomer criminals and their gangs. Quickly they realize that their prosecution by legal authorities and the harassment of their operations by police and civil authorities means that they will be back in jail soon. What they clearly see as necessary is a system that provides their organizations and gangsters with relative immunity from arrest, which only comes about through the collusion with politicians and police who, for a price, "protect" their criminal operations. They know they are going nowhere in crime without such political protection.

The Irish, Jews, and Italians in crime slowly developed such "insurance" when they reigned supreme in organized crime through arrangements with police and politicians that date from the mid-1800s. Arthur Schlesinger describes how this symbiotic relationship between politicians and criminals functioned in New York City in the 1860s:

> In the late sixties, the Tweed Ring began the process of mutual-defense pacts between politicians and the underworld, one partner receiving payoffs, the other protection: and the investigation of New York crime by a committee of the State Assembly in 1875 following the Ring's collapse documented emerging patterns of police-criminal cooperation. The center was an area between 24th and 40th Streets and Fifth and Seventh Avenues. (Schlesinger 1986, xxi)

Schlesinger also describes how the Police Inspector Thomas Byrnes worked out deals with criminals in the 1880s:

> Byrnes evidently conceived his mission as, above all, that of stopping depredations

against the wealthy and powerful in New York City. To accomplish this purpose he developed a complex system of treaties with the underworld by which, in effect, crooks would agree to practice their craft outside New York City or outside plush areas within the city. He built a network of informers whose interest it was to report on those who broke his rules; and, when the treaties were violated . . . the inspector had no hesitation about resorting to the third degree. (Schlesinger 1986, xvi)

The collusion with the local politicians guaranteed the criminals their freedom of action in gambling, vice, liquor, and drug rackets. When they were arrested, they "did little time" in jail, and what time they did do was spent in relative comfort for the "organization" took care of them.

According to Ianni,

The principle reason that the Italians and Irish were able to live as they did in prison, however, related to their connections and organization outside. Traditionally, white crime organizations protected their members from the authorities in every way possible. The white professional criminal has always been much less likely to go to jail in the first place. For the black or Puerto Rican criminal, prison is an inevitable stage of his career. If a member of a white crime network was convicted, both he and his family would be taken care of by the organization. The physical well-being of the men in prison was taken care of from the outside. (Ianni 1974, 183)

The ethnic gangster consequently realizes that he must work out reciprocal relationships with the ethnic politician for it is in the interest of each to develop such a symbiotic alliance. Ethnic crime and ethnic politics historically formed a working alliance that dates from the earlier part of the nineteenth century and has continued to the present. In New York, the Irish ranked as the most noteworthy of the early immigrant groups in both politics and crime, and their political and criminal expertise subsequently had been duplicated and imaginatively expanded by the Jews and the Italians. As each of these groups attained success and renown in politics and crime, so also did the entire ethnic group maneuver into the dominant society. The political affiliations and connections of the gangster provided the legal immunity so essential for the survival of the criminal and his organizations.

The gangster reciprocated by aiding the politician with "muscle" when necessary. He also provided him with large amounts of money necessary to run political campaigns, to bribe officials and potential opponents, to expand his political influence beyond the newcomer neighborhood. A working alliance consequently emerged in the former newcomer minority groups between ethnic crime and ethnic politics. Crime provided an enticing means of economic and social advancement, its success insured through the established though somewhat uneasy relationship with the local political structure.

The road to success for African-American, Hispanic, Asian, and other ethnic minority criminal operations entails the development of such political alliances. Those newcomer operations that either avoid such relations or are unable to foster them will fail, and their gangsters will be nothing more than the common prisoners who fill our jails; those organizations that successfully negotiate such political relationships will prosper as they eliminate their competitors and monopolize criminal enterprises.

The key to success will be the gang leader who sees that organized crime can only prosper with the tacit approval of political authorities, that is, politicians who will protect his interests and insure that organized crime functions in a stable, predictable environment. The most successful gangsters of the past—John Morrissey, Dion O'Bannion, Dutch Schultz, Meyer Lansky, Al Capone, Frank Costello—each had political allies in the urban political machines who forestalled and thwarted police and judicial action against them. Today's successful newcomer gangsters will have to do similarly if they are to survive and prosper and the lessons of America's ethnic past suggest that such individuals will surely emerge. What form they will take is unknown for the types of political organizations currently operative in urban centers are quite different from the Tammany-style machines of the past. Hence the major task of those syndicates seeking success involves the pioneering of new forms of police and political protection for their rackets that will guarantee them as much immunity from prosecution as did those political arrangements of former eras.

The "ideal" ethnic gangster thus will be poised for supremacy in the lucrative but violent world of contemporary organized crime, his ruthlessness and daring successfully documented from his past deeds, his ambitions and resourcefulness established by those who have dealt with him, his organizational abilities demonstrated in the gang he assembles and by his methods of disciplining and rewarding those who serve him in this gang, his contacts and associations with police, judges, and politicians insuring that his criminal enterprises operate without official interference. Those mobsters approximating these qualities will be criminal leaders of the future, duplicating and expanding the organized crime innovations of their predecessors from past ethnic minorities. They will have become successful in the American sense of the term, with large incomes, beautiful homes, stylish clothing and cars, with enormous power and influence not only in the criminal sphere but also in the political arena as well. Social honor and prestige will similarly accrue to them but only from within the newcomer communities. It will elude them as they seek the favorable recognition of the larger American society, for that society rejects criminals and their life-styles.

The Gangster's Social Honor within the Newcomer Community

How were the ethnic gangsters actually perceived within their own communities? How were they actually viewed by the larger nonethnic established society? Will current newcomer gangsters be able to achieve the social honor that eluded their predecessors?

As newcomer criminal syndicates achieve success in the realm of ethnic organized crime, their leaders become prominent notorious public figures, household names whose deeds and misdeeds attract enormous mass-media attention. Criminals in other societies emulate our American gangsters, mimicking their life-styles. This is evident in cultures clearly different from American culture. In Japan, for example, the *yakuza*—organized criminals—pattern themselves after the stereotypical American gangster:

> The yakuza . . . began to look different. Under the steady influence of the Americans, during and after the occupation [post World War II] the yakuza began to assume some of the characteristics of their American gangster counterparts. Yakuza who swore to uphold traditional values were as entranced with American styles as any Japanese. . . . Since yakuza didn't know any real American gangsters, they turned to the movies instead. . . . [They] took to dressing in dark suits, dark shirts, and white ties. Sunglasses were *de rigueur*, and in the 1960s, yakuza affected crewcuts. . . . To match their outfits, they affected a leer and a swagger that set them apart from the ordinary citizens. Yakuza leaders also acquired a taste for an important luxury that may seem ironic today—foreign (principally American) cars. Even today, yakuza leaders are among the few customers for large American sedans in Japan. (Kaplan and Dubro 1986, 89–90)

Currently however, few of the general public would recognize names such as Ellsworth "Bumpy" Johnson, Frank Matthews, Charles Lucas, Leroy "Nicky" Barnes, the Chambers Brothers, "Spanish Raymond" Marques, Jaime Herrera, "White Wolf" Chang An-Lo—all alleged gangsters associated with African American, Hispanic, and Chinese criminal organizations of the past twenty years. Many additional gangsters will be added to this list in the decades to come, some of whom will become famous as they establish total control in their sphere of influence within crime. Wealthy and powerful, they will seek to be accepted by the dominant American society, but such social honor will elude them just as it failed the gangsters of the past.

Al Capone for example, yearned for such social acceptance. Regarded by many as "owning" Chicago, he resented those who disdained his accomplishments: "I've been spending the best years of my life as a public benefactor. I've given people the light pleasures, shown them a good time. And all I get is abuse—the existence of a hunted man. I'm called a killer. Ninety percent of the people of Cook County drink and gamble and my offense has been to furnish them with the amusements. . . . Public service is my motto" (Kobler 1974, 209–10). Self-conscious about his Italian background, Capone required that his associates address him as Anthony Brown and that they have the trappings of upper-class decorum when they worked for him: "The Big Fellow hires nothing but gentlemen. They have to be well dressed and have to have cultured accents. They always have to say 'Yes Sir' and 'No Sir' to him" (Allsop 1961, 249). Yet the recognition they have lusted for never comes; in the eyes of the larger public they still are mobsters whose deeds have soiled their name.

There is one story, perhaps apocryphal, that Capone chose as bodyguards men who spoke impeccable English without a trace of an Italian accent, men who looked Anglo-Saxon rather than Italian. Another gangster, Frank Costello, is reputed to have sought counseling in the 1940s because he could not understand why the larger non-Italian community did not honor him for his work in assisting Italian newcomers in "making it" in America. The prestige so desired by gangsters never really comes; to the larger American audience they are public enemies rather than public heroes. Yet within their own ethnic newcomer community they are folk heroes. (See Appendix for a discussion of the status of the outlaw and the gangster as portrayed in American ballads and films.)

Ellsworth "Bumpy" Johnson illustrates the affection and pride that many in an ethnic minority community extend to its criminal "achievers." Reputed to be the top black organized criminal in Harlem in the 1950s and 1960s, Johnson worked under the control of the Italian mobs of East Harlem headed by "Fat Tony" Salerno, organizing the numbers racket, gambling, and narcotics dealing for them. Everyone in Harlem knew of Bumpy and most admired and respected him. He was perhaps the most famous of all black urban gangsters. The popular *Shaft* movies were based on his alleged exploits. When he died in 1968 of natural causes, Harlem genuinely mourned his loss. His obituary in the largest circulation Black newspaper in America, *The New York Amsterdam News*, eulogized him in a sympathetic fashion, proud of his achievements even though at times they were criminal:

Ellsworth "Bumpy" Johnson, 61, Harlem's most famous underworld figure, suffered a fatal heart attack early Sunday morning. . . . His funeral is expected to draw a large crowd of Harlem personalities, high and low. . . . Johnson had steered clear of the police since completing a 10-year stretch five years ago. Before last July, his last run-in with local police occurred in March, 1967 when they stopped him . . . for a traffic violation. He reportedly became loud and boisterous, and was arrested for disorderly conduct by a young patrolman who did not know him. . . .

The name of "Bumpy" Johnson was familiar in Harlem's night spots and restaurants. He was frequently seen with the area's night set and also with many of its politicians. . . . Bumpy served time in such famous prisons as Sing Sing, Danbury, Atlanta, and Levenworth, Danamora and Alcatraz. . . . But when "Bumpy" got out, he returned to Harlem like a conquering hero. The champagne bottles popped in many a popular Seventh Avenue night spot and old cronies and pals crowded around and welcomed Bumpy home. (*New York Amsterdam News*, 13 July 1968, 39)

The eulogies continued at his funeral at St. Mark's Episcopal Church in Harlem, with Reverend John Johnson emphasizing Bumpy's positive virtues. Speaking to the congregation, Fr. Johnson said,

He chose his career and followed it with his eyes open. He had a code of ethics. He was not a coward and he never betrayed a friend. He had good manners and was generous to a fault. . . . He decided early in life not to be a clown, a flunky, or a beggar. He despised phonies and hypocrites.

Maybe there was no other way for him to be a man but he had the capacity to undergo mental and physical strain on his person and he never cracked. (Walker 1968, 2).

Would that each of us would have such a memorial at our funeral!

I had the pleasure of meeting Bumpy in 1966. At that time I taught sociology at St. Francis College in Brooklyn. Among my students was a black Franciscan nun who taught in a parochial school in Harlem. Asking her about organized crime in Harlem, I was told about Bumpy and his fame in the area. Bumpy, as it turned out, had befriended her convent. Frequently appliances (e.g., refrigerators, washing machines, etc.) would be delivered and the nuns were never told who donated them. Presumably, they came from Bumpy. During snowstorms, Department of Sanitation trucks would plow out the convent parking spots while leaving the rest of West 124th Street deep in snow. Everyone "knew Bumpy was doing a favor" for the nuns who had spoken positively about him in a letter to the parole board.

On the occasion of a major convent anniversary, I had been invited to a party celebrating the event. The festivities were held outdoors in the convent front yard, and hundreds of people from Harlem attended— neighbors, clergy, police officials, politicians, professionals, judges— and Bumpy. Excitedly, I asked my nun friend to introduce me to him which she did. He truly was personable and friendly until I told him I was a sociologist interested in crime. That abruptly ended our conversation and Bumpy, probably correctly, ignored me for the duration of the party. It didn't take long for him to realize that I probably was up to no good, seeking to "interview" him as indeed I had every intention of doing!

The pride that the black community felt in Bumpy's success in the world of organized crime could be matched by any similar newcomer community. Men like him have done well in the eyes of their fellow newcomers. Even if many in the community did not agree with the methods employed by Bumpy and hundreds like him, they respected the fact that he "made it" to the top of his "profession" and could deal with anyone—high or low—on an equal basis.

The Lack of Social Status in the Larger Community

As the ethnic gangster reaches the top of the criminal success ladder, he discovers that he faces the same prejudice and discrimination that his newcomer community encounters. He may be rich and famous, yielding enormous power and political influence, but he still is despised by the larger society not only because of his criminal activities but also because of his minority status. He may have a fabulous home but it can only be located in certain "nouveau riche" neighborhoods, for he will be denied access to the established ones; he may wish to join elite country clubs but rarely will he be sponsored; he may wish to marry his children into established upper-class families but they will be summarily rejected. The newcomer ethnic criminal is an outcast from conventional society and his pariah status stems from the double rejection of his "profession" and his ethnic minority background. He differs little from his fictional counterpart depicted in the gangster films.

As a consequence the gangster learns that the success and respectability he craves are intimately connected to his ethnic status. If he is ever to be accepted, his ethnic group must first be acceptable to the larger society. The removal of the barriers to his ethnic group's social mobility thus becomes an important goal for the gangster, not because of some newly discovered interest in social justice, but because the group's acceptance improves his personal chances of true respectability.

America's ethnic gangsters consequently have often involved themselves in projects which not only helped their public image, but which also benefited the image of their ethnic group in the eyes of the larger American society. During the Depression, Al Capone sponsored dozens of soup kitchens in Chicago which fed thousands daily; Lucky Luciano and Meyer Lansky "volunteered" their mobs' services to United States Naval Intelligence during World War II to weed out espionage and sabotage on the New York waterfront; Jewish gangsters in the 1950s joined other Jews, avidly supporting the sale of Israeli war bonds and the United Jewish Appeal; in the 1950s the jewels of the Blessed Virgin statue were stolen from *Regina Pacis* chapel in Brooklyn, an affront not only to Italian Catholics but to Italian gangsters as well. They were returned a few days later and the thieves executed, reportedly by Joe Profaci's mob; in the late 1960s Profaci's successor, Joe Colombo formed the Italian-American Civil Rights League to protest and monitor alleged governmental discrimination against Italian Americans.

No doubt these activities of ethnic gangsters may have been self-serving, but they also aimed at improving the image of the ethnic group presenting it in a positive light as patriotic, compassionate, civic-minded, and disdainful of "disorganized" crime. The gangster could only benefit from the gradual social acceptance of the larger ethnic group in the American society. In this sense the ethnic criminal, clergyman, teacher, singer, basketball star, restaurant owner, and politician were "all in it together," their individual mobility tied to the general upward mobility of the entire ethnic minority. Each helped the other in some fashion, just as "one hand washes the other."

In the 1940s one such gangster, Frank Costello, used his political influence over New York's Tammany Hall Machine to insure the appointment of Italian judges to city and state courts. As Daniel Bell indicates this probably related more to his sense of ethnic social justice than to furthering of his criminal enterprises:

> A substantial number of Italian judges sitting on the bench in New York today are indebted in one fashion or another to Costello; so too are many Italian district leaders—as well as some Jewish and Irish politicians. And the motive in establishing Italian political prestige in New York was generous rather than scheming for personal advantage. For Costello it was largely a case of ethnic pride. As in earlier American eras, organized illegality became a stepladder of social ascent. (Bell 1960, 147)

As this mobility ensues, however, the ethnic-gangster rarely reaps its full rewards, for social respectability never comes to him as it does to those fellow ethnics in other legitimate endeavors. He remains an outcast, an eventual embarrassment to his ethnic group as well as a public enemy to the larger society. His hopes for respectability consequently rest with his sons and daughters who stand a slightly better chance of truly "making it" than did he but not necessarily. Al Capone's only child, "Sonny," suffered the stigma attached to his father's reputation. In 1937 he attended the University of Notre Dame, registering under his father's alias, Al Brown. He withdrew after a year when his actual identity became known, transferring to the University of Miami. By all reports he led a very honest, conventional life until 1965, when he was arrested for shoplifting in Hollywood, Florida. After receiving probation on this charge, he changed his name and has scrupulously avoided any public attention (Kobler 1971, 394).

Meyer Lansky perhaps the foremost Jewish organized criminal of the recent past could find a home nowhere. Rejected by the United

States, various Caribbean nations, and even by Israel, he became, for a time a man without a country. Yet his son, Paul, graduated West Point in 1954 and went on to pursue a career in the Air Force (Messick 1971, 200). The biographies of other noted gangsters would show similar odysseys, with status and respectability rarely accruing to them. Perhaps it would come to their children and grandchildren. Should current newcomer gangsters survive their climbs to power, undoubtedly they will find that their success also is hollow and disappointing.

Yet the long-term historical result entailed the gradual upward social mobility of the ethnic minority. Each of the modes of mobility—crime, politics, the professions—propelled the vast majority of its members towards the success they sought. Together all of them insured that the newcomer minority group would ascend and take a place in the American middle-class mainstream, the ethnic gangster, contributing perhaps unwittingly, to this process as did the ethnic business proprietor. But the long-term social honor would escape the ethnic gangster who would be relegated to the footnotes of history, a curious interlude in the mobility trek of the ethnic minority. His exploits and misdeeds are quickly repressed for every ethnic group prefers a romanticized view of its American origins rather than the more colorful if somewhat startling reality. Only the legends remain.

6

The Future of Ethnic Organized Crime

The foregoing analysis of ethnic organized crime in America has maintained that such crime provided a vehicle of upward mobility for lower-income ethnic minorities in their odyssey towards the fulfillment of the American Dream. Together with the other routes of mobility—labor, retail small business, the professions, the clergy, entertainment, and politics—ethnic crime enabled the bright ambitious "go-getters" to make something of themselves, and subsequently to assist the entire ethnic group in its ascent on the social ladder. As Ianni states,

> The degree and tenure of minority-group involvement in this business enterprise (organized crime) is basically a function of the social and cultural integration of the group into American society. At their first entrance in this society, immigrants and their children grasp at the immediate means of acquiring what the New World has to offer. As they are acculturated, their crimes become more American and in time merge into the arena of marginal legitimate business practice. Where one stops and the other begins is not always easy to see. (Ianni 1972, 61)

But what about the future? Will the former ethnic minority criminals simply graduate to white-collar crime and engage in a more "respectable" form of criminal activity? Will current ethnic minorities embark upon the well-trodden criminal paths of former minorities? Will crime be as important a mode of mobility among current newcomers as it had been for Irish, Jews, and Italians? Will state and federal prosecutors successfully destroy organized crime and eliminate once and forever the power of mobs? The answer to these questions ultimately rests upon the social conditions confronted by ethnic newcomers as they accommodate to the nation's metropolitan areas.

The Process of Urbanization and Industrialization

The social drama of newcomers trying to "make it" and assimilate into the American mainstream unfolds in the arena of the city, for the great waves of immigration are concurrent with America's massive urbanization and industrialization in the mid-to-late nineteenth century. In fact it was this phenomenal immigration that propelled America's industrial revolution. The ethnic and class conflict between newcomers and the established order became most evident in these cities. The success or failure of upward mobility of each ethnic minority directly encompassed this urbanization-industrialization phenomenon.

"Making it" in America primarily meant making it in the urban-industrial milieu. For upward mobility to take place, a rapidly expanding economic order must be present. This economic condition occurred in the established urban centers of the Northeast and Midwest in the late nineteenth century and subsequently diffused to the towns and embryonic cities of the rest of the nation. These rapidly growing towns, cities, and soon-to-become-cities, accounted for the vast material and economic success of America. Settling in these urban areas proved to be the central factor in the subsequent advancement of the newcomers, for they formed a great pool of unskilled labor, the vital ingredient necessary in that era's industrialization.

This access to the urban-industrial order provided the catalyst for subsequent ethnic group upward mobility, the necessary but not the sufficient condition for the movement of the ethnic growth out of the lower classes. How so? In the nineteenth and early twentieth centuries, American urban areas greatly increased because of extensive immigration, massive in-migration from local rural areas, and the net fertility increases of the urbanites themselves. With the resultant increase in population size and density, these cities expanded to the maximum potential of their existing social and economic resources.

Emile Durkheim's Contribution

As Emile Durkheim (1947) noted, this increasing population density provided the impetus for the initiation of the industrialization sequence. As a necessary (but not sufficient) condition for industrialization, this dense concentration of people in urban areas became the key to an understanding of the ethnic newcomers' subsequent rise in status. The eventual rise of lower-income newcomers from the depths of poverty depended primarily on this demographic factor, for it provided the foundation for subsequent mobility (Durkheim, 1947).

Industrialization therefore depends on this increased population density, which makes possible this dividing of the work task, and the presence of large numbers of ethnic newcomers in America's urban areas helped initiate the industrialization process. This process in turn launched the upward mobility of these newly arrived minorities, for they were better off economically in the long run as a result of the jobs undertaken.

The urban and industrial processes tend to coincide with each other even though they are distinct phenomena. In turn, the increased industrialization of the society spurred on the process of even greater urbanization. Since an ever-growing labor force fueled the expansion of manufacturing, this compelled continued rural-urban migrations. A cycle (increased population density> urbanization> industrialization) was established that eventually became self-sustaining to such a degree that continued population growth contributed to the solution of the problems of want and misery as a result of the material abundance created by industrialization of the society (Cochran and O'Kane 1977, 118; see also Matras 1973, 468).

What Groups Make It?

The access of newcomers to this urban industrial framework helps explain why certain groups succeeded more rapidly than others. How long a group had resided in America explains nothing of its success or failure in the mobility contest; how long the group had been exposed to the process of urbanization, either in America or elsewhere, proved to be the deciding factor. Those groups that had the longest encounter with America's urban industrial centers "made it"; those that failed to be included in the urban-industrial network suffered the consequence of continued lower-income status. Success or failure depended upon this access to the urban world. The majority of the members of nineteenth century immigrant groups (i.e., Irish, Germans, Swedes, Norwegians, Danes, Italians, Greeks, Chinese, Japanese, and Slavs) with the longest exposure to America's cities, achieved middle-class respectability, as did groups exposed to European town and city life (e.g., Jews); those who have only recently encountered urban life (post-World Wars I and

II) either here in America or elsewhere (i.e., African Americans, Puerto Ricans, Haitians, Colombians, etc.) are still "waiting on the ethnic line," still queueing for middle-class status.

Various native American Indian groups provide an illustration, as do American blacks prior to their massive migration from the rural South earlier in this century. The Indians have been on America's soil longer than any other group, yet are only partially urbanized and constitute the most impoverished group in the country. Excluded from meaningful participation in the nation's mainstream, many remain isolated in rural reservations far from the staging urban arenas where the trek from the bottom begins.

Until the interim between the world wars, blacks presented a similar situation. They have been here far longer than other groups. Only their massive out-migration from the rural South to the urban North commenced their upward mobility from the bottom layers of society—a process not yet completed but substantially under way. Their location in the industrial heartland of America has enabled a growing proportion of urban blacks to reach middle-class status and widen the socioeconomic gap between them and their rural counterparts who remain relatively fixed in lower socioeconomic positions. Their upward mobility and increasing middle-class status are largely dependent upon their location in the urban-industrial centers of America. Were they to have remained in southern rural regions, they would still be overwhelmingly lower class. Their current high rates of urbanization in both southern and northern centers, have changed this, with a corresponding increase in the number of blacks nearing middle-class status.

The Irish provide yet another example. Prior to the 1830s the majority of Irish Americans were Protestant in background and settled in small towns and rural areas, particularly in the South and the Midwest. During the American Revolution, these Irish comprised the backbone of the Continental Army. Their animosity to England was fueled by the fact that they were driven out of Ireland by the famines of the 1740s and by the oppressive economic policies of the British (Lee 1983, 46).

The bulk of Irish immigrants who immigrated to America after the 1830s were Catholic and, unlike Irish Protestants, settled in those areas soon to become the heart of the nation's industrialization—the large cities of the Northeast and the Midwest. This location enabled them to move slowly into the middle classes to such an extent that Irish

Catholics currently have higher average socioeconomic status than Irish Protestants. Citing recent National Opinion Research Center data, Fred Boal indicates

> one major factor can be suggested as lying behind these differences—the fact that the two groups are concentrated in different parts of the United States—over half the Irish Protestants are located in the "South" and seventy percent of the Irish Catholics are located in the Northeast and North-Central regions. . . . Thus the Catholics are predominantly large city dwellers in the north of the United States, the Protestants smaller city and rural dwellers in the South. Until recently . . . the south of the United States has been the poorest, least industrialized part of the county. The Irish Protestants, therefore, in their income and educational attributes are reflecting the general regional conditions they live in. Equally the Irish Catholics reflect their residence in areas where jobs are better paid and educational opportunities greater. (Boal 1977, 5)

The solution to the problem of how groups succeed is consequently embedded in the process of urbanization-industrialization, and in the response of, and reaction to, established groups in American life.

The Importance of Stable, Productive Employment

If these minorities find stable productive employment in urban areas, then the vast majority will have access to the success ethic of the larger society, and their involvement in organized crime will be minimal and short-lived. Such was the case with the German and Scandanavian newcomers of the nineteenth century, and such appears to be the case of those current newcomers who exhibited significant middle-class skills and cultural values before journeying to America (e.g., certain portions of Chinese, Japanese, Korean, Filipino, pre-1980 Cuban, Indian, Pakistani, and Soviet Jewish immigrants). For the most part these newcomers arrived legally and, as such, fulfilled current immigration statutes requiring skilled employment backgrounds.

What involvement these groups have in organized crime should be temporary, their sojourn lasting only as long as the larger ethnic group awaits full middle-class status and respectability. Having middle-class aspirations and more-or-less sophisticated urban life-styles, these newcomers waste little time moving up the social ladder. They opt primarily for the mobility routes of small retail businesses and the professions and quickly "make it" in America. In this sense they need not pursue organized crime in any large-scale manner, for other opportunities present themselves.

On the other hand, if the ethnic newcomers fail to find stable productive employment, to that degree they will not have viable access to the success demanded of them. In American society one's status and self-concept depend on this stable economic foundation. As Americans, we are not as interested in *who one is* as we are in *what one does*. A stable job thus becomes the sine qua non for self-respect, family stability, service to the community, and ultimately, upward mobility. Those with stable long-term employment thrive in our society; those without it—whether through their own fault or not—languish and fail to advance on the social ladder, oftentimes finding themselves enmeshed in a multitude of social and behavioral problems so familiar to any observer of their situation.

These incoming ethnic minorities to our metropolitan areas who lack middle-class skills and values are thus predisposed to difficulties in finding long-term stable employment. For the most part these are substantial portions of our African-American, Caribbean, South American, Central American, post-1980 Cuban, Vietnamese, Mexican, and Hong Kong Chinese urban newcomers. Many of these are illegal immigrants, who have largely emigrated from rural agricultural locales, arriving in our urban industrial centers, without appreciable economic skills. Like their Irish, Jewish, and Italian counterparts, they arrive and settle near the bottom of the social-class hierarchy; unlike their predecessors, however, they find few jobs awaiting them and languish in poverty because they either have no jobs or have ones that are marginal and low-paying. Ill prepared for industrial and postindustrial society, today's lower-class newcomers find that they are economically useless: they have no economic function in a society that has moved far beyond low-skilled employment.

The sad reality of our current economic situation is the relative disappearance of unskilled and semiskilled manufacturing jobs, jobs that had been the economic lifeline of earlier newcomer groups. Currently they are increasingly difficult to find and these present-day newcomers are destined to struggle to maintain a livelihood in such an atmosphere.

Yet these unskilled newcomers also wish to find success and are expected to be successful, to "be somebody." Like most of us, they want a decent job, a job which, as one commentator remarked, consisted in wearing a suit, having one's own office, and eating lunch daily in a restaurant. For all too many of the newcomers, this desire will never be fulfilled.

The Plight of Juan, Roberto, and Will

A generation ago, in the early 1960s, this employment plight was emphatically brought to my attention in my social work placement in New York City's Lower East Side. As a caseworker for Mobilization for Youth, the "granddaddy" of all the poverty programs that flourished in the Kennedy-Johnson era, I was responsible for helping lower-income Puerto Rican and black youth find jobs. One such youth, Juan (pseudonym) age nineteen, came to my office seeking employment. He had migrated from Puerto Rico ten years earlier and lived in dire poverty with his family—both parents and twelve brothers and sisters—in a three-room rat-infested apartment in the neighborhood. Juan was functionally illiterate, even though he stayed in high school until he dropped out at the tenth grade. He had never held a job in his life, though he clearly wanted one. Over time I learned that he wanted to be a private detective so he "could help people and catch bad guys." To realize this he sent a coupon from the back of a comic book to a mail order detective training outlet (along with $12 obtained from his father's welfare allotment) that promised to certify him as a "private eye." He was sent a cheap tin badge with PRIVATE DETECTIVE embossed on it, as well as a certificate that literally depicted a large eye and indicated that he was now a certified Private Eye! As I quickly learned, such pathetic scams were common.

Unable to find a job after weeks of trying, Juan decided to join the army and dutifully appeared at the Whitehall Testing Center in lower Manhattan for mental and physical testing, accompanied by his 20-year-old mentally retarded cousin Roberto who also sought to be inducted. Along with hundreds of other draftees and volunteers, Juan and his cousin took the mental and educational skills exams. After approximately thirty minutes of struggling to complete those, they were "politely" informed by the sergeant that they could go home, that they didn't have to complete the remaining portions of the testing. Both young men were ecstatic; as they later informed me they were convinced that they did *so* well on these exams that the Army, recognizing their abilities, exempted them while the other "dunces" had to take more tests. Only days later did they recognize the reality that their lack of literacy skills had doomed them to failure. "Things are so bad" said Juan, "that we can't even get drafted into the army!"

Repeated attempts to find employment met with repeated failures. I even brought Juan and Roberto to a building that Michael Harrington referred to as the "slave market," an edifice housing dozens of employment agencies that hired people for short-term, no-exit jobs such as dishwashers, floor sweepers, and so on. The "counselors" there were very polite to me, realizing that I was a social worker. No sooner had I left Juan and Roberto to be interviewed when the counselor threw both young men into the street telling them never to bring a social worker there again. So much for the "slave market."

For months I tried to find a job for another youth, Will, an eighteen-year-old black, but to no avail. Will's search for employment was no more productive than Juan and Roberto's search. Eventually a local supermarket manager agreed to hire him as a grocery bag loader. I still remember my feeling of pride that I had finally gotten him his first job. Yet Will didn't last long in this job—three hours was the total length of his employment. He was fired after he failed to return from his lunch hour. When I asked him what happened, he told me that he didn't know that he was supposed to return after his lunch: "The boss said, 'it's noon, you can leave now.'" Yet how was he to know what a lunch hour means, for he knew hardly anyone who worked. Consequently he would have no reason to know about lunch hours, coffee breaks, two-week vacations, arrive-at-nine and leave-at-five orientations.

Juan and his cousin's situation, as well as Will's, are probably worse than those encountered by most lower-income newcomers. Devoid of skills and opportunities, their chances of succeeding in American life by conventional means were indeed slim. What could I have told each of them? "Why not try to open your own little retail business?" "Have you thought of going to college, of being a lawyer, or priest or minister?" "Why not try your hand at professional sports, or at starting a rock group?" "Have you thought of running for political office down here in the Lower East Side?" Each of these options would have been out of the question for Juan, Roberto, and Will.

The world of productive labor, as our efforts demonstrated, also eluded them. Economic forces suggest that the labor market in the 1990s for the Juans, the Robertos, and the Wills of the nation, will probably be no better than currently is the case. Yet they, and many more like them, lust for the rewards of the American Dream, wanting to be looked up to by others, to have plentiful material possessions, to make something of themselves, to "be somebody."

Is it any wonder that crime presents itself as a viable alternative means of accomplishing these ends? Whether they are successful or not in criminal ventures is moot (the vast majority of them will not be successful criminals); for them the only realistic way to achieve their goals—goals instilled and encouraged by our society and made oh-so visible through television—is through crime. They know it, and we know it.

Crime as Work

Deprived of realistic opportunities to pursue stable, productive work, younger newcomers are attracted to criminal life-styles. For them, crime becomes their work, their occupation, their mechanism for establishing an identity, a way of "being somebody." Many newcomer criminals thus pursue their "career" with the same diligence and drive as would any successful businessman or lawyer. Their work habits, skills, and motivation are scarcely different from those of the rest of us in conventional society. Peter Letkemann has emphasized this arguing that we would be served better if we viewed crime as work, as an occupational pursuit similar to other occupations:

> Much contemporary research, particularly that having to do with the construction of typologies based on characteristics of criminals, proceeds on the assumption that knowledge of the criminal's background and characteristics will facilitate the control of criminal behavior. This approach need not be disparaged in order to make a case for alternative approaches. An occupational perspective seems to have obvious potential applied utility. To view crime as work demands that we look at it in terms of its viability as an occupation: skills required, training opportunities, effects of technological change, financial returns, and costs and risks involved. (Letkemann 1973, 163)

Thus, criminal newcomers adjust to the larger society and pursue the American Dream in their own way, perhaps risking life and limb, but adapting to the demands and rewards of their "job." The very fact that many continue to pursue lives of crime suggests that they are relatively content in it. As Ned Polsky notes, "one of the most genuinely appealing things about crime to career criminals and part-timers alike—though one would hardly gather this from criminology texts—is that for most crimes the working hours are both short and flexible" (Polsky 1967, 103). Were there no rewards, no status, no future in crime, few would continue to engage in it. Though these positives may be fantasies for most of our common criminals, their continuing quest for them fuels their criminal life-styles. For them, if only in their illusions, crime does pay. It fascinates the Juans, Robertos, and Wills of our lower-income communities, mesmerizing them with the allurements of success that they can scarcely obtain by legal methods.

Stable productive employment is the key to correcting the malaise of the American underclass—the millions of people who function, however inadequately, outside the mainstream. Programs giving the poor jobs are few and those that have been successfully implemented are even rarer. One such program has been created by David Riemer in a test site in Milwaukee, Wisconsin. Riemer noted in his analysis of Wisconsin's unemployment figures that the state could fill every single job tomorrow and would still lack jobs for 50,000 people. There are simply not enough jobs for the poor (Gunn 1990, 6). Poverty can only be reduced by creating jobs so the poor can function in the American mainstream. Riemer's welfare reform project in Milwaukee encourages welfare recipients to give up welfare benefits in exchange for a guaranteed job in the private sector, with subsidized guaranteed wages. Such initiatives aim at creating stable employment precisely among those peripheral to the economic mainstream (Riemer 1991). Riemer argues that the eradication of poverty requires three separate responses to the three tiers of poor in the United States:

> the first tier—poor people who cannot work or whose old age exempts them working—would receive a guaranteed annual income. Specifically, their SSI and Social Security paychecks would be supplemented to get them above the poverty line. For the other two tiers, work would be required as a condition for receiving help, and year-round work would be rewarded with an income above the poverty line. The second tier—consisting of poor people who can work but who cannot find

full-time, year-round work—would be offered community-service employment that would provide enough hours to work to plug the gap between their current level of employment and 35 hours of work per week for 52 weeks each year at the minimum wage. The third tier—persons who have dependent children and who already hold jobs . . . would be given a wage supplement . . . that would be sufficient to get their families above the poverty line. Like the guaranteed annual income, this approach would virtually eliminate poverty in the United States. Unlike the guaranteed annual income, it would give the poor what they want— jobs. (Riemer 1988, 185)

Yet few other significant public or private policy initiatives either on local or national levels have been introduced to implement such a solution. Few public figures are calling for the creation of jobs on a scale massive enough to help alter the deplorable future confronting those newcomers who are devoid of middle-class skills and values. Such a solution is beyond the thinking of liberals and conservatives alike who instead prefer feeble alternatives such as job training programs for nonexisting jobs, and educational programs that ignore the economic realities of inner-city poverty.

Without such an economic solution, the lower-income minority newcomers face a situation wherein they will find it increasingly difficult to find any viable employment needed to enable them to pull themselves out of poverty. As long as this remains the case, the continuation of ethnic newcomers in crime in general, and in organized crime in particular, seems inevitable.

Alternative Interpretations: Racism and Anomie

Few seem willing to recognize that the lack of productive employment is the fundamental problem confronting contemporary lower-income ethnic minorities. Many instead prefer to look elsewhere for the problem's source. In the past two decades it has become fashionable to view the plight of ethnic minorities in our urban centers as if it were an entirely new problem in American life. This is particularly apparent in relation to lower-income African Americans, whose social and economic problems are viewed as unique and fundamentally different from the predicaments of all previously lower-income minority groups.

Such thinking implies that the difficulties encountered by African American newcomers, are more complex and less amenable to solution, than the difficulties faced by the Irish, the Jews, the Poles, the Italians, and so on. This interpretation is somewhat myopic for it ignores the historical backgrounds of previous lower-income ethnic groups. Furthermore, it has led social observers to view the problem of lower-income blacks as essentially and fundamentally a problem of *racism*. As noted elsewhere, the argument of those favoring the uniqueness of the black situation runs as follows:

> The Negro cannot be likened to the immigrant groups of the nineteenth century simply because of his ascribed racial qualities. The former slave status and legal disenfranchisement from American social life have necessitated the realization that the Negro is in a category distinct from all previous societal rejects. His situation and problems are unique; they are literally larger and more incomprehensible than anything of a similar vein witnessed in our history, and the old answers will be irrelevant to the amelioration of the Negro's situation. (O'Kane 1969, 303)

This position betrays a very pessimistic view of lower-income blacks and their supposed uniqueness near the bottom of American social hierarchy, a view powerfully reinforced in the late 1960s with the so-called Kerner Report, written in response to the widespread urban riots in black neighborhoods of many of our cities. That analysis—*The Report of the National Advisory Commission on Civil Disorders* noted that

> racial discrimination is undoubtedly the second major reason why the Negro has been unable to escape from poverty. The structure of discrimination has persistently narrowed his opportunities and restricted his prospects. Well before the high tide of immigration from overseas, Negroes were already relegated to the poorly paid, low status occupation. . . . European immigrants, too, suffered from discrimination, but never was it so pervasive as the prejudice against color in America which has formed a bar to advancement, unlike any other. (*Report of the National Advisory Commission on Civil Disorders* 1968, 278–79)

Yet, as William J. Wilson emphasizes, "trotting out" the phenomenon of racism to explain the plight of the urban underclass does little to assist or ameliorate the situation:

> To suggest that the recent rise of social dislocations among the ghetto underclass is due mainly to contemporary racism . . . is to ignore a set of complex issues that are difficult to explain with a race-specific thesis. More specifically, it is not readily apparent how the deepening economic class divisions between the haves and the have-nots in the black community can be accounted for when this thesis is invoked.

. . . Nor is it apparent how racism can result in a more rapid social and economic deterioration in the inner city in the post-civil rights period than in the period that immediately preceded the notable civil rights victories. (Wilson 1987, 10–11)

Wilson further indicates that even if racism were to be eliminated, the conditions in the underclass would not change appreciably:

If you were to wave a magic wand, and there was no more racism, the situation of the ghetto underclass would not change significantly unless you did something about the economy and the communities they live in. (Wilson 1987, 26)

In addition, some social scientists generally indicated that the response to the situation where newcomers cannot succeed as a situation of anomie. Emile Durkheim explained the concept of anomie as a condition of personal disorientation which results when individuals function without attainable goals in a society lacking clear-cut norms, beliefs, and values. (Durkheim 1951, 246–57). Other social scientists have concentrated on the personal aspects of anomie, emphasizing such similar, but not identical, concepts such as anomia, alienation, self-isolation, rootlessness, powerlessness, and marginality, (cf. Srole 1956; Seeman 1959; Dean 1961.) In fact much of the literature relating to culture conflict focuses on this alleged disorganization of migrant groups including Park and Miller (1924, 61); Thomas and Znaniecki (1927, vol. 2, 1692–1700); Wirth (1931); Stonequist (1937, 10); Wirth (1938, 3–24). Lately however, another body of social science literature questions the idea that migration is disruptive and anomic: Cressey (1961, 38–40); Little (1965, 86); Zimmer (1970, 83); Berry (1973, 88). Bernard Rosen writes:

The migrant who finds work and makes a place for himself in the city will experience a psychological state denied most peasants—a sense of success. For he has in fact improved the conditions of his life. The sense of efficacy, a feeling that goals can be attained through one's own endeavor, has been identified as a salient difference between modern industrial man and the passivistic peasant. . . . For the migrant can see that an industrial city rewards competition and achievement and encourages independence . . . to a far greater extent than the rural community, where the hierarchical structure places a premium on passivity, conformity and obedience to authority. (Rosen 1973, 199)

In my own study of Spaniards migrating to the industrial city of Pamplona in northern Spain, I found no evidence of anomie or alienation among them. In fact, the migrants were remarkably well adjusted to life in Pamplona, more so than the Pamplonians who had lived their entire lives in that city! (O'Kane 1981).

Thus, as an explanation of the newcomers' behavior, anomie is faulty. The newcomers avoided the anomic response characteristic of Durkheim's analysis, turning neither against themselves nor their kin, not dissipating their talents and energies through self-pity and self-estrangement. Instead the hostility of the larger society fused and reinforced an ethnic identity in each group, insulating that group from the ravages of rootlessness. Suffering from prejudice and discrimination, they joined their fellow ethnics and slowly formed a healthy self-image intimately linked to their ethnic group membership. Whereas formerly they had identified themselves in a parochial fashion as Kerrymen, Calabrians, Silesians, Harlemites, or San Juanistas, now they identified themselves as Irish, Italians, Jews, African Americans, or Puerto Ricans. Seventy years ago, Robert Forester discussed the localized, provincial character of Italians both before and immediately after they immigrated to America:

> Observers have reported that they do not find Italians but rather Venetians, Calabrians, and so forth. Even the smaller unit, the village, clings to its identity. In Briey, in New York, in Buenos Aires, something like a street-by-street separation of the immigrants according to origin has been recognizable . . . most of all it is a thing so characteristically Italian that it is best denoted by the Italian name *campanilismo*: a loyalty to that which falls within the range of the village bell tower. This it is which spurs the immigrant to entrust his savings to his fellow townsman, rather than to a chartered but foreign bank, or to marry an immigrant girl deriving from his own neighborhood, or to write home asking that a girl from his village be chosen to traverse the seas to be his bride. But with this loyalty also goes marked hostility—at the least, indifference—to the immigrants from other parts of Italy. While conflicts of a sanguinary nature are one result of the curious situation so produced, a larger consequence is a patent disunity of the Italian population as such, mute evidence of the weakness of nationalist sentiment. (Forester 1919, 431)

Their common ethnic bond subsequently united the ethnic newcomers, precluding and effectively neutralizing the anomic self-estrangement reaction. Hence, the classic conception of anomie as originally developed by Durkheim in his explanation of certain groups in mid-nineteenth-century France cannot be applied to America's newcomers. Much of the social rhetoric that refers to newcomers as "anomic," "alienated from themselves," "estranged," "adrift in a meaningless world," and so on, is inaccurate nonsense.

Their marginality stems from a strong pervasive estrangement *from the larger dominant society*. They were thus alienated *from the society*, but not *from their inner selves nor from their own ethnic group*. This marginality has helped produce the creative people present in every ethnic minority. The ethnic group provided the economic, social, and psychological security so necessary for survival, comforting the newcomers in their rejection by the outside dominant groups in American life. Consequently the ensuing hostility of the dominant society forged a strong ethnic consciousness in the ethnic newcomers, a consciousness and identity insulating them from the negative consequences of the growing realization that middle-class status would be far more difficult to attain than they first had imagined. In turn, this group identity enabled the ethnic minorities to confront collectively a larger society that promised much but offered little.

The resulting security of "having one's own group," of knowing that "we" are just as good as "they," of realizing who one is and from where one came—all these factors helped insulate the ethnic newcomers from the painful realities of social exclusion. They provided newcomers with a sense of self and a group ethnic identity so necessary in their odyssey through American life. At times, ethnic intellectuals and polemicists who encouraged this ethnic identity have exaggerated its positive aspects, ignoring those group features that were received in a negative light. What Thomas Brown has said of Irish ethnic consciousness in the mid-1800s could easily be written of subsequent newcomer groups as well:

> The Irish-American apologist rarely concerned himself with the realities of the Irish-Catholic situation: the poverty and slums, the street gangs and saloons, the priest's influence and politicians' chicanery, the modest aspirations hard-working mothers held for their sons. The apologists preferred to speak of Irish glories. Because of its manifest and sometimes comical distortions and because it put aside problems that were matters of real concern, this propaganda was hardly influential outside the Irish-American community. Its importance lies in the power it had to give the immigrant and his sons a dramatic sense of participation in the American epic. It nourished egos suffering from a sense of humiliation. It assured the Irish poor that they had a stake in the nation's future. To those who branded them aliens, they could answer: "This is our country. We bought it dearly. We like it well, and we intend to stay." (Brown 1966, 30)

For those who may be surprised at some of the current excesses in African-American, Hispanic, and American Indian interpretations of their respective cultures, it may do well to remember that each incoming ethnic minority did similarly. One Irish-American enthusiast in the late 1800s, Martin O'Brennan, believed that Gaelic was the original language spoken in the Garden of Eden (Brown 1966, 32).

As an explanation of the social reaction of ethnic minorities to the dilemma of assimilation, the Durkheimian model of anomie, of rootlessness and normlessness, falters in other aspects as well, for the rules of how one should assimilate and achieve the American Dream were clear to all. American society in the nineteenth and twentieth centuries did not approximate the anomic model of a social order bereft of goals identifiable and clear-cut expectations of conduct. Americans' goals and promises were clear—the access to them was not.

Ethnic and Social Class Perspectives

A more fruitful avenue of inquiry entails viewing the plight of lower-income blacks in ethnic and social class terms rather than in racial and anomic terms. The pathos and problems that we see in the black underclass are consequences of lower-class membership and are not primarily related to racial factors; other nonblack lower-class groups suffer similar difficulties (e.g., Puerto Ricans, Columbians, Mexicans) while other nonblack racial groups have largely been spared these problems (e.g., Japanese). Viewing lower-income blacks in such a light enables us to compare and contrast them with similar ethnic minorities, both past and present. Furthermore, it enables us to isolate the crucial difficulty faced by all current lower-income minorities— the disappearance of unskilled and semiskilled employment, opportunities that in previous eras would have served as major vehicles of upward mobility. As these employment opportunities in unskilled jobs, relative to other types of jobs, began to diminish in the 1960s, 1970s, 1980s, and 1990s, rates of crime and family disruption markedly increased among all our lower-class minorities regardless of their racial characteristics, creating the bleak scenario that we see in lower-income communities across the land. The great gulf in American life is the gap between lower-income minorities and the more affluent middle and upper classes. Increasingly our more affluent groups, whether they be black, white, yellow, or red have little in common with their counterparts in the lower classes who are the same color as they.

The fundamental problem herein is the lack of stable employment. William J. Wilson has argued convincingly that the central problem faced by our inner-city ghetto residents is "joblessness reinforced by a growing social isolation in impoverished neighborhoods" (Wilson 1991, 9). Expanding on themes he developed earlier (1987), Wilson states that stable employment provides, not only necessary income, but also a coherent way of living a meaningful life. This absence of regular employment creates the vicious cycle in the lives of so many inner-city poor. The lack of jobs

> not only give rise to weak labor-force attachment, but increases the probability that individuals will be constrained to seek income derived from illegal or deviant activities. This weakens their attachment to the legitimate labor market even further. . . .

> Thus, in the absence of regular employment, what is lacking is, not only a place in which to work and the receipt of regular income, but also a coherent organization of the present. Regular employment provides an anchor for the temporal and spatial aspects of daily life. In the absence of regular employment, life, including family life, becomes more incoherent. (Wilson 1991, 10)

The consequences of this inability of poor males to find stable employment are everywhere apparent in our lower-income communities: long-term welfare dependency, collective despair, educational failure, family breakdown, unwed teenage mothers, alcoholism, drug abuse, crime, and violence.

Until American society creates an economic floor for this poorest segment of the nation through the provision of stable jobs, it will continue to fail in solving these enduring social problems. Those with stable jobs, irrespective of their race or ethnicity, have, and continue to abandon these ghetto areas in their pursuit of the American Dream. Their exodus creates a social and moral vacuum wherein the former tradition of law and order, respect for others, and civility quickly fall prey to the seamier segments of the community, the "riffraff" element that have made so many lower-income neighborhoods such dangerous places in which to reside.

The Enduring Vitality of Ethnic Organized Crime

This dearth of meaningful economic opportunities for the lower echelon of today's incoming groups—the nation's Juans, Robertos, and Wills—creates the fertile soil for the continuation of ethnic organized crime. The evidence presented in this analysis suggests that ethnic organized crime among current minority newcomers is flourishing and ever-expanding, with no end to it in sight. At a time when FBI and Department of Justice offensives against Italian organized crime are beginning to bear fruit, new ethnic mobs appear to fill the vacuum. Police and organized crime task forces scarcely know what to do about these new groups and have their hands full merely trying to describe these activities, let alone control them. With respect to certain groups (e.g., Chinese, Japanese, Vietnamese, and Soviet Jews), police even lack undercover agents who speak the same language as the newcomer criminals!

The prognosis for the elimination of ethnic organized crime is indeed grim. Compounding this reality is an equally depressing one: many of the former lower-income ethnic criminals have not necessarily become law-abiding citizens. Many simply have "moved up" to white-collar crime, and as such, have blended with the dominant groups in American life. Hence an unknown number of WASP, Irish, Jews, and Italian criminals can ply their criminal trade in an "acceptable" fashion, for, in spite of all the rhetoric, the American public isn't terribly worried about white-collar offenses. What concerns the public are crimes in the streets, and organized crime as the average American understands it—vice, thievery, gambling, narcotics, loan sharking, extortion, labor racketeering, contract killing, and so on. Of course, the ethnic groups involved in such crimes are precisely those newcomers who lack access to white-collar criminal ventures simply because they lack access to white-collar careers. If reputable official statistics on white-collar crime existed (they don't), we would undoubtedly find that African Americans have very low rates of stock embezzlement, Puerto Ricans low rates of insider trading stock abuses, Jamaicans low rates of antitrust offenses, and so on. Similar nonexisting data reporting the rates of WASP, Irish, Jewish, and Italian violations of these areas, would presumably show significant involvement.

We also constantly delude ourselves that ethnic organized crime is "on the way out." Each time a federal prosecutor obtains a conviction of a major organized criminal, reporters ask if that spells the end of organized crime in America. We often believe that organized crime can be eliminated, that we can return to some pristine, unspoiled past, where such crime did not exist.

Even objective observers of ethnic organized crime have succumbed to this fantasy. Herbert Asbury, perhaps, one of the most astute and informed observers labeled the last two chapters of his 1927 book *The Gangs of New York* in such a way as to suggest that this type of crime was nearing its end; chapter 15 he entitled "The Last of the Gang Wars," and chapter 16, "The Passing of the Gangster." Albert Fried in his remarkable study of Jewish crime in America, similarly alludes to the disappearance of Jewish newcomers in crime, viewing Meyer Lansky as the last of a dying breed:

> It is a fading memory enveloped in twilight now: the Lower East Side of Maier Luchowljansky's [Meyer Lansky] childhood, where Big Jack Zelig and his men (Lefty Louie, Whitey Lewis, and Gyp the Blood) still commanded the streets, taking up where Monk Eastman and Kid Twist had left off, where the whores and gun-molls and cadets and gamblers and guerrillas and life-takers, met at Segal's Cafe and in scores of hangouts like it, where youth gangs abounded on every block, where aspiring criminals learned the techniques of survival and with luck and audacity and brains achieved success as well. But the Lower East Side and every other urban ghetto—Chicago's and Philadelphia's and Cleveland's and Boston's and Detroit's and Newark's—once tenanted by Eastern European Jews are gone, and so are all the children of the underworld, those who fell in battle and those who died peacefully in the bosom of respectability, the anonymous mass and the privileged few. That past is vanquished. Meyer Lansky is the last of its heroes. (Fried 1980, 286)

Had Fried written his book a decade later, he undoubtedly would have noted that Lansky's demise represented only the end of an episode in Jewish crime, for the larger story continues, with up-and-coming Soviet Jewish criminals, such as Marat "the Georgian" Balagula pursuing promising futures in organized crime (Burstein 1986, 40).

As long as lower-income newcomers flock to our metropolitan centers, and discover that their access to the American Dream is severely hampered by the lack of meaningful employment and by the intransigence of the more established groups, then will ethnic organized crime persist and thrive. A solvable problem thus is in danger of becoming endemic to our society. The forms and modus operandi of ethnic crime will change, depending upon the cultural and social values of the newcomer minorities, the myriad criminal opportunities present to them, and the larger values of American society which require these newcomers to be successful, honest, and upright while providing few realistic opportunities to do so. The catalyst for the future evolution of ethnic organized crime lies precisely in our American social structure and well-meaning attempts to eliminate such crime cannot circumvent this reality. It's as American as apple pie.

Appendix
The Criminal in American Ballad and Film

The Criminal in American Culture

As outcasts, the rural social bandit outlaw and urban ethnic gangster occupy central places in American literature. We fear and despise them, but we endow them with mythical qualities, romanticizing their exploits even as we condemn them. We loathe their violence and amoral outlook on life, yet we admire these criminals, exhibiting enormous curiosity about their deeds. We voyeuristically examine these acts while we simultaneously decry them. We transform these criminals into figures larger than life, some anti-heroes, others genuine folk heroes. Who is unfamiliar with America's famous renegades—Billy the Kid, Jesse James, Al Capone, Bonnie and Clyde, Pretty Boy Floyd, Dutch Schultz? We write ballads and base movies on their lives; Billy the Kid even had a ballet composed in his "honor," by America's noted composer Aaron Copland.

The rural bandits of Texas and Missouri and the urban gangsters of New York and Chicago play crucial roles in our culture. They caricature who we are, where we came from, how we molded a nation from a wilderness, and how we assimilated millions of immigrant newcomers coming to our shores. The idealized gun battles of the Old West, the train robberies in Iowa, the bank holdups in Oklahoma, the beer wars of Prohibition, the gangland massacres, the crimes of the mafia—all remain crucial to our common mythologies as do the myriad noncriminal events that fill our history texts. Indeed Americans know more about the St. Valentine's Day Massacre than they do the Treaty of Versailles! These criminal events serve as moral lessons that remind us of the limits of acceptable behavior and illustrate the boundary line over which we must not cross.

The rural gangsters reflected the minimally organized rural farms and towns that spawned them. As social bandits they rarely engaged in *organized* crime, with its political protection, its use of extortion, infiltration of legitimate business, its large-scale organization with gangs of dozens if not hundreds of "soldiers." There was simply no need to organize on any large scale. The rural bandits' crimes involved robbery and violence. While often colorful and individualistic, these rural outlaws rarely seemed to have long-range goals; they lived for the moment and often died that way. On the other hand, the urban gangsters were invariably Catholic or Jewish, coming from recent immigrant stock, thoroughly urbane in their outlook and aspirations. Their deeds were less "colorful" than their rural bandit counterparts even though they were just as deadly.

The deeds of each—the outlaw and the gangster—are recorded in song and movies and constitute an important aspect of American mythology, so much so that it becomes difficult to conceive of our social history without these individuals.

The Outlaw Ballad and the Gangster Film

In the nineteenth and early twentieth centuries, the outlaw's status was reflected in the newspapers, dime novels, and songs of that era. The ballad became one mechanism wherein the exploits of the more famous bandits were recounted and extolled, with moral lessons emphasized, villains chastised, and virtues praised. These ballads confirmed the importance of the outlaw in the lives of ordinary common people, for they saw the Jesse Jameses and the Pretty Boy Floyds as glorifications of themselves—sharecroppers and poor folk—men who individually fought against great odds, who stood up for the poor of the land, bowing to no one. They embodied the rural, small-town Protestant ethic wherein individualism, loyalty, distrust of outside authority, and reliance on family and extended kin were honored virtues. True, they had gone astray, but they were forced to do so by circumstances beyond their control. Big bankers, eastern businessmen, "city slickers," railroad owners—all had created the milieu that "forced" outlaws to act the way they did—so say the ballads.

The deaths in the 1930s of Bonnie and Clyde, Pretty Boy Floyd, Ma Barker and her sons, Baby Face Nelson, and John Dillinger signify the waning of the era of the outlaw. The social banditry of the South and

Southwest gradually disappeared, pushed aside by the growing industrialization of American society (Hobsbawm 1981, 18).

The sixty-year period—from the 1870s era of Jesse James to the 1930s era of Pretty Boy Floyd—constituted a mere interlude between the nation's agrarian and industrial phases. A new era of urbanization characterized the nation, for the cultural, political, social, and demographic reference points had shifted slowly to the cities. The 1920s and 1930s tolled the death knell for the social bandits of the rural and small-town areas of the country, and the Bonnie and Clydes, and Pretty Boy Floyds comprised the last of a dying breed of violent but colorful outlaws.

As the rural bandit faded in the eyes of the American public, the urban ethnic gangster increased in stature. His status was rarely extolled in ballads but rather in the films of the twentieth century. Film was to the urban gangster what the ballad was to the rural outlaw—a medium that conveyed to the public the social location, moral virtues and vices, and official reaction to the criminal. For the ethnic gangsters of twentieth century urban America, the ballad played only a minor role: there are few such ballads honoring Lupo the Wolf, or Dion O'Bannion, or Hymie Weiss, or Dutch Schultz, or Bugsy Siegel, or Vito Genovese, though in the 1970s Bob Dylan composed one—"Joey" heralding the exploits of Crazy Joe Gallo. Yet films abound which depict the lives of such notorious ethnic gangsters as Al Capone, Legs Diamond, Lepke Buchalter, Machine Gun Kelly, Bugs Moran, Bugsy Siegel; many more films are fictionalized accounts which amalgamate actual incidents from the lives of numerous mobsters in telling a story (e.g., *The Godfather* and *Scarface*). Even the Broadway musical has been utilized in extolling the virtues and vices of the urban gangster as the short-lived 1989 production *Legs* would illustrate. The status and notoriety of the urban ethnic gangster owes a great deal to Hollywood, for the cinema created and popularized the legend of the gangster as the ballad had done previously for the outlaw.

Nineteenth Century Outlaw Ballads

This process of exalting America's criminals permeates our culture, embedded in ballads, stories, films, and folk wisdom. In the nineteenth century the gunslinger and the outlaw mesmerized the public's imagination. Billy the Kid, the Dalton gang, Sam Bass, Cole Younger, Jesse and Frank James—all became folk heroes to large segments of American society. Their actual deeds, often vicious and ruthless, were forgotten; their mythical deeds became legendary.

Billy the Kid

Billy the Kid exemplifies this transformation from renegade outlaw to folk hero. Born in New York City in 1859, William Bonney moved west with his family after the Civil War and quickly enmeshed himself in a life of crime. Reputed to have killed twenty-one men by the age of twenty-one, Billy the Kid established a reputation in the Southwest as a bloodthirsty, cold-blooded assassin. He worked as a gunslinger for the big ranchers in New Mexico in their feuds with the smaller, independent cattlemen. After these range wars Billy formed his own gang of cattle rustlers and robbers, chief among who were Tom O'Folliard and Charlie Bowdre (both eventually murdered). Billy's end came in 1881, ambushed by his one-time friend, Sheriff Pat Garrett.

Soon after his death the legend developed. To the common people of the Southwest, Billy represented the contempt that they felt towards official authority. Against all odds, Billy the Kid had survived in a world ruled by big cattlemen, bankers, politicians, and "the law." He became a hero, a friend to the poor, a handsome, sensitive, brave young man who assisted those in need. Stories and books have been written about Billy the Kid, most of which grossly distorted his life and deeds. Yet the romantic legend appealed to Americans more than the grim reality. The legend became embodied in ballads which glossed over his cold-blooded nature and emphasized his alleged virtues instead. The most famous of these is simply entitled *Billy the Kid*:

> I'll sing you a song of Billy the Kid
> I'll sing of the desperate deeds that he did,
> Way out in New Mexico, long, long ago,
> Where a man's only chance was his own forty-four.
>
> When Billy the Kid was a very young lad,
> In old Silver City he went to the bad,
> Way out in the West with a gun in his hand
> At the age of twelve years, he killed his first man.

Fair Mexican maidens play guitars and sing
A song about Billy, their boy-bandit king.
How ere his young manhood had reached its sad end,
He'd a notch in his pistol for twenty-one men.

'Twas on the same night when poor Billy died,
He said to his friends, 'I'm not satisfied.
There are twenty-one men I have put bullets through,
And Sheriff Pat Garrett must make twenty-two.'

Now this is how Billy the Kid met his fate,
The bright moon was shining, the hour was late;
Shot down by Pat Garrett, who once was his friend,
The young outlaw's life had now come to its end.

There's many a man with a face fine and fair,
Who starts out in life with a chance to be square,
But just like poor Billy he wanders astray
And loses his life in the very same way.

(Lomax 1960, 387)

Jesse James

Similar legends portray the life of Jesse James who "stole from the rich and gave to the poor." Regarded by many of the rural farmers of Kansas and Missouri as a modern Robin Hood, Jesse and his gang preyed upon the enemies of the common man—the banks and the railroads—and did so in a daring fashion. To the defeated Confederacy the James gang likewise represented the righteous vengeance heaped upon the businessman and their allies, groups who epitomized everything evil in the Southerner's mind. To these southerners Jesse, his brother Frank, and their allies the Younger brothers, Cole and Jim, were true heroes fighting for the oppressed and the downtrodden.

Yet the reality was somewhat different. Members of Quantrill's Raiders during the Civil War, Jesse and Frank James continued their guerrilla tactics after the war, plundering and looting, killing lawmen and innocent bystanders in the process. Yet the public's sympathy supported them particularly after 1875 when Pinkerton detectives bombed their mother's house, blowing off her right arm and killing Jesse and Frank's nine-year-old brother, Archie. According to Sifakis, "the incident stroked great resentment towards the Pinkertons and brought forth a rash of sympathy for the James boys, not only in Missouri but throughout the country. Lost in the shuffle of support for the outlaws was . . . their own long list of victims. The bungling Pinkertons had done as much as anybody to make them respectable" (Sifakis 1982, 370). Jesse continued his outlaw ways until his murder in 1882 at the age of thirty-four by one of his own gang members, Bob Ford, whose infamous deed plagued him until he also was assassinated in 1892 by Edward O'Kelly, a relative of Bob and Cole Younger. Following Jesse's death the legend continued to grow, portraying perhaps the best known American outlaw, as well as his killer, Bob Ford, "the dirty little coward that shot Mr. Howard [Jesse's alias] has laid Jesse James in his grave." Similar to ballads heralding Billy the Kid, ballads proliferated, enshrining Jesse James in folklore and legend. The most famous of these, *Jesse James*, celebrates his life. Samples of some of the verses follow:

Jesse James was a lad that killed many a man
He robbed the Danville Train
He stole from the rich and he gave to the poor
He'd a hand and a heart and a brain.

Chorus
Poor Jesse had a wife to mourn for his life
Three children they were brave
But the dirty little coward that shot Mr. Howard
Has laid poor Jesse in his grave.

It was Robert Ford, that dirty little coward
I wonder how he does feel
For he ate of Jesse's bread and he slept in Jesse's bed
Then he laid poor Jesse in his grave.

Chorus
Jesse James was a man, a friend to the poor
He'd never see a man suffer pain;
And with his brother Frank, he robbed the Chicago bank,
And stopped the Glendale train.
                    (Silber and Robinson 1967, 254)

The ballads of *Billy the Kid* and *Jesse James* illustrate the legendary qualities of the American outlaw. Despised by the established society, the outlaw and gangster are honored and romanticized by the common man reflecting his hostility and anger towards middle-class and upper-class America. A sense of powerlessness is placated by vicariously identifying with the superhuman qualities of these outlaws. It matters little that their exploits may have been criminal and vicious; what counts is the belief, often erroneous, that the outlaw stood up to oppression and did so in an honorable and noble fashion. His death, often at the hands of cowards and traitors, traumatizes his faithful admirers, as Hobsbawm notes in his discussion of these noble robbers: "For the bandits' defeat and death is the defeat of his people; and what is worse, of hope. Men can live without justice, and generally must, but they cannot live without hope" (Hobsbawm 1981, 51).

Sam Bass and Cole Younger

Similar ballads extolled the virtues of lesser-known desperados. Sam Bass, an outlaw, robber, pimp, and murderer in the 1870s was eulogized in *The Ballad of Sam Bass* following his death in 1878. Below are sample verses:

> Sam Bass was born in Indiana,
> That was his native home
> And at the age of seventeen
> Young Sam began to roam.

> Sam first came out to Texas,
> A cowboy for to be;
> A kinder-hearted fellow
> You seldom ever see.

The final verse berates Jim Murphy, a fellow gang member who betrayed Sam Bass to the Texas Rangers:

> Jim had borrowed Sam's good money
> And didn't want to pay;
> The only shot he fired for him
> Was to give poor Sam away.

> He sold out Sam and Barnes
> And left their friends to mourn;

> Oh, what a scorching Jim will get
> When Gabriel blows his horn!
>   (E. and C. Moore 1964, 344–45)

Cole Younger who rode with his three brothers in the Younger Brothers gang, terrorized Missouri, Kansas, Texas, and Minnesota in the 1870s along with their friends, Jesse and Frank James. Unlike many other famous outlaws, Cole Younger died a natural death in 1916 after serving twenty-six years in prison and starring in a Wild West show along with Frank James. Likewise his ballad *Cole Younger* illustrates some remorse over his criminal deeds, even as it extols his character.

> I am of a band of highwaymen;
> Cole Younger is my name
> And all my early depredations
> Have brought my friends to shame.
>
> 'We'll ride to avenge our father's death
> And try to win the prize
> We'll fight these anti-guerrilla boys
> Until the day we die.'
>
> It's aye, old boy, hand o'er your money;
> There's no time to delay
> For we are the noted Younger boys,
> Who spare not time to pray.
>   (E. and C. Moore 1964, 346–47)

Twentieth Century Outlaw Ballads

The twentieth century witnessed continued social banditry in the United States. The cowboy-outlaw had disappeared, replaced by new outlaws equipped with automobiles and submachine guns. Their modus operandi was similar to the James gang—robbing banks, gaining the sympathy and admiration of the average citizen; even their geographical areas of operation were similar—Missouri, Kansas, Texas, and Oklahoma. These gangsters operated in small gangs and focused their crime sprees in rural towns and small cities. Foremost among these were Bonnie Parker and Clyde Barrow—Bonnie and Clyde—Pretty Boy Floyd, Ma Barker and the Karpis-Barker gang, whose criminal activities in the 1930s gained them national and international notoriety. To my knowledge no ballads or feature films extol the merits of Ma Barker and her gang. Their "legend" is recounted indirectly in Raoul Walsh's 1949 classic film *White Heat* where Cody Jarrett's mother, Ma Jarrett, is the matriarch of a gang of killers.

Bonnie and Clyde

Bonnie Parker and Clyde Barrow captured the attention of the American public with their criminal activities in Texas, Missouri, Oklahoma, and Kansas at the height of the Depression. From 1930 to 1934 they robbed banks, service stations, and grocery stores killing over a dozen people in the process, many of them police. Their record of robbery, murder, and daring escapes from prison made them instant celebrities and national newspapers followed their exploits. Bonnie attracted particular notice in the newspapers, sending pictures of herself smoking cigars and toting a submachine gun. Clyde also exemplified heroic qualities that fascinated the public: "Clyde Barrow was cut from a heroic mold, unlike many other gangsters of the 1930s such as Baby Face Nelson, Pretty Boy Floyd and even John Dillinger. When trapped, he never abandoned his woman, after fighting his way back to her and leading her to safety" (Sifakis 1982, 85). Their end, like the end of their nineteenth-century predecessors, came in a brutal fashion, with Bonnie and Clyde ambushed by police in Gibland, Louisiana in 1934. Their epitaph commemorating their exploits was written by Bonnie months before her death. She called it the *Ballad of Bonnie and Clyde*, sample verses of which read:

> You've read the story of Jesse James
> Of how he lived and died;
> If you still are in need of something to read,
> Here's the story of Bonnie and Clyde.
>
> Now Bonnie and Clyde are the Barrow gang,
> I'm sure you all have read
> How they rob and steal and how those who squeal
> Are usually found dying or dead.
>
> There are lots of untruths to their write-ups,
> They are not so merciless as that;

And they fight because they hate all the laws,
The stool pigeons, spotters and rats.

They don't think they are too tough and desperate,
They know that the law always wins:
They've been shot at before, but they do not ignore
That death is the wages of sin.

Someday they will go down together
And they will bury them side by side
For a few it means grief, for the law it's relief
But it's death to Bonnie and Clyde.

                              (Burt 1958, 212–14)

Bonnie and Clyde have thus moved from history to legend, romanticized in song, and in films such as *The Story of Bonnie Parker* (1958) and Arthur Penns' monumental *Bonnie and Clyde* (1967) which show that though criminals can't win, their status depends on the manner in which they choose to lose.

Pretty Boy Floyd

Charles "Pretty Boy" Floyd emerged as a true hero to the poor of Oklahoma and surrounding states in the 1930s. Coming from poor farmer roots, Floyd began robbing banks and escaping jails in daring fashion. At times he would alert the sheriff of a small town that he would be coming to rob the bank, but most police were too fearful to stop him; they knew his reputation for violence. After robbing one bank, he encouraged his "rob from the rich, give to the poor" reputation by throwing money from his getaway car. Colorful as Pretty Boy was, he nevertheless was a vicious killer who often murdered in cold-blooded fashion. Yet these murders did little to turn away his admirers. When he was finally gunned down by Melvin Purvis' FBI men in 1934, he refused to tell them anything about his past crimes, allegedly saying, "I won't tell you nothing" before dying.

Pretty Boy Floyd's legend as a Robin Hood fighting the law and the big banks took shape even during his short life. The ballad *Pretty Boy Floyd* is perhaps the best known memorial to any criminal. Written by Woody Guthrie, the ballad ignores Floyd's senseless murders and concentrates on his generosity and hero-like qualities so admired by the sharecroppers of Oklahoma. Guthrie comments, "that's how it went with old Charley Floyd. He was born and raised right down in there where I was. I talked to lots of people that knowed him personal. Said he wasn't much of a bad feller. Fact, some of them respected him lots more than they did the sheriff and his deputies" (Lomax 1960, 427). Guthrie's ballad captures Floyd's legend:

> Come and gather 'round me, children
> A story I will tell
> About Pretty Boy Floyd, the outlaw
> Oklahoma knew him well.
>
> Then he took to the trees and timber
> To live a life of shame
> Every crime in Oklahoma
> Was added to his name.
>
> Yes, he took to the river bottom
> Along the river shore,
> And Pretty Boy found a welcome
> At every farmer's door.
>
> There's many a starving farmer
> The same old story told
> How the outlaw paid their mortgage
> And saved their little home.
>
> Yes, as through this world I've rambled
> I've seen lots of funny men
> Some will rob you with a six gun
> And some with a fountain pen.
>
> But as through your life you'll travel
> Wherever you may roam
> You won't never see no outlaw
> Drive a family from their home.
> (Lomax 1960, 227)

The Twentieth Century Gangster Film

As social banditry and rural outlaws gradually disappeared in American life after the 1930s, the public's fascination with the criminal focused on the ethnic gangsters of the nation's urban centers, a fascination illustrated in the dominant cultural medium of the city—the Hollywood movie. Urbanites had little use for the ballad, which played a minor role in the lives of the ethnic newcomers. Curious vestiges of such ballads remain however, for urban gangster "memorials" remain relatively rare. One such exception is the ballad *Joey*, composed by Bob Dylan in 1975, which chronicles the life and deeds of Joey Gallo, the leader of Brooklyn's Gallo mob in the 1960s and 1970s.

Like the outlaw ballads of rural America, Dylan's *Joey* romanticizes its hero, endowing him with honor, prestige, and ennobling traits, suggesting that his tragic status in life has redeemed him in the eyes of his followers. Like the balladeers of another era, Dylan views the criminal in his legendary form, a form only remotely related to the actual reality of crime. Yet such urban gangster ballads remain anachronisms. They are not part of the cultural style of twentieth-century newcomers who have opted for a different form of cultural expression. These ballads and folk tales represented the old world, the world of the rural villages and European towns they wished to forget. The newcomers embraced a modern urban world complete with new technologies and cultural media, among which the Hollywood film holds preeminent significance. The ethnic gangsters comprised an integral part of this urban world and the gangster film symbolically chronicled the criminals' peculiar version of the American Dream.

Just as the outlaw ballad extolled the virtues and vices of ruthless criminals, so also did the gangster movie. It chastised the gangster, depicting his corrupt deeds and murderous actions, presenting moral lessons that crime does not pay, that virtue triumphs in the end, and so on. Yet it also extolled the virtues of the gangster, showing his supposed warm, compassionate qualities, emphasizing his courage and dogged determination, arguing that, in the end, he actually may have been superior to those who defeated him. The gangster films which have become our nation's classics illustrate this ambivalent quality of the gangster, a man like the rest of us who simply went astray because of factors beyond his control.

Hundreds of feature films fit this gangster genre classification yet relatively few have extolled the ethnic gangster as a folk hero, a mythical figure praised for his behavior even though it be criminal. A sampling of these would include: *Little Caesar* (1930), *The Public*

Enemy (1931), *Angels With Dirty Faces* (1938), *The Roaring Twenties* (1939), *Kiss of Death* (1947), *On the Waterfront* (1954), *The Godfather I, II,* and *III* (1972, 1974, and 1990). Each illustrates this ambivalent nature of the ethnic gangster that has captured the American imagination. They portray "ideal" gangsters who, like Billy the Kid, Cole Younger, and Pretty Boy Floyd have sought "to be somebody," to make their mark, to be a success in a hostile, violent world. Indeed, the movie stars who portrayed the gangster in these films have themselves oftentimes represented the ideal stereotype of the criminal of that respective era. Actors such as Edward G. Robinson, James Cagney, Humphrey Bogart, Marlon Brando, Al Pacino, and Robert De-Niro have become the embodiment of the ideal gangster.

The ethnic gangsters of the 1920s and 1930s flourished in the world of Prohibition, illustrated in films depicting the chaos and violence of the beer wars and bootlegging rackets. Edward G. Robinson's portrayal of Rico in *Little Caesar*, James Cagney's numerous roles (e.g., Tommy Powers in *The Public Enemy*, Rocky Sullivan in *Angels with Dirty Faces*, Eddie Bartlett in *The Roaring Twenties*) exemplified the public image of the ideal gangster—one who was loyal to friends, sentimental in nature, ruthless in his pursuit of success, uncompromising with rival gangsters and police, sympathetic and loving toward his family, particularly his mother. The gangster of this era thought of himself as a "big shot" complete with his ever-present tuxedo and fancy night club life-style. Like Cagney's Rocky Sullivan, he would never die a "yellow rat." How this public stereotype meshed with the real life adventures of Dion O'Bannion, Al Capone, Hymie Weiss, Lucky Luciano and Bugsy Siegel is, of course, debatable. No matter, for the public preferred the elevated mythical status of the Hollywood gangster to the reality of actual criminals in the larger cities.

The ethnic makeup of the characters in these films is predominantly Irish and Italian, reflecting the ethnic makeup of organized crime in the 1920s and 1930s. Jewish characters on the other hand are noticeably absent in these films, a policy largely due to Hollywood producers, many of whom were Jewish, who wished to excise any reference to Jewish criminals because of fears of fueling anti-Semitic attitudes in the viewing public (Erens 1984, 138, 196). Hence Irish and Italian heroes and villains dominate the gangster films depicting the Prohibition era. The cast of gangsters in *Little Caesar* include Rico, Joe

Masera, Otero, Sam Vettori, and Flaherty. Cagney's cycle of gangster movies include characters such as Rocky Sullivan, Mack Keefer, Father Connolly, Tom Powers, and Matt Doyle. Their adversaries in these films are either other Irish and Italian gangsters, or WASP gangsters such as Frazier in *Angels with Dirty Faces*, portrayed by Humphrey Bogart.

The films of the 1940s portrayed gangsters of a different sort, where the ethnic background of the principle characters is muted and difficult to detect. This represents a reaction to the Nazi propaganda of the 1930s and early 1940s that advocated racial superiority. These films now depict the vicious, psychotic killer—one who belongs to a nondescript gang but who pursues his ends in a solitary, insane manner. The gangster's ethnicity is difficult, if not impossible, to detect. Richard Widmark's portrayal of Tommy Udo in *Kiss of Death* who kills an elderly handicapped woman by pushing her in her wheelchair down a flight of stairs serves as an example of the ruthlessness of the "new" gangster. So also does James Cagney's portrayal of Cody Jarrett in *White Heat* (1949) the psychotic killer whose only ambition is to make it to "the top of the world."

When Udo and Jarrett die violently, we don't mourn them as we would a Rico, a Rocky Sullivan, an Eddie Bartlett. Udo and Jarrett are true villains, bereft of any redeeming qualities and, as such, do not attain the mythical status of idealized gangsters. Unlike their cinematic predecessors they exhibit little that would endear them to the public. Were they real nineteenth-century outlaws, few ballads would be composed in their honor.

The 1950s witnessed the return of the ethnically-identifiable gangster. *On the Waterfront* presented the ethnic gangster in his infiltration of longshoremen by racketeers and unions. Again Irish and Italians predominate, with Jewish gangsters absent. The main figures are Irish characters: "Johnny Friendly" Scanlon (Lee J. Cobb), Terry Molloy (Marlon Brando) and his brother Charlie the Gent (Rod Steiger), Joey Doyle's sister (Eva Marie Saint), the Irish priest (Karl Malden); the subsidiary characters are Italians who play supporting roles as bodyguards (e.g., Tony "Two G's," etc.) The film presents two types of gangsters: the hardened, cynical gang leader—Johnny Friendly—and the young, malleable mob member Terry Molloy. In their ensuing struggle, Terry Molloy emerges the victor but only after he rejects the gang and listens to his girlfriend and the priest. His final victory comes about not because he testifies before the Waterfront Crime Commission but because he challenges Johnny Friendly with his fists, playing by the rules of the street. He becomes "somebody" instead of a "bum." The gangster hero thus becomes one who forsakes his criminal past and tries to live by society's rules, "infiltrating" legitimate society. The film ends with Terry Molloy making this crucial transition, a transition which in real life would indeed be very difficult.

In this era the ideal gangster's ambivalence about his criminality clearly shows. He yearns for a respectable life yet life's circumstances have made this improbable. Terry Molloy makes the transition from crime to respectability with the enormous support of a few loyal friends, but only after his brother and others he respects are murdered by the mob.

The 1960s evidenced the reappearance of the nonethnic criminal. The 1967 film *Bonnie and Clyde* portrays the nonethnic gangster, the rural WASP outlaws of an earlier era. In the leading roles Faye Dunaway and Warren Beatty depict two loners who, even though they belong to a gang, move in solitary fashion towards their inevitable destruction. The American audience's enthusiastic reception of the film suggests that the antihero gangster had achieved public status in the 1960s, for such tragic heroes dovetailed nicely with the antiauthority, rootless, anomic mood of that era. Ethnicity was not a salient feature in this or similar films.

This yearning for acceptance for social respectability, clearly presents itself in *The Godfather* films. More than any other films, *The Godfather I, II,* and *III* portray the ethnic gangster in historical perspective, with ethnicity in full flower. Irish, Jews, and Italians dominate the films and there is little attempt to conceal the ethnic makeup of the films' characters. The films, though fictional, represent a reasonable historical overview of Italian and Jewish organized crime in America; only the Prohibition era is absent in the films. Thus, the internecine wars among Italian gangsters in New York, the extension of organized crime to Las Vegas and the West, the Cuban casino operations, the warfare with Jewish gangsters—all are represented in some form in these films.

Many of *The Godfather* scenes reflect actual situations in American organized crime: the decapitated horse owned by the movie mogul Jack

Woltz relates to the "assassination" of the horse that killed "Nails" Morton in Chicago in 1924; the killing of Luca Brasi wherein his strong hand is pinned to a bar reminds us of how Dion O'Bannion was shot: one of his assassins shook his hand to prevent O'Bannion from drawing his revolver; the murder of Moe Green in Las Vegas is reflective of the murder of Bugsy Siegel in that same city, over the same dispute—control of the casino rackets in the 1950s; the murder of Inspector McCluskey indirectly relates to the alleged "mafia" murder of Chief David Hennessey in New Orleans in 1890; the concealment of the gun that killed McCluskey and Sollozzo the Turk in the restaurant toilet was an Irish mob trick employed in the New York beer wars of Prohibition; the move to gain Vito Corleone's godson Johnny Fontane a starring role is allegedly based upon Frank Sinatra's role in *From Here To Eternity*.

The "heroes" in *The Godfather* films clearly are the Corleones and their "soldiers." Don Vito Corleone, portrayed alternately by Robert De Niro and Marlon Brando, emerges as a modern-day avenger with his legendary actions winning the hearts of his fellow newcomer Italians, as well as the film's audiences. Vito Corleone exemplifies the virtues of the gangster beloved by the American public. He helps widows in need; he assists the Italian immigrant community in purging Black Hand extortionists; he exacts vengeance on those who have betrayed him, and on those who have dishonored and murdered his family. He simply perceives himself to be an honorable man worthy of respect, a true family man whom we in the audience admire. In his battles with corrupt Irish police, and murderous Italian and Jewish rivals, we cheer him, hoping he will emerge victorious, as he does.

Yet Vito Corleone yearns for a different life, one where he will be respected by the larger American society. He plans for his son Michael's future—perhaps a future as a United States senator. Societal forces prevent this. In the film's first sequel (*The Godfather Part II*) Michael ascends to the throne of criminal power. Having no illusions, he relates freely to others, befriending them and eliminating them at the proper moment. Michael Corleone and his arch rival, Hyman Roth (the fictional version of Meyer Lansky) scheme against each other until Roth finally is assassinated. Michael Corleone has now reached the top of the organized crime pyramid in virtual control of everything before him. Yet his success is hollow, his family decimated, his conquests meaningless. True success and respect so sought by both him and his father never come. He remains an isolated, brooding figure left alone in his affluence, with thoughts of what might have been, and memories of once-loved ones whom he has destroyed. He becomes a tragic hero, perhaps the fate of all our legendary gangsters, whether real or fictional, for the status, prestige and respectability offered by the American Dream elude the gangster.

In *The Godfather Part III* (1990) Michael Corleone is slowly redeemed as he finally becomes a legitimate billionaire pursuing fame and fortune in Rome and Sicily. Yet, he sees his power and status challenged by corrupt Vatican officials and ruthless mafiosi who become his opponents. In the ensuing struggle he again leads the remnants of his family, assisted by his sister, Connie, and his nephew, Vincent Mancini, in destroying his rivals. Yet, he ends up a broken man, helpless before his unfolding destiny as he witnesses the murder of his daughter.

Similar to the real-life gangsters they depict, the Hollywood mobsters never quite make it. In the hearts of the millions of Americans who admire them though, they become legendary successes. The fictional, legendary Jesse James, Billy the Kid, Pretty Boy Floyd, Rocky Sullivan, Vito and Michael Corleone, etc. are far more appealing to us than their actual historic counterparts.

The 1980s and 1990s illustrate the continuation of this status-seeking quest of the ethnic gangster, depicted most clearly in the 1986 film *The Untouchables*. As with the *Godfather* films, Irish and Italian heroes and villains abound, with Al Capone occupying center stage. His quest, like that of all newcomer criminals, entails the achievement of social honor in the eyes of the larger American public. Yet, like Vito and Michael Corleone, such acceptance is ephemeral and eludes Big Al. So also is it for the Cuban gangster, Tony Montana, in the late 1980s film, *Scarface*, which illustrates the rise of Hispanic gangsters as they vie violently with each other for control of the cocaine trade. Like his ethnic counterparts in earlier fictional films and real life situations, Montana dies violently, never achieving the total power he craved.

The salience of ethnicity is further exemplified in the films of the 1990s, with the fictional *Miller's Crossing* and the factual *Goodfellas* clearly depicting the conflict and cooperation of Irish, Jews, and Italians in organized crime. With these films, as well as the new African-American gangster genre (ex. *New Jack City*), the American public has been slowly exposed to the actual realities of ethnicity and crime in the larger society.

Bibliography

Abbott, Edith. 1924. *Immigration: Select Documents and Case Records.* Chicago: University of Chicago Press.

Abadinsky, Howard. 1981. *Organized Crime.* Boston: Allyn and Bacon.

Adamic, Louis. 1932. *Laughing in the Jungle.* New York: Harper and Brothers.

"AFT Targets Violent Jamaican Gangs in Nationwide Arrests." *International Association of Police Chiefs News* 1, 6 (November 1987):3.

Agueros, Jack. "Halfway to Dick and Jane." In *The Immigrant Experience: The Anguish of Becoming American*, edited by Thomas Wheeler, New York: Penguin Books, 1971:85–105.

Allsop, Kenneth. 1961. *The Bootleggers.* London: Hutchinson and Co.

Aristotle. 1941. *The Basic Works of Aristotle*, ed, Richard McKean, New York: Random House.

Arlacchi, Pino. 1986. *Mafia Business: The Mafia Ethic and the Spirit of Capitalism*, London: Verso.

Asbury, Herbert. 1929. *The Gangs of New York: An Informal History of the Underworld.* New York: Alfred Knopf.

Asbury, Herbert. 1936. *The French Quarter.* New York: Alfred A. Knopf.

Asbury, Herbert. 1942. *Gem of the Prairie: An Informal History of the Chicago Underworld.* Garden City, New York: Alfred A. Knopf.

Asbury, Herbert. 1968. *The Barbary Coast: An Informal History of the San Francisco Underworld.* New York: Capricorn Books.

Baltzell, E. Digby. 1964. *The Protestant Establishment: Aristocracy and Caste in America.* New York: Vintage Books.

Banfield, Edward. Review of *The Second Rebellion: The New York City Draft Riots of 1863* by James McCague, *New York Magazine* (29 July 1968) 37ff.

Barlow, Hugh. 1978. *Introduction to Criminology.* Boston: Little, Brown and Company.

Bell, Daniel. "Crime As An American Way of Life." *Antioch Review* 13 (September 1953):131–54.

Bell, Daniel. 1960. *The End of Ideology.* Glencoe, Ill.: The Free Press.

Berry, Brian. 1973. *The Human Consequences of Urbanization: Divergent Paths in the Urban Experience of the Twentieth Century.* New York: St. Martin's Press.

Block, Alan. "Aw! Your Mother's in the Mafia: Women Criminals in Progressive New York." *Contemporary Crises* 1 (1977):5–22.

Blum, Howard. "The War on 138th Street: Third, and Renegade, Gang Joined Drug-Empire Battle." *The New York Times*, 21 December 1978, A1; "Scene of the Battle Moves from Streets to the Courts" (22 December 1978):A1.

Blumenthal, Ralph, and Celestine Bohlen. "Soviet Emigre Mob Outgrows Brooklyn, and Fear Spreads." *The New York Times* (4 June 1989) 1.

Blumenthal, Shirley and Ozer, Jerome. 1980. *Coming to Ame'ica: Immigrants from the British Isles*. New York: Delacorte Press.

Boal, Fred. "Who Are the 'Irish Americans'?" *Fortnight: An Independent Review*. Dublin, Ireland: Issue No. 155, 14–27 (October 1977):14–27.

Bresler, Fenton. 1980. *The Chinese Mafia*. New York: Stein and Day.

Breasted, David. "Fear of a Negro Mafia Is Rising." *New York Daily News*, (31 July 1969):8.

Brogan, D.W. 1960. *Politics in America*. Garden City, N.Y.: Doubleday Anchor Books.

Brown, Claude, "Manchild in Harlem." *The New York Times Magazine* (16 September 1984):38.

Brown, Thomas. 1966. *Irish-American Nationalism*. New York: Lippincott Company.

Browning, Frank and John Gerassi. 1980. *The American Way of Crime*. New York: G.P. Putnam's Sons.

Bufferfield, Fox. "Chinese Organized Crime Said to Rise in U.S." *New York Times*, (13 January 1985):1.

"Bumpy Johnson Dead." *New York Amsterdam News*, 13 July 1968, 1.

Burgess, Thomas. 1913. *Greeks in America: An Account of Their Coming, Progress, Customs, Living, and Aspirations*. Boston: Sherman, French and Company.

Burstein, Daniel. "The Russian Mafia: A New Crime Menace Grows in Brooklyn." *New York Magazine* (24 November 1986):38–43.

Burt, Olive. 1958. *American Murder Ballads and Their Stories*. New York: Oxford University Press.

Byrnes, Thomas. 1969. *1886 Professional Criminals of America*. New York: Chelsea House Publishers.

Cagney, James. 1976. *Cagney by Cagney*. Garden City, N.Y.: Doubleday and Company.

Cloward, Richard. "Illegitimate Means, Anomie, and Deviant Behavior." *American Sociological Review*. 24 (April 1959):164–76.

Cloward, Richard and Ohlin, Lloyd. 1960. *Delinquency and Opportunity: A Theory of Delinquent Gangs*. New York: The Free Press.

Cochran, Lillian and O'Kane, James. "Urbanization-Industrialization and the Theory of Demographic Transition." *Pacific Sociological Review*. 20, 1 (January 1977):113–34.

Cole, Stewart and Cole, Mildred. 1954. *Minorities and the American Promise*. New York: Harper and Brothers.

Conzen, Kathleen. 1980. "Germans." In *Harvard Encyclopedia of American Ethnic Groups*, edited by Stephan Thernstrom, 406–25. Cambridge, Mass.: Harvard University Press.

Cressey, Donald. 1981. "Crime." In *Contemporary Social Problems*, edited by Robert Merton and Robert Nisbet, 21–76. New York: Harcourt, Brace and World Inc.

Curry, Jack. "Chinatown Leaders are Indicted in Gambling Ring." *The New York Times*, (1 September 1990):35.

Daily News, (specific dates and titles mentioned in text).

Daly, Michael. "Hunting the Wolf Packs," *New York Magazine* (3 June 1985):28–40.

Davie, Maurice. 1936. *World Immigration*. New York: The Macmillan Company.

de Crevecoeur, Michael Guillaume St. Jean. 1984. *Letters from an American Farmer*. Quoted In *Immigration As a Factor in American History*, edited by Oscar Handlin. Englewood Cliffs, New Jersey: Prentice-Hall, 1959:149.

Dean, Dwight. "Alienation: Its Meaning and Measurement." *American Sociological Review* 26 (1961):753–58.

Durkheim, Emile. 1951. *Suicide* (translated by J. Spaulding and G. Simpson). New York: The Free Press.

Durkheim, Emile. 1947. *The Division of Labor in Society*. New York: The Free Press.

Dylan, Bob. 1975. "Joey," song included in the album, *Desire*. New York: Columbia Records/CBS Inc.

Erens, Patricia. 1984. *The Jew in American Cinema*. Bloomington: Indiana University Press.

Forester, Robert. 1919. *The Italian Emigration of Our Times*. Cambridge, Mass.: Harvard University Press.

Fried, Albert. 1980. *The Rise and Fall of the Jewish Gangster in America*. New York: Holt, Rinehart and Winston.

Gannon, Bill. "DEA Hails Officers for Netting Drug 'Queenpin.'" *The Sunday Star-Ledger*, (4 December 1988),1:33.

Garis, Roy. 1927. *Immigration Restriction*. New York: Macmillan Company.

Glazer, Nathan. 1978. *Affirmative Discrimination: Ethnic Inequality and Public Policy*. New York: Basic Books.

Gordon, Milton. 1964. *Assimilation in American Life*. New York: Oxford University Press.

Graebner-Anderson, Annelise. 1979. *The Business of Organized Crime: A Cosa Nostra Family*. Stanford, Cal.: Hoover Institution Press.

Graham, Hugh and Ted Gurr. 1969. *The History of Violence in America: A Report to the National Commission on the Causes and Prevention of Violence*. New York: Bantam Books.

Grant, Madison. 1918. *The Passing of the Great Race*. New York: Charles Scribner's Sons.

Gross, Jane. "Speed's Gain In Use Could Rival Crack, Drug Experts Warn." *New York Times*, (27 November 1988), 1 and 26.

Gunn, Erik. "Unemployment: A New Way to Look at State's Low Jobless Rate." *Milwaukee Journal*, (October 31, 1990), 6 and 10.

Haberman, Clyde. "T.V. Funeral for Japan's Slain Godfather." *New York Times* (6 February 1985), 6.

Hamilton, Edith. 1951 "The Greek Way." In *Everyday Life in Ancient Times*, 69–201. Washington, D.C.: National Geographic Society.

Handlin, Oscar. 1957. *Race and Nationality in American Life*. Garden City, New York: Doubleday Anchor Books.

Handlin, Oscar. 1962. *The Newcomers*. Garden City, N.Y.: Doubleday Co.

Handlin, Oscar. 1979. *Boston's Immigrants*. Cambridge, Mass.: Harvard University Press.

Harrington, Michael. 1962. *The Other America*. New York: Penguin Books.

Harris, John. "Domestic Terrorism in the 1980s." *FBI Law Enforcement Bulletin* (October 1987):5–13.

Hartmann, Edward. 1948. *The Movement to Americanize the Immigrant*. New York: Columbia University Press.

Herberg, Will. 1955. *Protestant-Catholic-Jew*. New York: Doubleday Co.

Herskovitz, Melville. 1958. *The Myth of the Negro Past*. Boston: Beacon Press.

Higham, John. 1980. "Leadership" In *Harvard Encylcopedia of American Ethnic Groups*, edited by Stephan Thermstrom, 642–47. Cambridge, Mass.: Harvard University Press.

Hobsbawm, Eric. 1981. *Bandits*, revised edition. New York: Pantheon Books.

Hofstadter, Richard and Michael Wallace. 1971. *American Violence: A Documentary History*. New York: Vintage Books.

Howe, Irving. 1976. *World of Our Fathers: The Journey of the Eastern European Jews to America and the Life They Found and Made*. New York: Harcourt Brace Jovanovich.

Hunger Action Forum. 1990. 3, 2, Washington, D.C.: The Hunger Project.

Ianni, Francis. 1974. *Black Mafia: Ethnic Succcession in Organized Crime*. New York: Simon and Schuster.

Ianni, Francis and Elizabeth Reuss-Ianni. 1972. *A Family Business: Kinship and Social Control in Organized Crime*. New York: Russell Sage Foundation.

Kallen, Horace. 1924. *Culture and Democracy in the United States*. New York: Boni and Liveright.

Kaplan, David and Alec Dubro. 1987. *Yakuza: The Explosive Account of Japan's Criminal Underworld*. New York: Collier Books.

Katz, Jack. 1988. *Seductions of Crime: Moral and Sensual Attractions of Doing Evil*. New York: Basic Books.

Kelly, Robert. 1987. "The Nature of Organized Crime and Its Operations."

In *Major Issues in Organized Crime Control*, edited by Herbert Edelhertz, 3–49. Washington, D.C.: National Institute of Justice.

Kennedy, Ruby Jo Reeves. "Single or Triple Melting Pot? Intermarriage Trends in New Haven, 1870–1940." *American Journal of Sociology* 49 (January 1944):331–39.

Kennedy, William. 1978. *Legs*. New York: Penguin Books.

Kerr, Peter. "Chinese Now Dominate New York Heroin Trade." *The New York Times*, (9 August 1987), 1.

Kim, Illsoo. 1981. *New Urban Immigrants: The Korean Community in New York*. Princeton: Princeton University Press.

Kim, Illsoo. 1984 "The Korean Fruit and Vegetable Business: A Case Study." In *The Apple Sliced: Sociological Studies of New York City*, edited by Vernon Boggs, Gerald Handel, and Sylvia Fava, 107–17. South Hadley, Massachusetts: Bergin and Garvey Publishers.

Kobler, John. 1973. *Ardent Spirits: The Rise and Fall of Prohibition*. New York: G.P. Putnam's Sons.

Kobler, John. 1971. *Capone: The Life and World of Al Capone*. New York: G.P. Putnam's Sons.

Kusner, Kenneth. 1986. "Ethnicity and Business Enterprise: A Comment." In *Making It in America: The Role of Ethnicity in Business Enterprise, Education, and Work Choices*, edited by M. Stolank and M. Friedman, 43–54. Lewisburg, Pa.: Bucknell University Press.

Langton, Kenneth. 1969. *Political Socialization*. New York: Oxford University Press.

Larini, Rudy. "Mob Expert Sees Danger Lurking in 'New' Underworld." *The Sunday Star Ledger* (January 31, 1988), 1.

Lee, Alfred McClung. 1966. *Multivalent Man*. New York: George Braziller.

Lee, Alfred McClung. 1983. *Terrorism in Northern Ireland*. New York: General Hall, Inc.

Letkemann, Peter. 1973. *Crime as Work*. Englewood Cliffs, N.J.: Prentice Hall.

Levin, Mike and Krajicek, David. "Feds Catch Big One: He's King Kon." *Daily News*, (27 March 1988), 7.

Levin, Mike and Krajicek, David. "Heroin Biz Rooted in Asia." *Daily News*, (27 March 1988), 7.

Light, Ivan. 1972. *Ethnic Enterprise in America: Business and Welfare Among Chinese, Japanese, and Blacks*. Berkeley: University of California Press.

Lindsey, Robert. "They're Behind Bars But Not Out of Business," *The New York Times*, (2 June 1985), D:2.

Little, Kenneth. 1965. *West African Urbanization: A Study of Voluntary Associations in Social Change*. New York: Cambridge University Press.

Lomax, Alan. 1960. *The Folk Songs of North America*. Garden City, New York: Doubleday and Company.

Lorch, Donatella. "A Traditionally Insular Community Begins to Reach Out." *New York Times*, (28 October 1990) 4:20.

Los Angeles Times (Various dates and titles mentioned in text).

Lupsha, Peter. "Individual Choice, Material Culture, and Organized Crime." *Criminology* 19 (May 1981):3–24.

McAlary, Mike. 1990. *Cop Shot: The Murder of Edward Byrne*. New York: G.P. Putnam and Sons.

McCague, James. 1968. *The Second Rebellion: The New York City Draft Riots of 1863*. New York: Dial Press.

McKinley, James. "Missing Boy: Drug Trade Hits Again." *The New York Times*, (6 January 1990), 27–28.

Merton, Robert. 1957. *Social Theory and Social Structure* (revised edition). Glencoe, Ill.: The Free Press.

Merton, Robert and Kitt, Alice. 1950. "Contributions to the Theory of Reference Group Behavior." In *Continuities in the Social Research: Studies in the Scope and Method of 'The American Soldier'*, edited by R. Merton and P. Lazarsfeld, 40–105. Glencoe, Ill.: the Free Press.

Messick, Hank. 1971. *Lansky*, New York: G.P. Putnam's Sons.

Moore, Ethel and Moore, Chauncey. 1964. *Ballads and Folk Songs of the Southwest*. Norman: University of Oklahoma Press.

Mydans, Seth. "For Vietnamese, A Wave of Terror." *The New York Times*, (8 April 1991), A11.

Mydans, Seth. "As Cultures Meet, Gang War Paralyzes a City in California." *New York Times*, (6 May 1991), 1ff.

Nelli, Humbert. 1976. *The Business of Crime: Italians and Syndicate Crime in the United States*. New York: Oxford University Press.

O'Casey, Sean. 1957. *Juno and the Paycock: A Tragedy in Three Acts*. New York: St. Martin's Library.

O'Connor, Edwin. 1956. *The Last Hurrah*. Boston: Little, Brown and Company.

O'Kane, James. "Ethnic Mobility and the Lower-Income Negro: A Socio-Historical Perspective." *Social Problems* 16, 3 (Winter 1969):302–11.

O'Kane, James. "Economic and Non-Economic Liberalism, Upward Mobility Potential and Catholic Working-Class Youth." *Social Forces* 48 (June 1970):499–506.

O'Kane, James, Barenblatt, Lloyd, Jensen, Philip, Cochran, Lillian. "Anticipatory Socialization and Male Catholic Adolescent Socio-Political Attitudes." *Sociometry* 40, 1 (1977):67–77.

O'Kane, James. "The Ethnic Factor in American Urban Civil Disorders." *Ethnicity* 2 (Fall 1979):230–43.

O'Kane, James. 1981. *Pamplona: A Sociological Analysis of Migration and Urban Adaptation Patterns*. Washington, D.C.: University Press of America.

"Orientals Find Bias Is Down Sharply in U.S." *The New York Times* (13 December 1970), 1ff.

Park, Robert and Miller, Herbert. 1921. *Old World Traits Transplanted.* New York: Harper and Brothers.

Pennell, Susan, "'Ice': DUF Interview Results from San Diego." *NIJ Reports.* Washington, D.C.: National Institute of Justice, No. 221 (Summer 1990):12–13.

Peterson, Virgil. 1983. *The Mob: 200 Years of Organized Crime in New York.* Ottawa, Ill.: Green Hill Publishers.

Pileggi, Nicholas. 1985. *Wiseguy: Life in a Mafia Family.* New York: Simon and Schuster.

Piven, Frances and Cloward, Richard. 1971. *Regulating the Poor.* New York: Pantheon.

Polsky, Ned. 1967. *Hustlers, Beats and Others.* Chicago: Aldine Publishers.

President's Commission on Organized Crime. 1986. *Report to the President and the Attorney General, Volume 8, The Impact: Organized Crime Today.* Washington, D.C.: U.S. Government Printing Office.

Puzo, Mario. 1971. "Closing a Dream: Italians in Hell's Kitchen." In *The Immigrant Experience: The Anguish of Becoming American*, edited by Thomas Wheeler, 35–49. New York: Penquin Books.

Raab, Selwyn. "Gotti or No Gotti, The Mafia Looks Infirm These Days." *New York Times,* (18 February 1990), E6.

Raab, Selwyn. "A Battered and Ailing Mafia is Losing Its Grip on America." *New York Times,* (22 October 1990): 1ff.

Report to the National Advisory Commission on Civil Disorders. New York: Bantam Books, 1968.

Reuter, Peter. 1983. *Disorganized Crime.* Cambridge, Mass.: MIT Press.

"Riding A White Mare." *Time Magazine* (6 March 1989):33.

Riemer, David. 1988. *The Prisoners of Welfare.* New York: Praeger..

Riemer, David. "Jobs Are Too Few and Pay Too Little." *The Phildelphia Inquirer*, (24 February 1991), 9c.

Riordan, William. 1963. *Plunkett of Tammany Hall.* Lexington, Mass.: E.P. Dutton Co.

Rodriquez, Clara. 1974. *The Ethnic Queue in the U.S.: The Case of Puerto Ricans.* San Francisco: R and E Research Associates.

Rosen, Bernard. "Social Change, Migration and Family Interaction in Brazil." *American Sociological Review* 38 (1973): 198–212.

Rosenbaum, Ron. "Crack Murder: A Detective Story." *The New York Times Magazine*, (15 February 1987), 24.

Rosenbaum, Ron. "Update: Breaking the Crack Murders." *The New York Times Magazine*, (15 November 1987), 44.

Rosner, Lydia. 1986. *The Soviet Way of Crime.* New York: Bergin and Garvey.

Rudolph, Robert. "Drug Queen's Driver Played the White House." *The Star Ledger*, (24 November 1987), 22.

Sann, Paul. 1971. *Kill the Dutchman! The Story of Dutch Schultz*. New Rochelle, N.Y.: Arlington House.

Schlesinger, Arthur, Jr. 1969. "The Business of Crime." In *Introduction of 1886 Professional Criminals in America* by Thomas Brynes, xiii–xxvi. New York: Chelsea House Publishers.

Seeman, Melvin. "On the Meaning of Alienation." *American Sociological Review* 24 (1959):783–91.

Shaw, Clifford R. "Juvenile Delinquency-A Group Tradition." *Bulletin of the State University of Iowa*, No. 23, N.S. No. 700, 1933.

Silber, Irwin and Earl Robinson, eds. 1967. *Songs of the Great American West*. New York: The Macmillan Company.

Sifakis, Carl. 1982. *The Encyclopedia of American Crime*. New York: Facts on File Inc.

Slater, Marian. "My Son the Doctor: Aspects of Mobility Among. American Jews." *American Sociological Review* 34, 3 (June 1969): 359–73.

Spilerman, Seymour. "The Causes of Racial Disturbances: A Comparison of Alternative Explanations." *American Sociological Review* 35 (1970):627–49.

Srole, Leo. "Social Integration and Certain Corollaries: An Explanatory Study." *American Sociological Review* 21 (1956):709–16.

Stave, Bruce, ed. 1972. *Urban Bosses, Machines, and Progressive Reformers*. Lexington, Mass.: D.C. Heath.

Stolank, M. Mark, and Friedman, Murray, eds. 1986. *Making It in America: The Role of Ethnicity in Business Enterprise, Education, and Work Choices*. Lewisburg, Pa.: Bucknell University Press.

Stonequist, Everett. 1937. *The Marginal Man*. New York: Charles Scribner's Sons.

Sunday Star Ledger (specific dates and titles mentioned in text).

Sutherland, Edwin, ed. 1972. *The Professional Thief*. Chicago: University of Chicago Press.

Taylor, Carl S. 1990. *Dangerous Society*. East Lansing: Michigan State University Press.

Terry, Don. "In Chicago Courtroom, Nation's First Super Gang Fights for Life." *New York Times*, (19 May 1991):18.

Thomas, W.I. and Florian Znaniecki 1927. *The Polish Peasant in Europe and America*. New York: Alfred A. Knopf Inc.

Volsky, George. "Jamaican Drug Gangs Thriving in U.S. Cities." *The New York Times*, (19 July 1987), 17.

Walker Francis. 1959. "Immigration and Degradation." *Immigration As a Factor in American History*, edited by Oscar Handlin. Englewood Cliffs, N.J.: Prentice-Hall.

Walker, Jesse, "Bumpy's Death End of an Era." *New York Amsterdam News*, (20 July 1968), 1–2.

Warner, W. Lloyd, L.O. Low, Paul Lunt, and Leo Srole. 1963. *Yankee City*, (abridged edition). New Haven: Yale University Press.

Weinberg, S., and Arond, Henry. "The Occupational Career of a Boxer." *American Journal of Sociology* 57 (1952):460–69.

Wilkerson, Isabel. "New Studies Zeroing in on Poorest of the Poor." *The New York Times*, (20 December 1987), 26.

Wilkerson, Isabel. "Detroit Drug Empire Showed All the Traits of Big Business." *New York Times*, (18 December 1988), A1 and 42.

Winnick, Louis. "Yearning to Be Free." *The New York Times* (28 February 1988), D:25.

Wilson, William J. 1987. *The Truly Disadvantaged: The Inner City, The Underclass, and Public Policy*. Chicago: University of Chicago Press.

Wilson, William J. "Studying Inner-City Social Dislocations: The Challenge of Public Policy Agenda Research." *American Sociological Review* 56 (February 1991):1–14.

Wirth, Louis. "Culture, Conflict and Delinquency." *Social Forces* 9 (June 1931):484–92.

Wirth, Louis. "Urbanism As a Way of Life." *American Journal of Sociology* 44 (1938):3–24.

Wright, Carol, 1974. *The Working Girls of Boston*. Boston: Massachusetts Labor Department, 1889 pp. 114-118. In *The Ordeal of Assimilation: A Documentary History of the White Working Class, 1830s to the 1970s*, edited by Stanley Feldstein and Lawrence Costello. Garden City, N.Y.: Doubleday Anchor Books.

Zimmer, Basil. 1970. "Participation of Migrants in Urban Structures." In *Readings in the Sociology of Migration*, edited by C.J. Jansen, 71–83. Oxford: Pergamon Press

Index

Abadinsky, Howard, 72
Adamic, Louis, 7
Adonis, Joe, 72
Adonis Social Club, 73
African Americans, 94
Agueros, Jack, 36
Alcatraz prison, 134
Alger, Horatio, 8, 23
Allsop, Kenneth, 119
Alongi, Bob, ix, 5
Alterie, "Two Gun," 71
American Guards, gang, 56
American Native party, 13, 56
American Revolution, 142
Amerikanec, 7
Anastasia Albert, 68, 75
Anastasia family, 50
Anastasio, Anthony ("Tough Tony"), 50
Angels With Dirty Faces (film), 118, 123, 171
Anglo-Saxon beliefs, 12
Anomie, 149; various terms, 151
Anselmi, Albert, 71
Anticipatory socialization, 113
Aristotle, vi
Arlacchi, Pino, 88
Arond, Henry, 115–116
Aryan Brotherhood, gang, 128
Asbury, Herbert, 6, 44, 49, 68, 74, 157
Asians, 89
Asians, in Western states, 18
Assimilation process, 9
Atlanta Prison, 134
Ayers, Manny, ix

Baker, James "Halfback," 104
Balagula, Marat "the Georgian," 157
Baldwin, James, 42

Ballad of Bonnie & Clyde, 167–168
The Ballad of Sam Bass, 165
Baltimore, 1858 election riot, 54
Baltzell, E. Digby, 25
Banditos, gang, 128
Banfield, Edward, 57
Banton Posse, 104
Barbosa, Luiz, ix
Barenblatt, Lloyd, 113
Barker, Kate "Ma," 53, 160, 166
Barlow, Hugh, 58
Barnes, Leroy "Nicky," 95, 133
Barrow, Clyde, 53, 159, 160, 166
Bass, Sam, 162
"Battle Annie," gangster, 52
Beatty, Warren, 173
Bell, Daniel, 6, 25, 48, 53, 137
Benguerras family, 83–84
Bennett, Sue, ix
Bernstein, Abe, 75
Bernstein, Joe, 72
Berry, Brian, 151
"Billy the Kid" (song), 162, 163
Billy the Kid (William Bonney), 159, 175
Birchler, Mark, 95
Black and Tans, 2
Black Guerilla family, gang, 128
Black Islam, 103
Black Mafia, 88
Blacks (American & Caribbean), 89
Blackstone Rangers, 103
Blacks, victimization of, 13
Block, Alan, 52
Blood Tubs, gang, 13
Bloody Angle, New York City, 61
Blumenthal, Ralph, 93
Blum, Howard, 100

Boal, Fred, 143
Bogart, Humphrey, 171
Bohlen, Celestine, 93
Bolger, Jimmy, 59
Bonanno, Joe "Bananas," 76, 85
Bonney, William. *See Billy the Kid*
Bonnie & Clyde (film), 168, 173
Boo How Doy, 61
Bootlegging, 69
Born to Kill, 107
Bouras, Chelsais, 93
Bowdre, Charlie, 162
Bowery Boys, gang, 55–57
Boy Scouts, 77
Brady, "Yakey" Yake, 49
Brando, Marlon, 171, 174
Breasted, David, 97
Bresler, Fenton, 96
British social & political institutions, 12
Brogan, D.W., 45, 47
Brooklyn International Longshoremen's
    Association, 50
Brown, Al (alias), 137
Brown, Anthony, 133
Brown, Claude, 125, 127
Browning, Frank, 78
Brown, James, 103
Brown, Thomas, 153
Bruce, Lenny, 42
Bruno, Angelo, 93
Buchalter, Louis "Lepke," 69, 72, 74,
    161
Burgess, Thomas, 11
Burke, T.H., 12
Burstein, Daniel, 157
Burt, Olive, 168
Butterfield, Fox, 96
Byrne, Edward, 105
Byrnes, Thomas, 129

Cachie, Al, ix, 5, 124
Cadets, 63
Cagney, James, 112, 118, 171
Cali cartel, 106
Campanilismo, 151

Capone, Alphonse, 5, 49, 50, 68, 71,
    72–74, 77, 80, 84, 97, 98, 100, 109,
    112, 131, 133, 136, 137, 159, 161,
    171, 175
Capone, Sonny, 137
Caporasa, John, ix
Cartels, Colombian, 92
Castellano, Paul, 76
Castro, Fidel, 95
Cavendish, Lord Frederick, 2
Ceballos, Eucaris, 52
Cermak, Anton, 44
Chambers Brothers, 95, 133
Chan, Eddie (Chan Tse-Chin), 107
Chang, An-Lo "White Wolf," 133
Chang, Li Hung, 61
Chaplins, gang, 5
Chiang, Ching-Kuo, 106
Chicago Tribune, 70
China White, 96
Chinese Exclusion Act, 19
Chinese, victimization of, 13
Chink, Sadie, 52
Chu, J. Chuan, 96
Civil War, 57
Clergy, 28, 37
Clergy, African-American, 39
Clergy, Irish-Catholic, 37–39
Cloward, Richard, ix, 6, 25, 26, 27,
    36, 57
Cobb, Lee J., 172
Cochran, Lillian, 113, 141
Coll, Peter, 74
Coll, Vincent "Mad Dog," 60, 70, 73,
    74, 80, 86, 98
Colombo, Joe, 136
Colosimo, "Diamond Jim," 68
Conant, Lois, ix
Conforti, Rich, ix, 5, 123
Connolly, "Baboon," 49
Connolly, "Slops," 49
Continental Army, 142
Conzen, Kathleen, 54
Copeland, Aaron, 159
Copeland, John, ix
Corcoran, "Googy," 49

Corleone, Vito, 85
Corley brothers, 105
Costello, Frank, 68, 72–74, 75, 77, 84, 95, 131, 133, 137
Costello, Lawrence, 30
Coughlin "Bathhouse John," 20
Cowell, David, ix
Crack, 92
Crank, 92
Creighton, Robert, x, 94
Cressey, Donald, 151
Crime as work, 147–149
Crime, ethnic organized, 48
Crime, Italian, 66
Crime, organized, 28
Criminality, individual, 79
Criminality, stages, 79–82
Criminals, African-Americans, 93
Criminals, Chinese, 96
Criminals, Cuban, 95
Crips, gang, 128
Croker, Richard, 44
Cubans, Mariel newcomers, 90
Cucchi, Paolo, ix
Cuidad de Los Ninos, Peru, 50
Curley, Dan, 2
Curley, James, 44
Curry, Jack, 107

Daley, Richard, 44
Dalitz, Moe, 72, 75, 83
Dalton, gang, 162
Daly, Michael, 122
Danamora Prison, 134
Danbury Prison, 134
D'Andrea Tony, 68
Davidson, "Red Phil," 66
Davie, Maurice, 48
Dead Rabbits, 55–57
Dean, Dwight, 151
de Crevecoeur, Michael, 17
Demographic critical mass, 14
DeMora, James "Machine Gun" Jack McGurn, 71
DeNiro, Robert, 171, 174
Depression, 77, 167

DeSapio, Carmine, 44
de Stevens, George, ix
Diamond, Jack "Legs," 49, 60, 70, 73, 80, 86, 98, 100, 161
Differential association, 123
Dillinger, John, 160, 167
Dintino, Justin, 91
Discrimination, colonial period, 12
Discrimination, jobs, 11
Dog Posse, 103
Dominant groups, 9
Dooley, "Barefoot" Rafer, 119
Drew University, 25
Druci, Schemer, 70
Drugs, 99
Drugs & liquor, parallels, 97
Dubro, Alec, 98, 132
Duck, Mock, 61
Duggan, Jack, 2
Dunaway, Faye, 173
Dunkirk Posse, 103
Durkheim, Emile, 140, 151
Dutch Schultz, ix, 5, 69, 72, 73, 77, 80, 98, 100, 108, 131, 159, 161
Dylan, Bob, 161, 170

East New York Democratic Club, 45
Easter Rebellion, 2
Eastman, Monk, 65, 66, 157
Eastmans, gang, 65
Eighteenth Amendment, 69
El Quintos, gang, 15
El Rukns, gang, 103
Emerson, "Banjo" Pete, 49
Entertainment, 28, 40
Entertainment, ancient Greek, 41
Entertainers, black, 42
Entertainers, Jewish, 42
Erens, Patricia, 171
Erikson, Frank, 72
Eugnics movement, 18
Ethnic gang: criminal supremacy, 81
Ethnic gang: decline & fall, 81
Ethnic groups, characteristics, 9
Ethnic groups, hostility, 11
Ethnic minorities, new, 88–89

Ethnic Reactive Riots, 14

Farrell, Sadie "the Goat," 49
Father Divine, 39
Fay, Larry, 72
Federal Bureau of Investigation, 82, 103, 156, 168
Federal Drug Enforcement Administration, 93
Fein, "Dopey Benny," 66
Feldstein, Stanley, 30
Fella, Mike, ix, 5
Fitzpatrick, Richie, 66
Five Points section of New York City, 44, 55–57, 65
Ford, Bob, 164
Ford brothers, 49
Forester, Robert, 152
Four Seas Gang, 106
Fort, Jeff, 103
Floyd, Charles "Pretty Boy," 159, 166, 168, 175
Flegenheimer, Arthur (see Dutch Schultz)
Flying Dragons, gang, 107
Francia, Rafael, ix
Franzese, Mike, 94
Franzese, "Sonny," 94
Fratiano, Jimmy "The Weasel," 85–86
Freeman, "Pop," 105
Fried, Albert, 53, 63, 66, 76, 157
Friedenfels, Roxanne, ix
Friedman, Murray, 28
From Here to Eternity (film), 174

Gabriel, Bob, ix
Gaelic language, 154
Galante, Carmine, 76
Gallo gang, 76
Gallo, Joey, 76, 87, 161, 170
Gambino, Carlo, 5, 75, 76, 84, 85, 108
Gangs, Brooklyn, 5
Gangs, Irish, 55–60
Gang That Couldn't Shoot Straight, 85
Gannon, William, 53
Garden of Eden, 154
Garis, Roy, 18

Garrett, Sheriff Pat, 162–163
Garvey, Marcus, 39
Genna Brothers, 68, 71, 80, 98, 100
Genovese, Vito, 75, 85, 100, 105, 161
Gerassi, John, 78
Germans, victimization of, 13
Ghost Shadows gang, 107
Giancana, Sam "Momo," 76
Glazer, Nathan, 12
Godfather (film), 49, 78, 85, 161, 175
Goodfellas (film), 121, 175
Gophers, The, gang, 59
Gordon, Milton, 21
Gordon, Waxey, 69
Goth, John, 85
Graebner-Anderson, Annelise, 83–84
Graham, Hugh, 13
Gray, James, ix
Gray, Kathy, ix
Gray, Robert "Cornbread," 105
Great Famine, 12
Green, Danny, 59
Gross, Jane, 92
Grubbs, Helen, ix
Gunn, Erik, 148
Gurr, Ted, 13
Gusenberg, Frankie, 70
Guthrie, Woody, 168

Haberman, Clyde, 97
Hague, Frank, 44
Hamilton, Edith, 41
Handlin, Oscar, 35, 39, 41, 54
Harrington, Michael, 146
Harris, John, 103
Hart-Cellar Act, 19, 90
Hartmann, Edward, 9
"Hell Cat Maggie," gangster, 52
Hell's Angels, gang, 128
Hell's Kitchen, 59
Hennessy, David, 67
Herberg, Will, ix, 6, 21, 25
Herrera, Jaime, 133
Herskovitz, Melville, 17, 18
Hertz, Rosie, 52
Highman, John, 35

Highbinders, 62
Hill, Henry, 121
Hip Sing, tong, 61, 106
Hispanics, 89
Hoboken, 1851 anti-German prejudice, 59
Hobsbawm, Eric, 161, 165
Hodgkins, Rebecca, ix
Hofstadter, Richard, 13
Holy Name Cathedral, 71
Hoover, J. Edgar, 91
Horowitz, Harry "Gyp the Blood," gangster, 66, 157
Howe, Irving, 40, 42
Hudson Dusters, gang, 59
Huff, Boo Boo, 72
Hughes, Jack, ix, 123–124
Hunger Action Forum, 117
Hutson, Jean, ix
Huvane, Steven, ix

Ianni, Francis, 6, 53, 65, 83, 86, 87, 127, 130, 139
Ice, 92
Ida "the Goose," gangster, 49
Immigrants, Chinese, 32, 33, 60–62
Immigrants, Eastern & Southern European, 62
Immigrants, German, 53–54
Immigrants, Irish-Catholic, 12, 54–55
Immigrants, Korean, 33
Immigrants, occupations of, 20
Immigrants, Scandinavian, 54
Immigration Restriction League, 18
Industrialization, 94, 139
Innovation, 26
Intellectual nativism, 17
Inter-Ethnic gang rivalry, 80
Irish, Catholic, 143
Irish, Protestant, 143
Irish, victimization of, 13
Italian-American Civil Rights League, 136
Italians, victimization, 13

Jackson, Jesse, 39

James, Archie, 163
James, Frank, 162, 166
James, Jesse, 49, 161, 164, 175
Jefferson Avenue, 4, 5
Jensen, Phil, ix, 113
Jew, Vincent, 106
Joey (ballad), 170
Johnson, Ellsworth "Bumpy," 133, 134, 135
Johnson, Rev. John, 134
Johnson, Nucky, gangster, 72, 147
Johnston, George S., ix
Juno and the Paycock, vi

Kallen, Horace, 21
Kaplan, David, 97, 132
Karpis-Barker gang, 166
Katz, Jack, 121
Kearney, Denis, 60
Kelly, Addie Mae, ix
Kelly "Honest" John, 60
Kelly, Machine Gun, 49, 161
Kelly, Robert, 94, 97
Kelly, "Shanghai," 60
Kenna, "Hinky Dink," 70
Kennedy, Ruby, 21
Kennedy, William, 74
Kerner Report, 150
Kerr, Peter, 86
"Kid Glove" Rosie, gangster, 52
Kim, Illsoo, 33
King, Martin Luther, 39
Kiss of Death, film, 172
Kitt, Alice, 113
Kleinschmidt, "Black" Lena, 52
Know-Nothings (see American Native party)
Kobler, John, 72, 97, 119
Kon, Johnny, (Yu-Leung Kon), 96
Krajicek, David, 97
Ku Klux Klan, 18
Kusmer, Kenneth, 32, 42

Labor, skilled and unskilled, 28, 29
La Cosa Nostra, 59, 91
Langton, Kenneth, 114

Lansky, Meyer, 50, 69, 72, 74, 75, 77, 81, 95, 98, 100, 131, 136, 157, 174
Lansky, Paul, 138
La Nuestra Familia, gang, 128
Larini, Rudy, 91
Lazar, Sam, 72
Lazia, John, 68, 72
Ledeen, Lydia, ix
Lee, Alfred McClung, ix, 21
Lee, Tom, 61
Lefty Louie, gangster, 157
Legs, play
Letkemann, Peter, 147
Levenworth Prison, 134
Levin, Mike, 97
Lewis, Whitey, gangster, 157
Licavelli mob, 59
Light, Ivan, 32, 34, 62
Lincoln, Abraham, 14
Lindsay, Mayor John, 87, 128
Lindsey, Robert, 128
Little Ceasar (film), 170
Little Italy of New York City, 65
Little, Kenneth, 151
Liu, Henry, 106
Lomax, Alan, 163
Lonegan, Richard "Peg Leg," 60, 72, 74, 98
Lorch, Donatella, 108
Louisville, 1855 election riot, 54
Lower East Side of New York City, 65
Lucas, Charles, 95
Luchese, Thomas "Three Fingers Brown," 75
Luciano, Charles "Lucky," 63, 68, 69, 72ff, 77, 81, 84, 95, 98, 100, 136, 171
Lupo, Ignazio "Lupo the Wolf," 68, 161
Lupullos, 83
Lupsha, Peter, 87, 88

Machine, political, 44
Mafia, 67, 88, 92, 99, 159
"Mafia," Cleveland, 82
Mafia, new, 87

Malden, Karl, 172
Mandebaum, Marm, 52
Marcello, Carlos, 76
Marielitos, 95
Marques, "Spanish Raymond," 133
Mason, Howard "Pappy," 105
Massachusetts Bay Colony, 12
Massa, Paula, ix
Masseria, Joe "the Boss," 68
Matranga, crime faction, 67
Matras, Judah, 141
Matthews, Frank, 95, 133
McAlary, Mike, 105
McCague, James, 57
McErlane, Frank, 72
McGriff, Kenneth "Supreme,"105
McKinley, James, 103
McLaughlins, The (gang), 59
McManus, "Eat 'Em Up" Jack, 49, 60
Meagher, Mike, ix
Means, illegitimate, 26, 27
Means, legitimate, 26, 27
Medellin cartel, 106
Medill School of Journalism, 77
Melting pot thesis, 16, 20, 21
Merton, Robert, 26, 113, 114
Messick, Hank, 138
Mexican Mafia, gang, 128
Mexicans, 93, 94
Mexicans, victimization of, 13
Meyer, Evelyn, ix
Mickens, Tommy "Tony Mantana," 105
Milano, Frank, 83
Miller, Gerald "Prince," 105
Miller, Herbert, 151
Miller's Crossing (film), 175
Mills, Jim, ix
Mobility upward, 21
Mobilization for Youth, 145
Moore, Chauncey, 166
Moore, Ethel, 166
Moran, Bernadette, ix
Moran, George "Bugs," 49, 70, 71, 98, 161
Moran, Tom, ix
Moretti, Willie, 76

Morrissey, John, 57, 59, 131
Morsink, Hans, ix
Morton, Samuel "Nails," 70, 174
Murder Inc., 75
Murphy, Jim, 165
Mydans, Seth, 108

Narcotics, 76
National Opinion Research Center, 143
Nation, gang, 128
Native Americans, 142
Nativism, 12
Nativistic riots, 13
Nelli, Humberto, 63, 67
Nelson, George "Baby Face," 160, 167
Newcomers, reasons for coming, 7
Newcomers, Soviet Jewish, 93–94
Newcomers, Upward Mobility, 8
Newgate Prison, 48
New Jack City (film), 176
New York Amsterdam News, 134
New York City Draft Riot, 14, 57
New York City, mayoralty election of 1956, 56
New York City Police Department, 5
New York State Organized Crime Task Force, 94
Nicholas, Lorenzo "Fat Cat," 105
Nicky Louie, gangster, 107
Nitti, Frank, 72
Noe, Joey, 73
Noland, Alice, 73
Northsides, gang, 70, 80

O'Bannion, Dion, 50, 60, 70, 77, 86, 98, 100, 108, 131, 161, 171, 174
O'Brennan, Martin, 154
O'Brien, Pat, 118
O'Casey, Sean, vi
Ocasio, Oscar, 102
O'Connell guards, 55–57
Oden, Tom, ix
Odessa gangsters, 93
O'Donnell, Pat, 3
O'Donnells, gang, 71, 98, 100
Odum, H.W., 17

O'Folliard, Tom, 162
Ohlin, Lloyd, 26, 27, 57
O'Kane, family, ix
O'Kane, James, 23, 44, 57, 113, 141, 151
O'Kane, Matilda, ix
O'Kelly, Edward, 164
Old Bailey Prison, 48
Old West, 159
Ollom, John, ix
Omerta, 85
Ong, "Uncle Benny" (Fei Lo Chat), 107
On Leong, tong, 61, 106, 107
On the Waterfront (film), 172
Organized crime, ethnic, 1
Organized criminal accommodations, 81
Orgen, "Little Augie," 74
Outlaws, gang, 128

Pacino, Al, 171
Pagans, gang, 128
Pamplona, Spain, 151
Pappas, Mitzi, ix
Parker, Bonnie, 53, 159, 160, 166
Park, Robert, 151
"Pat O'Donnell" (song), 3
Patriarca gang, 85
Patriarca, Raymond, 76
Pax Caponeana, 5, 98–99, 109
Peers, Roseanna, 52
Peetros, Harry, 93
Penn, Arthur, 168
Pennell, Susan, 92
Peterson, Virgil, 56
"Phoenix Park Murders" (song), 2
Pileggi, Nicholas, 121
Pinkertons, 163
Piven, Frances, 36
Plug Uglies, gang, 55–57
Plunkett, George Washington, 44, 116
Police precinct, 5, 90
Politics, vi
Politics, ethnic, 43
Politics, ethnic, reasons for "semi-legitimacy," 44

Politics, urban, 28
Polsky, Ned, 148
Pony Down, 104
Pool, Bill "the Butcher," 49
Population density, 141
Potato Bag Gang, 93
Powell, Adam Clayton, 39, 44
President's Commission on Organized Crime, 105, 107, 128
"Pretty Boy Floyd" (song), 169
Pretty Rob, 104
Prize fighters, various ethnic groups, 43
Prizzi's Honor (film), 85
Profaci, Joe, 76, 136
Professions, 28, 34
Professions, choice of various ethnic newcomers, 37
Professions, learned, 35
Professions, semi, 35
Prohibition, 58–59, 69, 75, 76, 94, 97, 98, 100, 119, 171, 173, 174
Provenzano, crime faction, 67
Public Enemy (film), 170
Public opinion of immigrants (late 1800s–early 1900s), 16
Puritan ethic, 9
Purple Gang of Detroit, 75
Purvis, Melvin, 168
Puzzo, Mario, 30

Quantrill's Raiders, 163

Raab, S., 85
Rabbis, 40
Racism, 149ff
Racketeer Influence Corrupt Organizations Act (RICO), 78, 85
Radical movements, social work, 36
Rastafarian religious cult, 104
Ravage, Marcus, 63
Reader, Jonathan, ix
Rebellion, 26
"Red Rocks," gangster, 46
Regina Pacis, chapel, 136
Reles, Abe "Kid Twist," 75
Religion, ethnic clergy, 25

Report of the National Advisory Commission on Civil Disorders, 150
Retreatism, 26
Reuss-Ianni, Elizabeth, 65, 139
Reuter, Peter, 88
Riemer, David, 148
Riemer, Neal, ix
Rio, Johnny, 72
Riordan, William, 116
Ritualism, 26
Roache Guards, 56
Roaring Twenties (film), 171
Robinson, Earl, 164
Robinson, Edward G., 171
Robinson, Jackie, 42
Rock, Joe, 73
Rock, John, 73
Rodriquez, Clara, 142
Rome, ancient, 99
Rosen, Bernard, 151
Rosen, "Nig," 72
Rosenbaum, Ron, 104
Rosenberg, "Lefty Louis," gangster, 66
Rosner, Lydia, 93
Rothkopf, Lou, 72
Rothstein, Arnold, gangster, 73, 75, 98
Routes of mobility, 28
Routes of mobility, semi-legitimate, 43
Ruch, Jean, ix
Rudolph, Robert, 52
Rynders, Captain Isiah, 57

"Sadie, the Goat," gangster, 52
Saint, Eva Marie, 172
Salerno, "Fat Tony," 134
Saltis, Joe, 72
Saltis-McErlane Mob, 71
Sanford, General Charles W., 56
Sann, Paul, 73
Scalish, John, 71, 83
Scarface (film), 161, 175
Scarfo Gang, 85
Schlesinger, Arthur, 26, 53, 129
Schwartz, Charlie, 72
Scientific racism, 15
Seeman, Melvin, 151

Shaft (film), 134

Shapiro, Jacob "Gurrah," gangster, 74

Shaw, Clifford, 120

Sheer, Thomas L., 86

Shower Posse, 103

Shtetl, 37, 63

Sicilian Black Hand criminals, 67, 68

Siegel, Benjamin "Bugsy," gangster, 49, 60, 72ff, 77, 81, 98, 161, 171, 174

Sifakis, Carl, 61, 71, 163, 168

Silber, Irwin, 164

Sinatra, Frank, 170

Sing Sing Prison, 113, 119, 134

Skinner, Claude, 105

Slater, Marian, 37

Small businesses, retail, 28, 32

Smallwood, Donny, 104

Smith, Al, 15, 47

Social Register, 50

Social Security system, 45

Soloman, "King," gangster, 72

Spangler Posse, 103

"Spanish Mary," gangster, 52

Speed, 92

Sports, professional, 42–43

Starr, Bell, 53

Steiger, Rod, 172

Stolank, M., 34

"Stompers," gang, 15

Stonquist, Everett, 151

Story of Bonnie Parker (film), 168

Srole, Leo, 151

Structural Pluralism, 21

St. Clair, "Madam Queen" Stephanie, 52

St. Francis College, Brooklyn, 135

St. Mark's Episcopal Church, Harlem, 134

St. Valentine's Day Massacre, 71, 98, 159

Sue Yop, tong, 61

Sullivan, "Big Tim," 60, 70

Sum Yop, tong, 61

Sutherland, Edwin, 123

Tammany Hall, 44, 45, 47, 57, 65, 70, 116, 131, 137

Taylor, Carl, 104

Tel Aviv Posse, 103

Teresa, Vincent, 76, 85

Terranova, Ciro, 68

Terry, Don, 103

Texas Syndicate, gang, 128

Thomas, W.I., 151

Tong Ons, 106

tongs, 62, 96

Tong wars, 61–62

Torres, Gumersindo, 102

Torrio-Capone gang, 71

Torrio, Johnny, 68, 71, 72

Toy, Fung Jing "Little Pete," 61

Trade union movement, 31

Trafficante, Santo, 76

Treaty of Versailles, 159

Tweed Ring, 129

Twenty-First Amendment, 101

United Bamboo, gang, 106

United Jewish Appeal, 136

United States Dept. of Justice, 156

United States Naval Intelligence, 136

University of Miami, 137

University of Notre Dame, 137

Untouchables (film), 49, 78, 175

Urban bosses, 45–48

Urban ethnic diversity, 4

Urbanization, 94, 139

Urbanization and industrialization, 55

Upper caste, 17

Unwashed masses, 16

Vaccarelli, Paolo "Paul Kelly," 65

Vach, "Cyclone Louie," 49

Valachi, Joe, 76, 85

Valdo, crime victim, 102

Vitoffsky, "Charlie the Cripple," 49

Volsky, George, 103

Vox Populi, trade unions, 31

Wah Ching, gang, 105

Walsh, Danny, 60

Walker, Jesse, 134
Wallace, Michael, 13
Walsh, Mike, 57
Walsh, Raoul, 167
Ward boss, Tammany Hall, 105
Water House Posse, 103
Weidenbaum, Paul, ix, 5, 124
Weinberg, S., 115–116
Weiss, Hymie, 70, 71, 98, 161, 171
Wescott, Roger, ix
Westies, gang, 59
West Point, 138
Wheeler, Thomas, 30
Whitehall Testing Center, 145
White Heat (film), 167
White Hand, Irish gang, 72
Wice, Paul, ix
Widmark, Richard, 172
Wild Bunch, gang, 104
"Wild Colonial Boy" (song), 1
Wilkerson, Isabel, 95
Williamsburg, Brooklyn: 90th Precinct, 124, 125
Wilson, William J., 150, 155

Winnick, Louis, 6, 19
Winter, Howard, 59
Wirth, Louis, 151
Wolf packs, 122
Wood, Fernando, 57
Woo, Kok Leung, 97
Workman, Charlie, 75
Wright, Carol, 29

Yakuza, 97, 132
Yale, Frankie, 68, 71
Yamaguchi-gumi, 97
Young, Andrew, 39
Young Boys Inc., 104
Younger, Cole, 162, 166

Zelig, Big Jack, 66, 157
Zerelli, Joe, 75
Zimmer, Basil, 151
Znaniecki, Florian, 151
Zwieback, Max "Kid Twist" gangster, 66, 157
Zwillman, Abner "Longy," gangster, 69, 72ff